Grant Corner Inn

BREAKFAST, BRUNCH & BEYOND

New & Revised Cookbook

■

Louise Stewart & Pat Walter

With Special Illustrations by
Garth Williams

OLMSTEAD
PRESS

SELECT REGISTRY
DISTINGUISHED INNS OF NORTH AMERICA

With much appreciation to Anne Marshall,
for the many hours of testing, creating, editing and mothering our cookbook.

With many thanks to Judy Allison, whose endurance in the final hour saved our sanity!
And special thanks also to Suriya, Geri, Lucy, Cricket and all the wonderful Grant Corner Inn staff.

Published in 2000 by Olmstead Press: Chicago, Illinois
and Select Registry, Distinguished Inns of North America: Marshall, Michigan

Original cover art by Laura Wilk
Cover designed by Hope Forstenzer

Updated and additional text designed and typeset by
Syllables, Hartwick, New York, USA

First Edition published in 1986 by Grant Corner Inn
Secretarial Services by Bell's Exec
Design by Webb Design Studio/Taos
Calligraphy by Suriya

Printed and bound in the USA by Sheridan Books, Ann Arbor, Michigan

ISBN: 1-58754-005-3 • Library of Congress Card Number: 00-104128

Editorial Sales Rights and Permission Inquiries should be addressed to:
Olmstead Press, 22 Broad Street, Milford, CT 06460
Email: editor@lpcgroup.com

Manufactured in the United States of America
1 3 5 7 9 10 8 6 4 2

Substantial discounts on bulk quantities of Olmstead Press books are available to corporations, professional
associations and other organizations. If you are in the USA or Canada, contact LPC Group,
Attn: Special Sales Department, 1-800-626-4330, fax 1-800-334-3892, or email: sales@lpcgroup.com.

To Bumpy
For the Joy
You Have Brought
into Our Lives

With gratitude for the gifts
of love from my family

Motivation .... Daddy
Perseverance ... Mother
Sensitivity .... Helen
Sense of Humor .... Jack

In memory
of those happy years together
at Camelback Inn,
where "genuine hospitality"
became our way of life.

ASIDES

PANCAKES & WAFFLES

MUFFINS

Tangerine Bran Muffins
Bran Marmalade Muffins
Peanut Butter Bran Muffins
Cocoanut Tea Cakes
Gingerbread Muffins
Oatmeal Maple Muffins
Maple Spice Muffins
Chocolate Orange Muffins
Pumpkin Streusel Muffins
Blue Corn Muffins
Rice-Corn Muffins
Chocolate Cherry Muffins
Chocolate Macaroon Muffins
Chocolate Chip Muffins
Bacon Cheese Muffins
Jalapeño Cheese Muffins
Poppy Seed Banana Muffins
Blue Corn Honey Sesame Muffins
Cranberry Pumpkin Muffins
Raspberry Almond Muffins
Kahlua Muffins

pages 153-180
YEAST SPECIALTIES

Herbal White Bread
Vanilla-Glazed Raisin Bread
Anadama Bread
Honey- Wheat Bread
Oatmeal Bread
7-Grain Loaf
Sourdough Wheat Loaves
Cheddar Bread
Honey-Wheat English Muffins
Jam and Cheese Loaf
Cinnamon Twist Coffee Cake
Swedish Tea Ring
Golden Apricot Twist
Poppy Seed Ring Cake
"Cheese Danish" Coffee Cake
Chocolate Babka
Chocolate Bread
Fresh Blueberry Kolacky

Martha's Hot Cross Buns
Almond Fans
Almond Heaven
Apple Cinnamon Twists
Old-Fashioned Cinnamon Rolls
Orange-Raisin Cinnamon Rolls
Rum-Butter Sticky Buns
Gooey Pecan Buns
Orange Whole Wheat Sticky Buns
Aunt Helen's Orange Rolls
French Quarter Beignets
Biscochito-Nuts (New Mexican
    Raised Doughnuts)
Cocoanut Cream Buns
Apricot Bran Bread

pages 181-210
MORE FROM OUR PASTRY BASKET

Lemon Cashew Bread
Toasted Almond Apricot Loaf
Orange-Pecan Bread
Tropical Tea Bread
Tish's Zucchini Bread
Applesauce Spice Bread
Date Walnut Bread
Walnut Mocha Bread
Dutch Honey Spice Bread
Pumpkin Raisin Bundt Bread
Gingerybread
Boston Brown Date Bread
Cherry Coffee Cake
Apple Coffee Cake
Pear Streusel Roll
Joannie's Apricot Lattice Cake
Strawberry Rhubarb Crumb Cake
Strawberry-Macaroon Puff
Peach Pocket Cake
GCI Blueberry Cobbler Cake
Blueberry-Almond Coffee Cake
Blackberry Crumb Kuchen
Raspberry Streusel Coffee Cake

Camelback Inn Sunday Coffee
    Cake
Poppy Seed Coffee Cake
Super Carrot Coffee Cake
Sour Cream Streusel Coffee Cake
Kugelhopf
Tropical Torte
Almond Puff Pastry
Peachy Cornbread
Apricot or Raspberry Piroshki
Josephine's Biscotti
Currant Scones
Tender Buttermilk Biscuits with
    Three-Fruits Butter
Grandmother Stewart's Raisin
    Biscuits
Cheddar-Chive Biscuits
Bacon Parmesan Popovers
Geri's Sopaipillas
Pineapple Fritters
Fresh Apricot Beignets
Mother's Jam Cake
Pumpkin Raisin Bread
Aunt Helen's Grand Marnier Cake
Chocolate Zucchini Bread
Lemon Mango Bread

pages 211-218
JELLIES & PRESERVES

Lucy's Apricot Jam and Variations
Plum Jam
Strawberry Jam
Betsy's Orange-Strawberry
    Preserves
Cran-Orange Relish
Grant Corner Inn Peach Butter
Baked Apple Butter
Blueberry Chutney
Plum-Cherry Chutney
Gourmet Chutney
Red or Green Pepper Jelly
Pickled Watermelon Rind

Because of Grant Corner Inn's 7000-foot location. I'd like to provide you with my notes on high-altitude baking.

First of all, the items that could be most affected are those baked with the ingredients of baking powder and/or soda (quick breads, coffee cakes, muffins, pancakes and waffles). Secondly (to minimize your fears), many of those particular items from this cookbook have been tested at various altitudes, and no alterations were necessary. My recommendation for anyone in a lower altitude is to follow our recipes just as they are. Should any problems occur, try the following adjustments:

1) Decrease baking powder and soda ¼ teaspoon for every teaspoon called for. (This adjustment should be sufficient, but if not, go on to the next steps.)

2) By very small amounts, a) decrease flour, b) decrease eggs and c) increase butter uniformly.

3) Decrease oven temperature (by not more than 25 degrees).

INGREDIENT HELPER

1 tablespoon = 3 teaspoons

16 tablespoons = 1 cup

½ stick butter = ¼ cup or 4 tablespoons

1 stick butter = ½ cup or 8 tablespoons

A Visit to Grant Corner Inn

Lush delicate branches of giant weeping willow trees partially conceal the grand manor home proudly displaying the neat wooden placard, "Grant Corner Inn, Bed and Breakfast, Public Welcome, Breakfast and Sunday Brunch." An established Santa Fe landmark, located just two blocks from the historic plaza and next door to the world-renowned Georgia O'Keeffe Museum, the Grant Corner Inn seems to emanate a feeling of mature contentment. The grace and grandeur of a by-gone era draws passerbys naturally up the garden walk. Sounds of gentle guitar music, relaxed laughter and chatter and the sweet aromas of baking contribute to the Inn's enticing ambiance. Over the years thousands of guests have been charmed by Grant Corner Inn's friendly service and fine food.

The Walter family, Pat, Louise (or "Wiggy") and Elena (or "Bumpy"), opened Grant Corner Inn December, 1981. The photographs in the Inn's foyer trace the history of the home's origin from 1905, when it was built for the Winsor family, to years later, when it became the home of the Robinson's and then when it became a boarding house in the 40s and 50s. The Walters continue to welcome guests in grand style. Louise, hostess and interior designer, oversees with a keen eye for detail learned from her life at Camelback Inn and from her parents who were Camelback's founders and innkeepers for thirty years. Pat, with ancestors from Walter's Brewery in Colorado, contributes his artistic talents in building and food creation. Bumpy delights the guests with her youthful energy and ever-sparkling graciousness. The fifteen members of the Inn staff are complimented continuously for their warm and efficient service.

Appropriately, the new edition of *Grant Corner Inn, Breakfast, Brunch and Beyond* comes on the eve of the Inn's 20th year in business. This milestone anniversary brings with it a renewal that is evident in every facet of the Inn's operation. The guest rooms, through the design efforts of Pat and Louise,

Pat Walter, Elena (Bumpy) Walter and Louise Stewart

retain character and personality, while offering every state of the art, comfort and luxury. Walls have been removed to increase the size of individual rooms. Shared baths are "a thing of the past." Jacuzzi tubs, cushy robes, air-conditioners, refrigerators and computer outlets are a few of the additions.

Rabbits continue to play a major role in the Inn's décor. They are soft, whimsical, friendly and definitely, rejuvenating. They are everywhere, except on the menu!

The Grant Corner Inn kitchen has also been involved in the fervor of revitalization. A recent remodel included all new appliances. Fresh, innovative food still lures guests and local residents to daily breakfast and Sunday brunch. Holiday and special occasion dinners have become increasingly popular. Diners plead for the old favorite recipes, but sometimes see them used in new combinations. Steadfast and true, Lucy continues to bake fresh breads and create jellies and relishes in many variations. Pat has injected his free spirit and culinary expertise to enhance and elevate the Grant Corner Inn dining experience. The new last chapter, "Beyond Brunch," is a tribute to his talents.

Please enjoy and celebrate the rebirth of Grant Corner Inn's Cookbook, entitled *Grant Corner Inn, Breakfast, Brunch and Beyond*!

Visit the Inn in Santa Fe at:
Grant Corner Inn
122 Grant Avenue
Santa Fe, NM 87501
800/964-9003

www.grantcornerinn.com
Email: gcinn@aol.com

Grant Corner Inn Crew, 1999

Eye-
Openers

Calligraphy by Suriya

Graphics by Louise

GRANT CORNER INN ORANGE FRAPPÉ

Serves 6

4 cups fresh-squeezed orange juice

juice of one lemon

1 large banana

6 strawberries, fresh or frozen

¼ cup whipping cream

6 ice cubes

fresh mint for garnish

Blend ingredients on high for one minute. Serve in frosted, stemmed goblets, garnished with fresh mint leaves.

Cook's Note: The fruit frappé has become very popular at Grant Corner Inn. Each morning the fruit blend changes. Any fresh fruit that is too ripe for the guest room fruit baskets finds its way to the blender for frappé. Preparation is simple, and infinite flavors are possible. The cook only needs to taste as he goes. The beauty in these drinks is that they usually need no sweetener other than the natural fruits. My one "hint" is that they be served very, very cold. During breakfast we keep prepared frappé and glasses in the freezer; then blend each frappé to order.

■

CRANBERRY-BANANA FRAPPÉ

Serves 6

2 cups Cranapple juice

1 cup fresh-squeezed orange juice

¼ cup whipping cream

1 tablespoon lemon juice

2 bananas

¾ cup crushed ice

fresh mint for garnish

Combine all ingredients in blender container with crushed ice. Blend on high speed one minute. Serve in frosted, stemmed goblets, garnished with sprigs of fresh mint.

■

MELON COOLER

Serves 2

½ ripe, sweet cantaloupe, peeled and chunked

1 banana

1 teaspoon lemon juice

5 ice cubes

1 cup cream, whipped

thin melon slices, skin on, for garnish

Blend cantaloupe, banana, lemon juice, and ice cubes for one minute on high. Add whipped cream and give mixture several short pulses, until cream is incorporated. Serve in frosted, stemmed goblets, garnished with half a melon slice.

■

PIÑA COLADA COOLER

Serves 2

¼ cup fresh pineapple chunks

1 teaspoon fresh lime juice

¼ cup pineapple juice, chilled

1½ teaspoons canned cream of cocoanut

5 ice cubes

fresh pineapple wedges for garnish

Blend all ingredients for one minute on high

until smooth and creamy. Pour into stemmed, frosted goblets and garnish with wedges of fresh pineapple.

■

HELEN'S BANANA FRAPPÉ

Serves 2

1 banana, peeled and sliced

2 tablespoons fresh orange juice

2 tablespoons apple juice

2 tablespoons plain yogurt

2 teaspoons wheat germ

2 teaspoons Lecithin powder

5 ice cubes

orange slices for garnish

Blend all ingredients one minute on high until smooth and creamy. Pour into frosted, stemmed goblets and garnish with orange slices.

Cook's Memory: My sister, Helen, at about age 12, began to take an interest in health (long before the interest was fashionable). She taught herself yoga, frequented health food stores, made her own yogurt and constantly lectured to the family (mostly me!) on nutrition.

■

RASPBERRY FIZZ

Serves 2

½ cup fresh or frozen unsweetened raspberries

½ cup apricot nectar, chilled

5 ice cubes

1 tablespoon powdered sugar

½ teaspoon lemon juice

¼ cup chilled club soda

lime slices for garnish

Blend raspberries, nectar and ice on high until smooth. Add powdered sugar and lemon juice and blend another 30 seconds. Stir in club soda. Pour into frosted, stemmed goblets and garnish with slices of lime.

■

STRAWBERRY FLIP

Serves 2

1 cup fresh strawberries, capped

1 banana

1 teaspoon lemon juice

½ cup strawberry nectar, chilled

2 tablespoons sour cream

1 cup crushed ice

fresh strawberries for garnish

Blend all ingredients for one minute on high. Pour into frosted, stemmed goblets and garnish with whole strawberries.

■

EGGNOG

Serves about 16

6 eggs, separated

¾ cup sugar

½ cup milk

½ cup bourbon

½ cup cognac or brandy

½ teaspoon salt

3 cups whipping cream, softly whipped

freshly grated nutmeg

In medium bowl beat together egg yolks, sugar and milk until thick and foamy. Whisk in bourbon and cognac. Chill 2-3 hours or overnight.

In medium mixing bowl beat egg whites with salt until stiff, but not dry, peaks form. Gently fold whites and whipped cream into liquor base; chill 1-2 hours.

Stir through mixture before dipping by the punch-cupful. Dust with freshly grated nutmeg.

∎

SPICED PEACH SMOOTHIE

Serves 2

1 large, ripe peach, peeled, pitted and sliced

¼ cup plain yogurt

1 teaspoon mild honey

¼ cup peach nectar

⅛ teaspoon cinnamon

5 ice cubes

cinnamon for garnish

Combine all ingredients in blender container.

Blend on high for one minute, or until smooth and creamy. Serve in frosted, stemmed goblets, garnished with a dusting of cinnamon.

∎

HOT CRANBERRY CUP

Serves 2

¾ cup apple cider

¾ cup cranberry cocktail

6 whole cloves

6 whole allspice

2 sticks cinnamon

Bring all ingredients to a boil; turn down heat, cover and simmer 20 minutes. Pour into mugs and garnish with cinnamon sticks.

∎

MULLED APPLE CIDER

Serves 2

2 cups apple juice, preferably unfiltered

¼ cup brown sugar

1 tablespoon lemon juice

1 stick cinnamon, broken into pieces

5 whole cloves

10 whole allspice

cinnamon sticks for garnish

Combine all ingredients in small saucepan. Heat to boiling, cover, and reduce heat. Simmer 15 minutes. Strain into mugs; garnish with cinnamon sticks.

∎

BEEFY TOMATO STARTER

Serves 2

⅓ cup beef boullion

1⅓ cups V-8 juice

2 teaspoons fresh lemon juice

¼ teaspoon celery salt

dash Worcestershire sauce

dash Louisiana-style hot sauce

celery sticks for garnish

Mix all ingredients in small saucepan. Bring to a boil, then lower heat and simmer 1 minute. Serve hot, garnished with celery sticks.

■

OLD-TIME HOT CHOCOLATE

Serves 2

⅓ cup sugar

1 tablespoon light brown sugar

¼ cup Dutch-process cocoa

2¼ cups milk

¼ teaspoon vanilla extract

pinch of salt

¼ cup whipped cream

shaved chocolate for garnish

Combine sugars, cocoa in a medium saucepan. Slowly add enough milk to form a smooth paste, then add rest of milk along with vanilla extract and salt. Cook over medium heat, stirring constantly until mixture is just about to boil. Pour into cups and garnish with dollops of whipped cream and shaved chocolate.

■

CORTÉS HOT CHOCOLATE

Serves 6

6 cups milk, divided

3 ounces Mexican chocolate
(Cortés and Ibarra are popular;
or substitute 3 ounces unsweetened chocolate,
½ cup sugar and 1 drop almond extract)

pinch cinnamon

pinch salt

cinnamon sticks for garnish

In medium saucepan bring ½ cup milk to a boil; break up chocolate and dissolve in milk, stirring, over low heat. Add remaining milk and slowly bring to a boil, stirring, adding cinnamon and salt when mixture is close to boiling.

Remove from heat and beat until frothy with a rotary beater or molinillo (a carved wooden beater twirled between the palms of the hands to froth chocolate).

Garnish each mugful of chocolate with a cinnamon stick.

Cook's Note: Pat's Aunt Dora and Uncle Ignacio Cortés have the Cortés Chocolate Company in San Juan, Puerto Rico. We always stock up on this delicious chocolate when we're visiting Puerto Rico.

■

HOT VANILLA

Serves 2

2 cups milk

4 teaspoons mild honey

1 teaspoon vanilla

cinnamon, allspice and nutmeg for sprinkling

Bring milk to boil in small saucepan; stir in honey. Beat to a froth with whisk or egg beater; pour mixture into large mugs. Stir in ½ teaspoon vanilla into each mug; sprinkle with spices and serve hot.

■

HERITAGE SPICED TEA

makes approximately 12 cups

2 lemons

1 orange

2½ sticks cinnamon, broken into pieces

1 tablespoon whole cloves

12 cups water, divided

3 tea bags

Squeeze lemons and orange, setting aside juice. Place rinds of fruits in top of double boiler, along with cinnamon, cloves, sugar and 4 cups water. Bring to a boil, cover, and let stand for one hour. In meantime, boil 8 cups water, remove from heat and add tea bags. Let steep 3 minutes. Remove teabags. Strain citrus-sugar mixture into tea; add reserved citrus juice. Serve hot in tea cups, garnished with floating thin lemon slices.

■

CAFE LATTÉ

Serves 4

1 cup very hot freshly-made espresso coffee

3 cups hot steamed milk

powdered sweet chocolate for topping

For each serving, rinse a heatproof 8 or 10-ounce glass with hot water. Pour in ¼ cup espresso and ¾ cup hot milk. Stir, then top with powdered chocolate.

■

VIENNESE MOCHA

Serves 2

¼ cup half and half

¾ cup milk

2 tablespoons sugar

2 teaspoons Dutch-process cocoa

¾ cup freshly brewed strong coffee

¼ cup whipped cream

cinnamon

In a small saucepan over medium heat, stir together half and half, milk, sugar, and cocoa until blended. Bring mixture to a boil, then add coffee. Pour mocha into mugs or cups and top with whipped cream.

■

APPLE-CINNAMON FRAPPÉ

Serves 4 to 5

2 cups apple juice

²/₃ cup milk

¼ cup B&B Liqueur

1 large banana, peeled

1 tablespoon fresh lemon juice

1 teaspoon ground cinnamon

1 teaspoon ground nutmeg

about 6 ice cubes

fresh mint and additional nutmeg for garnish

Blend all ingredients in blender for about 1 minute until pureed. Serve in frosted goblets. Garnish with a mint sprig and ground nutmeg.

Cook's Note: The liqueur can certainly be omitted, leaving still a delicious drink!

■

ARIZONA TANGERINE SMOOTHIE

Serves 6

2 cups fresh tangerine juice

1 cup fresh orange juice

½ cup half and half

2 bananas

½ cup orange sherbet

¾ cup crushed ice

Blend all ingredients in blender until well mixed. Serve in frosted goblets. Garnish with fresh strawberries.

Cook's Memory: With this recipe comes a beautiful memory of the fragrance of spring citrus blossoms driving down Camelback Road in Phoenix, AZ.

PEAR LIME FRAPPÉ

Serves 6

2 cups pear nectar

½ cup fresh lime juice

¼ cup fresh orange juice

1 cup whole milk

1 cup chopped, peeled fresh pears

1 banana

¾ cup crushed ice

fresh mint for garnish

Combine all ingredients in blender with crushed ice. Blend on high speed one minute. Serve in frosted, stemmed goblets, garnished with sprigs of fresh mint.

Cook's Note: This recipe originated to satisfy our St. Patrick's Day diners.

■

Fresh
&
Fruity
Starters

ARIZONA FRUIT PLATE

Serves 4

4 small bunches red seedless grapes

1 egg white, beaten to a froth

superfine granulated sugar

3 large oranges, peeled, seeded and sliced

8 Sphinx dates, pitted

8 large pecan halves

Dip grape bunches in egg white; roll to coat thoroughly, then shake off excess. Quickly dip in sugar, rolling to coat and shaking off excess. Place on baking sheet and chill 10 minutes.

Meantime, arrange other fruit; fan orange slices along one side of dessert plate. Stuff dates with pecans and arrange 2 on each plate. Garnish with grapes.

Cook's Memory: This fruit plate is reminiscent of the wonderful fresh fruit served at Camelback Inn in the winter. (Canned fruit was always taboo!) I am often homesick for date palms and citrus orchards and especially the scent of citrus blossoms in the spring.

■

HONEY CREAM FRUIT SKEWERS

Serves 8

2 kiwis, each peeled and cut into 8 wedges

¼ cantaloupe, cut into 8 chunks

¼ honeydew melon, cut into 8 chunks

¼ pineapple, cut into 8 chunks

8 strawberries

Honey Cream Sauce:

½ cup honey

¼ cup fresh lemon juice

¼ teaspoon paprika

½ cup heavy cream, whipped

Divide fruit among eight bamboo skewers, threading fruits so that kiwis wind up on both ends. Chill in refrigerator while you make Honey Cream Sauce.

Blend honey, lemon juice and paprika in small bowl. Fold in whipped cream, cover and chill before using.

■

CURAÇAO ORANGES AND KIWIS

Serves 4

2 large oranges, peeled and sliced

2 ripe kiwis, peeled and sliced

4 teaspoons Curaçao liqueur

fresh mint sprigs for garnish

For each serving, arrange orange and kiwi slices on dessert plate, fanning them out and alternating fruits. Sprinkle with Curaçao. Garnish with a fresh mint sprig.

■

CHAMPAGNE CANTALOUPE WITH BERRIES

Serves 4

2 small, ripe cantaloupes

1 half-pint raspberries

2 cups Champagne, chilled

2 tablespoons Chambord liqueur, optional

Cut cantaloupes in half. Scoop out seeds. Divide raspberries among the four halves. Pour ½ cup Champagne into each and, if desired, drizzle with Chambord.

■

HAWAIIAN MELANGE

Serves 4

1 ripe mango, peeled, pitted and diced

1 ripe papaya, peeled, seeds reserved, diced

1 ripe banana, peeled and sliced

¼ ripe pineapple, chunked

1 cup whipped cream

½ cup mayonnaise

1 starfruit, sliced

In medium bowl combine mango, payaya, banana and pineapple; chill 10 minutes.

In small bowl gently fold whipped cream into mayonnaise, then fold dressing into chilled fruit. Mound into footed glass dessert dishes and top with a starfruit slice and a sprinkle of papaya seeds.

■

HONEY NUT BANANAS

Serves 4

4 ripe, firm bananas

juice of 1 lemon

¾ cup mild honey

1 cup toasted peanuts or almonds, finely chopped in processor

Peel and cut bananas in half lengthwise; immediately coat with lemon juice. Dip each half in honey, then roll in nuts. Arrange 2 halves on each serving plate.

■

GINGER-HONEY PINEAPPLE BOATS

Serves 4

1 large pineapple, quartered lengthwise, leaves left on

½ teaspoon ground ginger

¼ teaspoon salt

¼ teaspoon paprika

¼ cup vegetable oil

2 tablespoons lemon juice

1½ tablespoons honey

lime slices for garnish

For each serving, cut flesh from pineapple rind in one piece, then slice crosswise into 8 pieces; chill.

Into jar with lid place ginger, salt, paprika, oil, lemon juice and honey. Shake well to mix.

Serve each pineapple quarter with 2 tablespoons dressing; garnish with lime slices.

■

STRAWBERRIES ZABAGLIONE

Serves 6

1 quart strawberries, washed and chopped

4 egg yolks

3 tablespoons sugar

¼ cup Grand Marnier liqueur

½ cup heavy cream, whipped

Divide strawberries among 6 stemmed balloon wine glasses; chill.

Beat egg yolks with whisk in top saucepan of double boiler until thick and lemon-colored. (You may use a portable electric mixer, if desired.) Gradually add sugar, beating (or whisking) until mixture is fluffy and mounds when whisk or beater is raised. Place double boiler saucepan over simmering water; slowly add Grand Marnier. Continue beating until mixture is airy and mounds, about 5 minutes. Remove from heat and set in pan of ice-cold water. Continue beating until mixture cools. Gently fold in whipped cream. Refrigerate until ready to serve.

Mound zabaglione over strawberries; serve immediately.

■

ORANGE SURPRISE

Serves 4

2 bananas, sliced

juice of 1 orange

1 cup fresh or frozen strawberries

2 tablespoons sour cream

1 egg white

½ cup whipped cream

1 tablespoon Grand Marnier

4 oranges, pulp removed
and shells cut with jigsaw edges

orange sections for garnish

Into blender container put bananas, orange juice, strawberries, sour cream, egg white, whipped cream and Grand Marnier. Blend on high speed until ingredients are pureed.

Pour fruit mixture into prepared orange shells and freeze until slushy. Garnish with orange sections.

■

FRESH FRUIT GRANOLA PARFAIT

Serves 6

6 medium strawberries, sliced

½ cup blueberries

1 banana, sliced

2 cups plain yogurt

3 tablespoons honey

1½ cups Granola

Mix fruits in small bowl. Divide half the fruit among 6 parfait glasses or stemmed goblets. Top with half the yogurt mixed with honey, then half the granola. Repeat layers, ending with granola on top.

■

GRANOLA

Makes 10 cups

¾ cup vegetable oil

¼ cup honey

1 cup packed brown sugar

1 teaspoon vanilla

½ teaspoon salt

8 cups rolled (not quick) oats

¾ cup almonds, toasted

½ cup sunflower seeds, toasted

½ cup flaked (dry) cocoanut

Preheat oven to 325 degrees.

In medium saucepan stir together oil, honey, brown sugar, vanilla and salt. Heat, stirring until brown sugar melts. Oil and sugar will remain separate.

In very large bowl stir together oats, toasted nuts, sunflower seeds and cocoanut. Pour on liquids, stirring well to distribute. You may need to use your hands.

Spread mixture onto foil-lined baking pans. Bake 10-15 minutes at 325 degrees, stirring often, until cereal is golden brown. Allow to cool thoroughly before storing in airtight container.

■

SOUR CREAM AMBROSIA

Serves 6

3 oranges, peeled and sectioned

½ pound green seedless grapes

½ cantaloupe, chunked

¼ pineapple, chunked

½ cup shredded moist cocoanut

¼ cup pecans, chopped

1 cup sour cream

1 tablespoon honey

¼ teaspoon vanilla

pomegranate seeds for garnish

In medium bowl mix fruits, cocoanut and pecans. Stir together sour cream, honey and vanilla and mix well into fruits. Serve in footed glass dessert dishes, garnished with pomegranate seeds.

∎

MOTHER'S SUMMER JELLIED FRUIT

Serves 4-5

2 envelopes unflavored gelatin

¼ cup sugar

1½ cups fresh orange juice

½ cup fresh lemon juice

3 bananas, sliced

2 peaches or nectarines, peeled and sliced

1 cup green seedless grapes

2 plums, pitted and sliced

2 teaspoons Grand Marnier

½ cup whipped cream

1 teaspoon grated orange rind

In medium bowl stir together gelatin and sugar. In small saucepan heat citrus juices to just below boiling; pour into gelatin and stir well to dissolve. Pour mixture into a 1½-quart glass bowl. Chill 30 minutes, or until gelatin is semi-set. Add fruit and stir gently. Chill until firm.

Fold Grand Marnier into whipped cream. Serve jellied fruit in footed glass goblets topped with a dollop of cream and a sprinkling of orange rind.

Cook's Memory: When Camelback was closed during the summer months, Mother prepared dinner once a week at our summer house in La Jolla. We especially enjoyed her jellied fruit, served either as a salad or dessert. The leftovers were always gobbled up as a snack or breakfast. During my brother's lifeguard days, he would have no trouble eating the amount of the above-mentioned recipe in one sitting!

∎

POACHED PEARS WITH RASPBERRY SAUCE

Serves 6

6 firm ripe pears
(Bartletts are particularly good)

¼ cup lemon juice

2 cups fresh or frozen raspberries

1 cup fresh orange juice

½ cup lime juice

¾ cup powdered sugar

mint leaves for garnish

Poach the pears: peel and core pears, leaving stems intact. Cut a thin slice off bottom of each pear and stand them upright in a large saucepan. Add lemon juice, then add cold water to cover pears. Bring to a boil; reduce heat and simmer, covered, until pears are tender, about 25 minutes. Drain and chill at least 3 hours.

Make the sauce: put raspberries, orange juice, lime juice and powdered sugar in blender. Blend on high speed 1 minute, or until pureed.

Place each pear in a low glass dessert dish. Pour about ⅓ cup raspberry sauce over each; garnish by inserting stem of mint leaf at base of each pear stem.

■

BROILED ORANGE SLICES

Serves 4

2 large oranges

2 tablespoons butter

2 tablespoons packed light brown sugar

½ teaspoon curry powder

Preheat oven broiler.

Slice off ends of oranges; slice each fruit into 4 ½-inch slices. Lay slices on greased baking sheet. Dot with butter, then sprinkle with brown sugar and curry powder.

Broil slices 6 inches from heat source about 4 minutes, or until sugar is bubbly.

■

BROILED GRAPEFRUIT

Serves 6

3 Texas ruby-red or Indian River
pink grapefruit

¾ cup packed light brown sugar

Preheat oven broiler.

Cut grapefruit in half and separate fruit from membranes using serrated grapefruit knife or small paring knife. Sieve about 2 tablespoons brown sugar over each half.

Broil halves 6 inches from heat until topping is bubbly.

Variation: Sprinkle each half with 2 teaspoons Amaretto before broiling.

■

BROILED CINNAMON PEARS

Serves 6

½ cup packed brown sugar

⅛ teaspoon cloves

¼ teaspoon nutmeg

3 ripe pears, peeled, halved and cored

½ stick butter, melted

½ cup heavy cream

cinnamon for garnish

Preheat oven broiler.

In small bowl combine brown sugar, cloves and nutmeg, stirring well. Place pear halves round-side-down in buttered baking dish. Brush generously with butter, then sprinkle with brown sugar mixture.

Broil pears 6-8 inches from heat 3-4 minutes, or until brown sugar is bubbly and caramelized.

Remove from heat, place on serving plates and spoon cream into pear halves. Dust with cinnamon and serve hot.

■

AMARETTO PEAR COMPOTE

Serves 4

4 pears, peeled, cored and chopped

¼ cup packed dark brown sugar

juice of 2 oranges

juice of 1 lime

¼ cup water

1 teaspoon cinnamon

3 tablespoons Amaretto liqueur

½ cup heavy cream, whipped

¼ cup sliced toasted almonds

In medium saucepan combine pears, brown sugar, citrus juices, water and cinnamon. Simmer, stirring occasionally, for about 30 minutes, or until pears are very tender. Mash pears with a fork until sauce is chunky. Add Amaretto.

Serve warm, topped with whipped cream and sliced almonds.

■

WARM CURRIED FRUIT COMPOTE

Serves 8

1 15-ounce can peach halves

1 small can pineapple chunks

1 6-ounce bag dried apricots

1 cup prunes

1 cup dried apple rings

1 cup packed dark brown sugar

1-1½ teaspoons curry powder, to taste

½ stick butter

Drain peaches and pineapple into small saucepan. Set aside fruit; bring juices to a boil. Remove from heat and add apricots, prunes and apple rings; let soak about a half hour.

Mix fruits in buttered 2-quart baking dish. Sprinkle with brown sugar, then with curry. Dot with butter.

Bake at 350 degrees 30-35 minutes, or until bubbly and sugar has caramelized. Spoon into footed dessert dishes and serve warm.

Cook's Note: This is a perfect fall brunch dish, deeply satisfying and a good complement to hearty dishes and hearty appetites!

■

PAT'S CINNAMON BANANAS

Serves 4

juice of 1 lemon

2 tablespoons milk

4 ripe, firm bananas

1 cup cornflake or other cereal crumbs

2 teaspoons cinnamon

2 tablespoons sugar

butter for sautéing

orange and kiwi slices for garnish

In low, wide bowl mix lemon juice and milk. Peel bananas and slice in half lengthwise; immediately place in bowl and coat with lemon juice mixture. Set aside.

In plastic bag mix cornflake crumbs, cinnamon and sugar. One by one, shake banana halves in bag to coat with crumbs. Refrigerate coated banana uncovered for 15 minutes.

In large sauté pan heat butter over medium-high heat. Sauté bananas until browned and crispy, gently turning once. Arrange 2 halves on each plate; garnish with orange and kiwi slices.

■

APPLESAUCE COMPOTE

Serves 6

6 medium red or green cooking apples. peeled and diced

2 teaspoons cinnamon

1/4 teaspoon nutmeg

1/4 teaspoon allspice

1/2 stick butter

1/4 cup half and half

1 cup whipped cream for topping

Bring apples and 1 cup water to a boil in medium saucepan; cover and cook on low heat until tender. Drain.

Using potato masher, mash apples into a chunky puree. Add cinnamon, nutmeg, allspice, vanilla and butter; stir to mix and melt butter. Add half and half.

Serve warm in stemmed compote dishes, topped with whipped cream and a sprinkle of nutmeg.

■

BAKED GRANOLA APPLES

Serves 4

4 Macintosh. Granny Smith or other cooking apples

cinnamon

1/2 cup Granola (see page 26)

approximately 3 tablespoons butter

1 tablespoon currants

2 tablespoons packed light brown sugar

heavy cream for pouring

Preheat oven to 375 degrees; generously butter 4 6 x 6-inch squares of aluminum foil.

Core apples and make a cross-like cut about halfway through them; gently pull quarters out to enlarge openings.

Sprinkle apples with cinnamon. Place each on a square of foil; bring foil halfway up sides to form a cup with edges. Divide half the granola among apples; top with a teaspoon butter for each. Sprinkle currants on butter, then sprinkle on remainder of granola. Divide brown sugar among apples; top each with another teaspoon butter.

Arrange apples in large baking dish; carefully pour in boiling water around apples to reach about halfway up; try to avoid pouring water inside foil cups.

Bake at 375 degrees for 50 minutes to 1 hour. or until apples are tender when pierced with fork. Serve warm with heavy cream.

■

BRANDIED APPLE DUMPLINGS

Serves 4

2 cups all-purpose flour

2 teaspoons baking powder

¼ teaspoon baking soda

1 teaspoon salt

1 tablespoon sugar

¼ cup shortening

⅔-¾ cup milk

4 medium-size red baking apples (McIntosh or Roman Beauty are nice), cored but not peeled

¼ cup packed light brown sugar

3 tablespoons butter

¾ teaspoon cinnamon

1 tablespoon brandy

Hard Sauce for topping warm dumplings

Preheat oven to 350 degrees. Generously grease a baking sheet.

Into medium mixing bowl sift flour, baking powder, baking soda, salt and sugar. Using fingers or pastry blender, cut in shortening until mixture resembles coarse meal. Stir in milk just until dry ingredients are moistened.

Turn out onto floured surface and knead 6 times. Roll out to 12x12-inch square; cut into four 6x6-inch squares.

For each dumpling, place an apple on a dough square. Stuff with 1 tablespoon brown sugar, then with generous 2 teaspoons butter. Sprinkle with cinnamon, then with brandy.

Draw corners of dough up to meet at top of apple.

Twist corners together and seal seams. Prick all over with a fork. Brush with milk, if desired, and sprinkle with sugar for crisp, shiny crust.

Bake apples at 350 degrees for 30-35 minutes, or until golden brown. Serve warm topped with a generous dollop of Hard Sauce.

HARD SAUCE

¼ stick unsalted butter, very soft but not melted

¾ cup sifted powdered sugar

¼ teaspoon vanilla

1 teaspoon brandy

In small mixing bowl beat butter with electric hand mixer until light and fluffy. Add powdered sugar 1 tablespoon at a time, beating after each addition until light and fluffy. Beat in vanilla and brandy, drop by drop. Sauce should be fairly solid, but still spoonable.

■

CAMELBACK INN'S BANANA DAINTIES

Serves 4 to 6

4 very ripe bananas

2 cups whipped cream

½ tablespoon orange or lemon juice

sugar

fresh fruit for garnish (cherries, peaches,etc.)

Peel and scrape bananas. Put through strainer. Add juice. Mix very lightly and then fold in whipped cream. Sugar to taste. Serve in glasses and garnish with sections of fruit.

■

CRANBERRY APPLESAUCE

Serves 10

1 cup sugar

1 cup water

2 cups cranberries

1 ¼ cups sugar

2 cups water

¼ teaspoon cinnamon

8 medium apples, peeled and cut into wedges

Boil together for 5 minutes the 1 cup of sugar and water. Add cranberries and cook until the skins pop making sure not to overcook. Set aside.

In large pan, boil sugar, water and cinnamon 10 minutes (do not boil hard). Add apples and cook until tender. Set aside to cool slightly. Stir together.

■

LEMON SPANISH CREAM

Serves 4 to 6

½ cup sugar

1 envelope unflavored gelatin

⅛ teaspoon salt

1 ¼ cups milk

3 eggs

⅓ cup lemon juice

2 teaspoons lemon rind, grated

Mix sugar, gelatin and salt and put in top of double boiler. Stir in milk and place on medium heat for about 3-6 minutes until gelatin dissolves. Set aside.

Separate eggs. Beat yolks with fork in medium bowl. Gradually stir hot milk mixture into yolks. Pour mixture back into top of double boiler and cook over hot (not boiling) water stirring constantly until mixture forms a thin coating on a metal spoon (about 10 minutes.)

Remove mixture from heat. Stir in lemon juice and rind. Chill until thick, but not set. Beat egg whites until stiff; fold into custard mixture. Pour into 1-quart mold; chill until firm. Remove from mold and garnish with orange sections, fresh strawberries and mint sprigs.

■

PLUM MOUSSE WITH CRÈME ANGLAIS

Serves 6 to 8

2 envelopes unflavored gelatin

6 plums

lemon juice from 2 lemons

½ cup cranberry juice

5 eggs, separated

1 cup sugar, divided

1 cup heavy cream, whipped

Crème Anglaise

Sprinkle gelatin over lemon juice and let soften (about 10 minutes). Add cranberry juice and stir over low heat until gelatin is dissolved. Set aside.

Peel and slice 3 plums. In blender or food processor, combine plums and gelatin mixture; puree.

In medium bowl beat egg yolks with ½ cup sugar. Slowly add pureed mixture and stir. In another bowl beat egg whites until stiff. Beat ½ cup sugar into egg whites. Stir egg whites into pureed mixture and then fold in whipped cream.

Chill mousse at least 3 hours. Serve with Crème Anglaise and garnish with remaining sliced plums and fresh mint sprigs.

CRÈME ANGLAISE

2½ cups milk

1 vanilla bean

¾ cup sugar

6 egg yolks

2½ teaspoons cornstarch

Boil milk with vanilla bean for about a minute, and then remove the vanilla bean. Beat sugar and egg yolks together until thick. Add the cornstarch. Slowly add the boiled milk. Continue mixing until blended. In heavy enameled saucepan, cook mixture over low heat stirring constantly until sauce thickens (or will coat the back of a spoon). Do not let sauce boil. Strain through a sieve and refrigerate.

Cook's Memory: One of my most favorite desserts of my mom's was a version of this made with grape juice Try it that way too!

■

ORANGE MOUSSE PARFAIT WITH BANANAS AND BLACKBERRY SAUCE

Serves 4 to 6

1 cup fresh orange juice, strained

8 tablespoons sugar (divided)

1 envelope unflavored gelatin

3 eggs, separated

3 tablespoons fresh lemon juice

1 cup chilled whipped cream

3 bananas, sliced

Sprinkle gelatin over lemon juice and let soften (about 10 minutes). Add orange juice and stir over simmering water in double boiler until gelatin is dissolved. Cool.

In another bowl, beat egg yolks with 4 tablespoons sugar. Add gelatin mixture and stir. Beat egg whites until stiff with 4 tablespoons of sugar. Add whipped cream to egg yolk mixture and fold in meringue. Chill about 2 hours.

Layer sliced bananas and mousse in parfait glasses with Blackberry Sauce ribboning through. Garnish with fresh blackberries and mint sprigs.

BLACKBERRY SAUCE

Makes 1 ½ cups

1 10-oz. Package frozen blackberries, thawed

2 tablespoons lemon juice

2 tablespoons powdered sugar

In blender combine berries, lemon juice and sugar. Strain to remove seeds.

■

GRANDMA SHOE'S OMELET

Makes 4 omelets

8 eggs, separated

pinch of salt

¼ cup red currant jelly

1 cup grated Cheddar cheese

1 tablespoon powdered sugar for garnish

Preheat oven to 400 degrees. Butter 4 small (6-inch) cast iron skillets.

Beat egg whites until stiff, not dry, peaks form. Beat yolks with salt, then fold in whites. Divide eggs among the four skillets. Cook on medium heat about 4-5 minutes, or until a lifted edge is browned.

With a spoon make a small cavity in the middle of each omelet; into each drop a spoonful of currant jelly. Sprinkle cheese over omelets and transfer to oven.

Bake about 10 minutes, or until eggs are set and slightly puffed. Invert omelets onto warmed plates and dust with powdered sugar.

Cook's Memory: "Grandma Shoe" was my mother's mother, Mabel Shoemaker. She and I shared a room from the time I was about four until I was six, so we became great pals. She was bedridden with arthritis by that time, but that didn't prevent us from talking constantly. She would tell me about the omelets she loved to make, and about how she made everyone tiptoe past the oven so her masterpieces wouldn't fall! The above recipe is my interpretation of one Grandma Shoe might have made.

■

OMELET PAT

Makes 4 omelets

½ 10-ounce package frozen spinach, cooked according to package directions, drained and squeezed dry in paper towels

4 ounces cream cheese, softened

1 clove garlic, minced

½ teaspoon salt

pinch pepper

1 tablespoon chopped cilantro

½ cup (2 ounces) grated Monterey jack cheese

½ stick unsalted butter, divided

10 eggs, beaten

cilantro sprigs for garnish

In medium bowl combine spinach, cream cheese, garlic, salt, pepper, cilantro and cheese, beating well to blend; set aside.

Melt 1 tablespoon butter in omelet pan over medium-high heat until foaming subsides. Pour in ¼ beaten eggs and allow to set 30 seconds. Lift edges of omelet, allowing uncooked egg to run underneath.

Spoon ¼ of spinach filling along center of omelet; cover pan and turn off heat. Allow to set 30 seconds. Fold omelet sides over center and flip onto heated plate. Repeat with other 3 omelets. Garnish with cilantro sprigs.

Cook's Memory: My husband's many recipes are scattered throughout the cookbook. Self-taught in the kitchen, Pat is very creative and loves to cook. His love for garlic (and olive oil too) came from his summers spent in Puerto Rico. Pat is always "Chef" for our weekend brunches.

■

STRAWBERRY OMELET

Serves 4

8 eggs

4 teaspoons butter

8 large fresh strawberries, sliced

½ cup sour cream

¼ cup packed light brown sugar

fresh lemon juice for sprinkling

sifted powdered sugar for topping

Beat eggs just until whites and yolks combine. For each omelet, melt 1 teaspoon butter in 6-inch omelet pan and swirl to cover bottom and sides. Pour in ¼ egg mixture and allow to set 45 seconds. Lift up edges and let uncooked egg run underneath. When omelet has set, arrange 2 slices strawberries in fan shape around edge of half the omelet. Spoon 2 tablespoons sour cream on top, then sprinkle with 1 tablespoon brown sugar. Fold unfilled half over, then slide out onto warmed plate. Sprinkle with a few drops lemon juice; dust with powdered sugar.

∎

SPINACH-BACON OMELET WITH HOLLANDAISE

Makes 4 omelets

1 10-ounce package frozen chopped spinach

8 slices bacon, fried crisp, drained, then processed until finely chopped

1 dozen eggs

4 tablespoons parsley, finely chopped

4 teaspoons butter for greasing pan

parsley for garnish

Hollandaise Sauce

Cook spinach in ¼ cup water in covered saucepan just until it breaks apart with fork. Cook another minute; drain, cool slightly, then squeeze spinach in paper towels to remove most of liquid. Chop through spinach several times.

Combine spinach, bacon, eggs and parsley in medium bowl, beating well to mix completely.

Melt one teaspoon butter in omelet pan until foaming subsides. Pour in ¼ of the spinach-egg mixture and allow to set 45 seconds to 1 minute. Lift edges all around, allowing uncooked egg to run underneath. When omelet is cooked, fold in half and slide at once onto warmed plate. Repeat 3 times. Pour about 2 tablespoons Hollandaise Sauce along center of each omelet. Garnish with parsley.

HOLLANDAISE SAUCE

½ cup butter, lightly salted

juice of ½ lemon

2 tablespoons water

4 egg yolks

pinch of cayenne pepper

In the top of a double boiler melt butter; add lemon juice and water. Add egg yolks. Make sure your double boiler pot does not touch the hot water. Whisk ingredients until thickened. Add cayenne, stir and serve immediately.

Cook's Note: This is our version of the famous omelet served at Clyde's, a landmark eatery in Georgetown.

∎

HEARTY PANCETTA POTATO OMELET

Serves 4

2 ¼-inch slices pancetta
(Italian cured, unsmoked rolled bacon),
diced, or 8 slices hickory-smoked bacon, diced

4 small new potatoes, boiled in their jackets,
sliced ¼-inch thick

2 green onions, thinly sliced,
including some green tops

¼ teaspoon pepper

½ teaspoon salt

8 eggs

4 teaspoons butter

In medium sauté pan over medium heat sauté pancetta or bacon until crisp. Remove from pan and drain pan of all but 3 tablespoons fat. Over medium-high heat sauté potatoes and onions in fat until crusty and browned. Season with pepper and salt. Set aside.

In medium mixing bowl beat eggs just to combine yolks and whites. For each omelet, melt 1 teaspoon butter in 6-inch omelet pan, swirling to cover sides and bottom. Pour in ¼ of beaten eggs. Allow to set, then lift edges to allow uncooked egg to run underneath. When eggs are nearly set, spoon on ¼ of filling. Fold omelet and slide onto warmed plate.

■

GIGI'S CHILE CON QUESO OMELET

Serves 4

1 medium onion, chopped

1 clove garlic, minced

2 tablespoons butter, divided

1 16-ounce can whole tomatoes, drained and chopped

1 4-ounce can chopped green chiles, drained

1 tablespoon all-purpose flour

½ cup half and half

salt and cayenne pepper to taste

¼ pound (1 cup) shredded mild Cheddar cheese

12 eggs

chopped cilantro and jalapeño slices
for garnish

Sauté onion and garlic in 1 tablespoon butter until transparent; add tomatoes and simmer until thick, about 15 minutes. Add chiles; set aside.

In small saucepan melt remaining 1 tablespoon butter; add flour and stir over medium heat 4 minutes. Gradually add half and half, stirring until mixture is smooth and thick. Season to taste with salt and cayenne; handful by handful add the cheese, stirring between additions to smooth.

Stir the cheese mixture into the tomatoes and chiles; cover and set aside.

For each omelet; pour ¼ beaten eggs into seasoned omelet pan over medium-high heat. Let set 1 minute, then lift edges all around, allowing uncooked egg to run underneath. Fill each omelet with chile con queso, fold in half and transfer to serving plate. Top with more chile con queso, chopped cilantro and jalapeño slices.

Cook's Note: I have tasted Chile Con Queso made many different ways, but Gigi's is always tops!

■

MORAVIAN FRITTATA

Serves 6

1 large potato, baked at 425 degrees, 55 minutes

1 large cooking apple (Roman Beauty or Macintosh is good)

2 tablespoons olive oil

1 tablespoon butter

2 scallions, finely sliced

1 teaspoon sugar

¾ teaspoon salt

½ teaspoon pepper

6 eggs

½ cup milk

Cheddar Sauce (see recipe page 65)

fresh unpeeled apple slices for garnish

Preheat oven to 350 degrees.

Coarsely chop potato and apple. In medium ovenproof skillet, heat olive oil and butter over medium-high heat. Add scallions and sauté 1 minute. Add potato, apple and sugar and sauté, stirring often until nicely browned. Mix in salt and pepper.

In small bowl beat eggs with milk. Pour over vegetable-fruit sauté. Bake at 350 degrees 30-35 minutes, or until eggs are set and frittata is slightly puffed. Cut into wedges and serve with Cheddar Sauce. Garnish with a fan of fresh apple slices.

Cook's Note: My cousin, Joannie, recently visited her daughter in North Carolina and came back with descriptions of this wonderful frittata.

■

FRITTATA CON COZZE-BIG SUR MUSSEL OMELET

Serves 2-4

1½ dozen small mussels

½ cup water

1 slice lemon

3 tablespoons olive oil

2 scallions or 1 small leek, chopped

1 clove garlic, minced

½ teaspoon dried chervil (or 1 tablespoon fresh)

4 eggs

salt and freshly ground pepper to taste

Scrub the mussels. Place them in a pot with water and lemon. Cook over high heat for 5-7 minutes. Remove the mussels as they open. Do not overcook.

Heat 2 tablespoons of the oil in a skillet and slowly saute the scallions and garlic until wilted. Stir in the shelled mussels and chervil. Beat the eggs in a bowl with the salt and pepper.

Stir the mussel mixture into the eggs. Heat the remaining tablespoon of oil in a small skillet until quite hot. Add the egg mixture. Lower heat and cook slowly until golden on the bottom and firm enough to turn. Flip the omelet and continue to cook until the omelet is set, but still moist within. This can be eaten hot or at room temperature. To serve, cut into wedges.

Cook's Note: My friend, Ciss, fixes this frittata at her home in Big Sur where she often gathers fresh mussels. She recommends it served with crusty French bread, sweet butter and a salad of sliced beefsteak tomatoes, fresh basil, marjoram, cracked black pepper and a good olive oil.

■

CHICKEN MOUSSE FRITTATA

Serves 6

2 chicken breasts, skinned, boned,
coarsely chopped

¼ cup cream

½ teaspoon salt

¼ teaspoon pepper

pinch nutmeg

4 eggs, divided

1 cup milk

1 tablespoon butter

3 large or 4 medium shallots, thinly sliced

1 small zucchini, cut into 1½ x ⅛-inch julienne

1 carrot, cut into 1½ x ⅛-inch julienne

Spinach-Watercress Sauce

Preheat oven to 325 degrees. Generously grease an 8 or 9-inch round layer cake pan.

Combine chicken breasts and cream in bowl of food processor outfitted with steel knife. Process until chicken is pureed; add salt, pepper, nutmeg and egg yolks. Process to combine. Replace top and process, pouring milk through feed tube until mixture is smooth. Set aside.

Melt butter in medium sauté pan. Sauté shallots, zucchini and carrot 4 minutes. Arrange vegetables on bottom of prepared pan.

In medium mixing bowl beat egg whites until stiff but not dry. Fold into chicken mixture. Pour chicken over vegetables, smoothing top.

Set cake pan into larger pan and fill with 1 inch of water. Carefully transfer to oven. Bake at 325 degrees for 25-35 minutes, or until set and slightly puffed. Remove from water bath and allow to cool 7 minutes. Then unmold onto platter. Cut into 6 wedges and serve each with a generous dollop of Spinach-Watercress Sauce.

SPINACH-WATERCRESS SAUCE

1 10-ounce package frozen spinach, cooked just until spinach is thoroughly heated, then squeezed dry in paper towels

handful watercress leaves

2 tablespoons olive oil

½ teaspoon Dijon mustard

½ teaspoon dried basil

½ teaspoon tarragon

2 teaspoons lemon juice

1 tablespoon chopped chives

1 small shallot, coarsely chopped

1 anchovy filet or ½ teaspoon anchovy paste

¼ teaspoon Tabasco sauce

6 tablespoons whipping cream

Combine all ingredients in blender container and blend on high speed until pureed, scraping down sides often.

Cook's Note: This is a featherlight concoction, perhaps more "mousse" than frittata.

■

VEGETARIAN BRUNCH TORTE

Serves 6

8 eggs

½ cup milk

1½ cups cream cheese, softened

¼ cup roasted, salted sunflower seeds

½ teaspoon finely chopped parsley

½ teaspoon chives

½ teaspoon oregano

cherry tomatoes for garnish

Preheat oven to 350 degrees. Grease three 9-inch pie plates.

Beat eggs well; add milk and blend. Divide egg mixture equally among pie plates. Bake at 350 degrees for 15 minutes, or until eggs have set. Cool 5 minutes.

Beat cream cheese with sunflower seeds, parsley, chives and oregano.

Unmold the 3 baked omelets. Place one on warmed platter. Spread with half the cream cheese mixture. Top with second omelet, spread- ing other half of cream cheese on top of that. Top with third omelet.

Cut torte into wedges and serve immediately, garnishing with cherry tomatoes.

Cook's Note: Our vegetarian guests also like this torte filled with cream cheese and jam.

■

QUICHE LORRAINE CUPS

Serves 4

4 Basic Crepes (see page 130)

1 small onion. finely chopped and sauteed in 1½ teaspoons butter

4 slices bacon, fried crisp and crumbled

1 cup (¼ pound) grated Gruyère or Emmenthaler cheese

2 tablespoons all-purpose flour

¼ teaspoon salt

¼ teaspoon nutmeg

¼ teaspoon pepper

3 eggs, beaten

1½ cups milk

orange and grapefruit segments for garnish

Preheat oven to 350 degrees. Generously butter 4 small ovenproof bowls.

Fit cooled crepes into prepared bowls, forming tulip-shaped cups. Divide the onion and bacon among cups. Over that sprinkle cheese.

In medium mixing bowl stir together flour, salt, nutmeg and pepper. Beat in eggs and milk to form smooth custard. Divide among cups.

Bake at 350 degrees for 25-30 minutes. or just until quiche filling is firm. Cool 5 minutes before gently slipping cups out of bowls. Garnish with fruit segments.

■

POTATO BROCCOLI QUICHE

Serves 6

1 large baking potato

1 10-ounce package frozen broccoli spears

2 tablespoons butter

1 medium onion, finely chopped

1 clove garlic, minced

¼ red bell pepper, finely diced

3 tablespoons fresh homemade
or commercial salsa

2 tablespoons finely chopped parsley

1½ cups half and half

3 eggs

1 cup (¼ pound) grated Cheddar cheese

1 9-inch pie shell, blind-baked
at 450 degrees for 7 minutes

Cut potato into quarters and bring to a boil in small saucepan with just enough salted water to cover. Boil, covered, for 20 minutes or until tender. Set aside.

In another small saucepan bring broccoli to a boil with 2 tablespoons water. Cover and cook just long enough to separate and heat broccoli through. Drain and chop coarsely; set aside. Preheat oven to 375 degrees.

Melt butter in small sauté pan. Sauté onion and garlic until transparent; add red pepper and sauté another minute.

In medium bowl combine potatoes, broccoli, sautéed vegetables, salsa and parsley. Correct seasonings and spoon into prebaked pie shell. In small bowl beat half and half with eggs. Sprinkle

Cheddar over vegetables in pie shell and pour custard over all.

Bake quiche at 375 degrees for 50 minutes to an hour, or until top is browned and knife inserted at center comes out clean.

■

SWISS SHIRRED EGGS

Serves 4

2 tablespoons butter

½ pound ham, finely chopped

1 medium onion, finely chopped

½ cup finely chopped parsley

1½ cups (6 ounces) grated Swiss or Jarlsberg
cheese, divided

4 eggs

1 cup Basic White Sauce

2 tablespoons Parmesan cheese

½ teaspoon nutmeg

apple slices dipped in lemon
for garnish

Preheat oven to 375 degrees. Generously grease 4 individual ovenproof ramekins.

In medium sauté pan melt butter; sauté ham and onion 4 minutes; turn off heat and stir in parsley.

Divide ham mixture among ramekins, then top with 1 cup grated Swiss cheese. Make a well in center of each; break an egg gently into each.

Bake eggs at 375 degree for 15 minutes, or until eggs have set and cheese is melted and bubbly.

Heat White Sauce in small saucepan; gradually add remaining ½ cup Swiss cheese, whisking between additions to keep sauce smooth. Add Parmesan and nutmeg. Top baked eggs with Swiss cheese sauce and garnish each with apple slices.

BASIC WHITE SAUCE

Makes about 1 cup

2 tablespoons butter

2 tablespoons all-purpose flour

1 cup milk

salt, white pepper, nutmeg
and cayenne pepper, to taste

In small saucepan melt butter over medium-high heat; stir in flour and cook, stirring occasionally, 4 minutes. Whisk in milk gradually, cooking until thickened. Add seasonings.

■

TOMATO-BAKED EGGS

Serves 6

6 medium, ripe tomatoes

salt and pepper

6 eggs

Blender Bearnaise for topping

fresh tarragon sprigs
and black olives for garnish

Preheat oven to 375 degrees. Butter a baking sheet.

Slice off tops of tomatoes and scoop out pulp, leaving ¼-inch thick shell. Drain upside down 5 minutes, then sprinkle insides with salt and pepper.

Carefully break an egg into each shell. Bake on prepared sheet for 25-30 minutes, or until egg whites have set and tomato shells are tender.

Top with generous spoonful of Blender Bernaise and garnish with tarragon sprigs and black olives.

BLENDER BERNAISE

Makes about 2 cups

10 egg yolks

2 tablespoons tarragon vinegar

½ teaspoon salt

⅛ teaspoon cayenne pepper

1 teaspoon dried tarragon, divided

2 sticks unsalted butter

1 shallot, minced

Combine egg yolks, vinegar, salt, cayenne and ½ teaspoon tarragon in blender container. Blend on high speed 30 seconds.

In small saucepan melt butter. Add shallot and sauté until transparent. Turn blender on and add melted butter through top, at first a few drops at a time, then in thin stream once mixture "catches" (emulsifies); "catching" will take about a minute. When sauce is thickened, stir in remaining ½ teaspoon tarragon. Serve warm.

■

BAKED EGGS ITALIANO

Serves 6

½ stick butter

3 medium zucchini, coarsely chopped

½ pound mushrooms, sliced

2 cloves garlic, minced

½ pound bulk breakfast sausage

¼ teaspoon basil

¼ teaspoon Italian seasoning

salt and pepper to taste

2 cups (½ pound) grated Mozzarella cheese

6 eggs

Preheat oven to 375 degrees. Generously grease 6 individual ovenproof ramekins.

In medium sauté pan melt butter; add zucchini, mushrooms and garlic and sauté 4 minutes, or until zucchini chunks are crisp-tender. Drain, transfer to medium bowl and set aside.

In same sauté pan slowly cook sausage until browned, breaking up large chunks with a fork. Drain off grease and add sausage to vegetable mixture; add spices, salt and pepper.

Divide mixture among prepared ramekins; make a depression in middle of each and into it carefully break an egg. Sprinkle ramekins with cheese.

Bake at 375 degrees for 10 minutes, or until eggs have set. Top with Marinara Sauce.

MARINARA SAUCE

1 tablespoon good quality olive oil

2 tablespoons chopped onion

½ clove garlic, minced

¼ green pepper, finely chopped

1 15-ounce can whole tomatoes, drained and coarsely chopped

1 7-ounce can tomato sauce

2 tablespoons red wine

pinch sugar

¼ teaspoon fennel seeds, crushed

¼ teaspoon oregano

salt and pepper to taste

Heat olive oil in medium sauté pan over medium-high heat. Add onion, garlic and green pepper and sauté until transparent, about 1 minute. Transfer to medium saucepan and add tomatoes, tomato sauce and wine. Simmer over low heat 5 minutes; add sugar, fennel, oregano, salt and pepper. Let simmer another ½ hour, or until sauce is thickened.

■

BAKED EGGS CARUSO

Serves 4

2 tablespoons olive oil

1 clove garlic, minced

½ pound chicken livers, coarsely chopped

3 ribs celery, cut into ¼-inch slices

½ green pepper, coarsely chopped

1 medium onion, coarsely chopped

1 15-ounce can Italian pear or regular tomatoes, coarsely chopped, juice reserved

¾ teaspoon thyme

pinch sage

salt and pepper to taste

4 eggs

Caruso Sauce

Preheat oven to 400 degrees. Generously grease 4 small ovenproof ramekins.

In medium sauté pan heat oil over medium-high heat. Sauté garlic 1 minute, then add chicken livers and turn heat to medium. Let livers sauté without turning 4 minutes, or until almost cooked through. Stir, then add celery, green pepper and onion; cook, stirring often, 7-8 minutes, or until vegetables are crisp-tender.

Add tomatoes, tomato juice, thyme and sage; stir and cook over medium heat until most of liquid has evaporated. Flavor to taste with salt and pepper.

Divide chicken liver mixture among ramekins; make a depression in each and into it carefully break an egg. Bake at 400 degrees 10-12 minutes, or until egg whites have set. Remove from oven and top each with 2 tablespoons Caruso Sauce.

CARUSO SAUCE

1½ tablespoons olive oil

1 clove garlic, minced

1 7-ounce can tomato sauce

1 teaspoon red wine vinegar

1 teaspoon basil

1 tablespoon finely chopped parsley

¼ teaspoon grated orange rind

salt and pepper to taste

In small saucepan heat oil over medium-high heat. Sauté garlic 1 minute, then stir in tomato sauce, vinegar, basil, parsley and orange rind. Turn heat down to medium and cook uncovered 20 minutes, or until sauce has thickened. Season to taste with salt and pepper.

■

EGGS MAGNOLIA

Serves 6

3 tablespoons butter, divided

1½ tablespoons all-purpose flour

1 cup milk

¾ cup (3 ounces) grated Swiss cheese

salt and pepper to taste

6 ounces mushrooms, thickly sliced

1 can (14 ounces) hearts of palm, sliced ¼ inch

3 English muffins, halved and toasted

6 ¼-inch slices Canadian bacon,
lightly sautéed and kept warm

6 hard-cooked eggs, each cut into 4 slices

1 hard-cooked egg, sieved for garnish

finely chopped parsley for garnish

In medium saucepan melt 1 tablespoon butter.

Add flour and cook over medium heat 4 minutes, stirring occasionally. Stir in milk gradually; cook over low heat until thickened. Add cheese a handful at a time, stirring to melt each handful before the next is added. Season with salt and pepper to taste; cover and set aside.

In medium sauté pan melt remaining 2 tablespoons butter. Sauté mushrooms over medium-high heat until golden brown. Add hearts of palm and cook until warmed through. Stir vegetables into cheese sauce; set aside and keep warm.

For each serving, place an English muffin half on serving plate; cover with Canadian bacon slice, then with 4 egg slices. Spoon on sauce; garnish with sieved egg and parsley.

■

KEWPIE'S BAKED EGGS WITH SHRIMP

Serves 6

3 onions, finely chopped

3 green peppers, finely chopped

4 tablespoons olive oil

3 medium tomatoes, peeled,
seeded and finely chopped

salt, pepper and chile powder

12 large eggs

6 large shrimp, cooked and shelled

Preheat oven to 350 degrees. Sauté onions and green peppers in oil one minute. Add tomatoes; cook until softened. Season with salt, pepper and chile powder.

Spoon a little sauce into the bottom of six individual baking dishes or ramekins. Slip 2 eggs from their shells into each dish. Place a shrimp in the center of each, then bake at 350 degrees for 10 minutes, or until eggs are set.

Cook's Note: This recipe may also be made in one large baking dish, proceeding as with individual dishes.

Cook's Memory: Ethel Hulbert Renwick is a world-renowned author, lecturer and nutritionalist. "Kewpie," as I know her, has always been a special part of my family. To put it in food terms, "She has been along side the Stewarts through thick and thin!"

■

SCOTCH EGGS

Serves 8

1 pound bulk breakfast sausage, hot or mild

¼ teaspoon basil

¼ teaspoon cayenne pepper

1 tablespoon grated onion

6 hard-cooked eggs, shelled

⅔ cup all-purpose flour

2 eggs, beaten

1 cup fine saltine cracker crumbs vegetable oil for deep frying

Preheat oil in deep fryer to 370 degrees.

In medium bowl combine sausage, basil, cayenne and onion, mixing well. Divide into six portions; form each into a patty. Place an egg on each and mold sausage mixture around egg, making sure eggs are totally covered.

Roll the eggs in flour to lightly coat, shake off excess. Dip eggs into beaten egg, then roll in cracker crumbs.

Deep fry the eggs in oil for 5-6 minutes, or until sausage coating is a deep brown.

■

EGGS FLORENTINE

Serves 8

2 tablespoons unsalted butter

2 tablespoons all-purpose flour

1 cup milk

½ teaspoon freshly grated nutmeg

½ teaspoon salt

¼ teaspoon white pepper

1 tablespoon olive oil

1 clove garlic, minced

2 10-ounce packages frozen spinach, cooked according to package directions, drained and squeezed dry in paper towels

4 sourdough English muffins, split and toasted

8 soft-poached eggs

2 cups Hollandaise Sauce (see page 39)

In small saucepan melt butter over medium heat. Add flour and stir to combine; cook 4 minutes. Gradually add milk, stirring constantly; stir in nutmeg, salt and pepper. Set aside.

In medium sauté pan heat olive oil over medium heat; sauté garlic 1 minute. Add spinach and mix thoroughly.

Add spinach to white sauce and stir well to combine.

To assemble each portion, put 1 English muffin half on warmed plate. Spoon over it about ¼ cup spinach mixture. Top with poached egg and Hollandaise Sauce.

■

PAT'S EGGS BENEDICT

Serves 6

6 poached eggs

3 English muffins, split

6 ¼-inch slices Canadian bacon

6 ¼-inch slices firm unpeeled fresh tomato

3 tablespoons butter, melted, divided

1 clove garlic, pressed

¾ teaspoon basil

pinch rosemary, crushed between the fingers

1 tablespoon parsley, finely chopped

2 tablespoons grated Parmesan cheese

⅛ teaspoon cayenne pepper

orange slices and paprika for garnish

1½ cups Quick Hollandaise Sauce

Toast English muffin halves. Keep warm in oven.

Sauté Canadian bacon slices until golden brown on both sides. Transfer to oven to keep warm.

Prepare the herbed tomatoes: mix 2 tablespoons butter, garlic, Parmesan cheese, basil, rosemary, parsley and cayenne in small bowl. Pour 1 tablespoon butter into large skillet. Sprinkle some of butter-herb mixture in skillet, top with tomato, then sprinkle with remainder of herb mixture. Sauté tomatoes on both sides until heated through but not mushy.

Assemble the eggs: in each small buttered ramekin, place 1 English muffin half. Top with Canadian bacon slice, then tomato slice, then poached egg. Spoon generous 4 tablespoons Hollandaise Sauce over each, sprinkle with paprika and garnish with orange slices.

QUICK HOLLANDAISE SAUCE

Makes about 1½ cups

5 egg yolks

1 tablespoon lemon juice

¼ teaspoon salt

⅛ teaspoon cayenne pepper

dry mustard and white pepper to taste

1 stick unsalted butter

In blender container combine egg yolks, lemon juice, salt and other spices. Blend on high speed 1 minute.

In small saucepan melt butter. Turn on blender and add butter through top, a few drops at a time at first, then in thin stream once mixture thickens and "catches" (emulsifies). Serve warm.

Variation: Sometimes we gild the lily a bit and layer in 2 steamed fresh asparagus spears as we're putting together the Benedicts. Let the tops poke out from under the mantle of Hollandaise Sauce.

■

TARRAGON EGGS

Serves 6

¾ stick (6 tablespoons) unsalted butter

1 pound fresh mushrooms, sliced

3 tablespoons minced onion

1½ tablespoons tarragon vinegar

1 teaspoon dried tarragon

½ teaspoon salt

1 cup heavy cream

6 poached eggs

Preheat oven to 350 degrees. Butter 6 individual ovenproof ramekins.

In large sauté pan melt butter; sauté mushrooms. Remove mushrooms from pan and set aside. To pan add onion, vinegar and tarragon; boil rapidly until liquid evaporates. Add salt.

Pour cream into pan and cook over high heat, stirring until reduced by ¼ and thickened.

Divide the mushrooms among the ramekins; set an egg at the center of each. Spoon about 2 tablespoons tarragon sauce over each egg. Bake at 350 degrees for about 6 minutes, just until heated through.

■

HUEVOS DE LA CASA

Serves 6

Filling:

½ stick butter

6 mushrooms, thinly sliced

1 clove garlic, minced

1 tablespoon sherry

2 tablespoons finely chopped parsley

2 tablespoons finely chopped cilantro

pinch Adobo seasoning (available in Latin American grocery stores; or substitute 1 pinch each garlic powder, black pepper and oregano)

12 eggs

5 tablespoons butter, divided

6 8-inch whole wheat or regular flour tortillas, warmed

1 cup sour cream

1 cup red pepper or jalapeño jelly

paprika for garnish

Make the filling: in medium sauté pan melt butter over medium-high heat until foaming subsides; add mushrooms and garlic. Sauté 1 minute, then add sherry, parsley, cilantro and Adobo seasoning. Sauté another minute. Beat eggs in medium bowl; add sautéed mixture and set aside.

Melt the butter. Brush each tortilla with a little butter, using about 3 tablespoons in all. Spread each with about 4 teaspoons sour cream, then dot with pepper jelly, spreading jelly to form thin layer.

For each entrée: melt 1 teaspoon butter in 8-inch sauté pan. Pour in ⅙ egg-mushroom mixture; cook over medium heat until set. Flip omelet, cook briefly on other side, then slide onto prepared tortilla and roll jellyroll fashion. Turn out onto heated plate.

Brush rolls with remaining melted butter and sprinkle with paprika.

■

HUEVOS RANCHEROS

Serves 6

6 blue corn (or regular corn) tortillas, steamed

3 tablespoons butter, melted

2½ cups Pat's Refried Beans (see page 84)

¾ cup Pat's Chunky Salsa (see page 74)

6 eggs, fried sunnyside up

¾ cup sour cream

1½ cups (6 ounces) grated
longhorn Cheddar cheese

paprika and cilantro leaves for garnish

Preheat oven to 375 degrees. Generously butter 6 individual ovenproof ramekins.

For each serving, place 1 tortilla in prepared ramekin. Spread with generous ⅓ cup Pat's Beans; top with 2 tablespoons Pat's Salsa. Layer on a fried egg, then 2 tablespoons sour cream, then a generous sprinkling of grated cheese.

Bake at 375 degrees for 8-10 minutes, or until cheese is melted and bubbly. Serve hot, garnished with paprika and cilantro leaves.

■

HUEVOS CON ESPÁRRAGOS

Serves 6

¾ stick (6 tablespoons) unsalted butter, divided

10 fresh mushrooms, sliced

1 tablespoon finely chopped parsley

½ clove garlic, minced

4 tablespoons all-purpose flour

2 cups milk

½ teaspoon salt

2 cups asparagus tips, steamed until tender-crisp

6 hard-cooked eggs, sliced

2 tablespoons fresh bread crumbs

1 cup (¼ pound) grated Monterey jack cheese

Preheat oven to 350 degrees. Generously grease a 2-quart glass baking dish.

In small sauté pan melt 2 tablespoons butter. Sauté mushrooms 1 minute, then add parsley and garlic; sauté another 2 minutes. Set aside.

In medium saucepan melt remaining 4 tablespoons butter. Stir in flour and cook 4 minutes over low heat. Gradually add milk, stirring to smooth; add salt. Bring cream sauce to a boil; stir in asparagus tips, cover, and remove from heat.

Beginning with cream sauce, layer prepared pan alternately with sauce, egg slices and mushrooms, ending with sauce. Sprinkle casserole with bread crumbs and cheese. Bake at 350 degrees for about 15 minutes, or until top of casserole is browned.

■

GREEN CHILE STRATA

Serves 6

6 flour tortillas

12 roasted, peeled, chopped green chiles or

4 cans chopped green chiles, drained

4 cups (1 pound) grated Monterey jack
cheese 5 eggs, beaten

2 cups milk

1 teaspoon salt

Preheat oven to 350 degrees. Generously grease a 9 x 13-inch baking pan.

Cover bottom of baking pan with tortillas, cutting tortillas to fit without overlapping. Sprinkle with ½ the chopped chiles, then with half the cheese. Repeat layers, ending with cheese.

In medium bowl combine eggs, milk and salt. Pour over layered ingredients. Let stand in refrigerator at least ½ hour; overnight is fine.

Bake at 350 degrees for 30 minutes, or until strata is slightly puffed and bubbly. Cool 5 minutes, then cut into squares.

∎

CHEESE-CHORIZO STRATA

Serves 4

¼ pound Chorizo sausage, cooked and drained

¼ cup chopped mild green chiles

¼ fresh jalapeño, minced, optional

¼ pound Monterey jack cheese, cut into
¼-inch cubes

3 cups French bread cubes

4 eggs

¾ teaspoon cumin powder

½ teaspoon salt

½ teaspoon pepper

2 ⅔ cups milk

½ stick butter, melted

Pat's Chunky Salsa
for topping (see page 94)

Generously grease 4 individual ovenproof ramekins or one 2-quart casserole dish.

For each small dish; spread ¼ chorizo over bottom. Top with chiles and jalapeños, if desired. Sprinkle with ¼ cubed cheese, then with ¼ French bread cubes.

In medium mixing bowl whisk eggs; add cumin, salt and pepper, whisking to combine. Whisk in milk.

Drizzle each dish with melted butter, then divide egg-milk mixture among them. Chill at least 2 hours, preferably overnight.

Preheat oven to 300 degrees; set ramekins in pan of hot water and bake at 300 degrees 45-50 minutes, or until puffed and set. Serve with Pat's Chunky Salsa.

Cook's Note: If you're baking the strata in one large dish, increase oven time to 1½ hours.

∎

SOUTHWESTERN EGGS BENEDICT

Serves 4

8 poached eggs

4 English muffins, split

8 spicy sausage patties (or chorizo)

3 tablespoons butter, melted

4 cups Roasted Roma Tomato Salsa

1½ cups Lime Jalapeno Hollandaise Sauce

½ cup pinon nuts for garnish

Toast and butter English muffin halves. Keep warm in oven. Saute sausage until cooked through and browned on both sides. Keep warm.

Assemble the eggs: in each buttered ramekin, place on English muffin half. Top with sausage, salsa, egg and Hollandaise. Garnish with pinon nuts and serve immediately.

ROASTED ROMA TOMATO SALSA

Makes 4 cups

¼ cup olive oil + 1 tablespoon

½ yellow onion, chopped

2 pounds Roma tomatoes, blackened

4 teaspoons minced roasted garlic

½ cup fresh cilantro, minced

4 Chipotle chiles, chopped

¼ cup red wine vinegar

1 tablespoon salt

1 tablespoon sugar

Saute onion in 1 tablespoon of olive oil for 10 minutes. Transfer onion, half of blackened tomatoes and garlic to food processor and pulse until chopped, not pureed. Add cilantro and chiles, pulse just to mix.

Peel, seed and chop remaining pound of tomatoes and fold together with remaining ¼ cup olive oil, vinegar, salt and sugar.

LIME JALAPENO HOLLANDAISE SAUCE

Makes approximately 1 cup

2 teaspoons jalapeno chile peppers, chopped

1 tablespoon lime juice, freshly squeezed

¼ teaspoon salt

1 stick unsalted butter, melted

In a food processor place the egg yolks, jalapeno chile peppers, lime juice and salt. Puree them together so that they are smooth. With the food processor constantly running, slowly add the butter. Puree the mixture for 1 minute or until it is thick. Heat the sauce so that it is warm.

■

BACON PIE WITH TOMATILLO SAUCE

Serves 4 to 6

8 slices bacon

5 slices bread, cut into cubes

2 cups Swiss cheese, grated

1 cup mild Cheddar cheese, grated

½ cup roasted Anaheim chiles, peeled, seeded and chopped

3 eggs, beaten

2 cups heavy cream

1 teaspoon salt

½ teaspoon nutmeg

Preheat oven to 350 degrees. Cook bacon until crisp and break into pieces. Sprinkle on bottom of 1 ½ quart shallow glass dish. Place bread on top of bacon. In bowl, combine cheeses, chiles, eggs, cream, salt and nutmeg. Pour into baking dish. Bake for approximately 35 minutes or until set.

TOMATILLO SAUCE

1 ½ pounds tomatillos, husks removed

3 cups water

1 onion, minced

¼ cup blanched almonds, chopped

1 tablespoons olive oil

1 tablespoon fresh cilantro, chopped

1 jalapeno, seeded and chopped

2 cups chicken broth

In saucepan place tomatillos and water. Bring water to boil. Lower heat and simmer until they are tender, about ½ hour. Drain tomatillos and puree in blender. Set tomatillos aside.

In large saucepan, sauté onion and almonds in olive oil until almonds are slightly browned. Stir in cilantro and jalapeno. Stir in the tomatillos and chicken broth. Simmer, stirring occasionally for approximately ½ hour. Serve hot. This sauce keeps well for several days.

■

HUEVOS LOCOS

Serves 6

12 eggs

12 small blue corn tortillas

1 15-oz can corn

1 cup chopped green chile

1 medium white onion, chopped

1 cup vegetable oil

2 cups Cheddar cheese, grated

½ cup sour cream

1 avocado, sliced

paprika for garnish

PICO DE GALLO

4 medium tomatoes

4 green onions

1 green pepper

1 bunch cilantro

1 small jalapeno

1 clove garlic, minced

juice from 1 lime

1 tablespoons balsamic vinegar

First make Pico de Gallo: chop tomatoes, onions, green pepper, cilantro and jalapeno. Mix together. Add lime juice, garlic and vinegar. Mix well, cover and refrigerate.

Cut tortillas in small strips. Fry in ½ cup hot oil and drain on paper towel. Drain beans, corn and green chile. Mix together. Fry onions in ½ cup hot oil. Mix onions with bean-corn mixture. Beat eggs. Scramble eggs with corn mixture and tortillas. Serve in individual ramekins. Melt cheese on top. Serve with Pico de Gallo, a dollop of sour cream, sliced avocados and a sprinkle of paprika.

∎

CORN PIE

Serves 6

4 large eggs

2 cups fresh or frozen corn

1 cup chopped apples

1 cup whole milk

1 tablespoon flour

1 tablespoon sugar

pinch salt

½ cup grated Cheddar cheese

Separate eggs. Beat together egg yolks, milk, flour, sugar and salt. Add corn and apples. Beat egg whites. Mix in cheese. Pour into 8-9" greased pie pan (or individual ceramic ramekins). Bake at 350 degrees for 40-45 minutes until golden and set. Serve with drizzled warm maple syrup.

∎

SQUASH POTATO CHEESE STRATA WITH MELON SALSA

Serves 4

5-6 new potatoes, cooked and sliced thin

2 zucchini, sliced

½ red onion, chopped

½ red pepper, chopped

1 clove garlic, minced

1 teaspoon dried Italian seasonings

¼ cup olive oil

1 ¼ cups milk

4 eggs

1 ½ cups grated Monterey Jack cheese

4 oz. cream cheese, in small chunks

pinch salt and pepper

Grease glass pie pan. Line pan with potatoes so they form a crust for the pie. Sauté zucchini, onion, pepper, garlic and Italian seasonings in olive oil. Spread this mixture over potatoes. Beat eggs and milk together and pour over vegetables. Add cheeses. Bake at 350 degrees for one hour or until knife inserted in center comes out clean. Serve with Melon Salsa.

MELON SALSA

Makes approximately 5 cups

1 cup cantaloupe, seeded, rind removed and diced

1 cup honeydew melon, seeded, rind removed and diced

1 cup medium red bell pepper, seeded and diced

2 jalapeno chile peppers, seeded and finely chopped

½ cup scallions, thinly sliced

½ cup fresh cilantro, chopped

1 lemon, freshly squeezed

In a medium bowl place all the ingredients and mix them together. Cover the bowl with plastic wrap and refrigerate the salsa for 30 minutes.

■

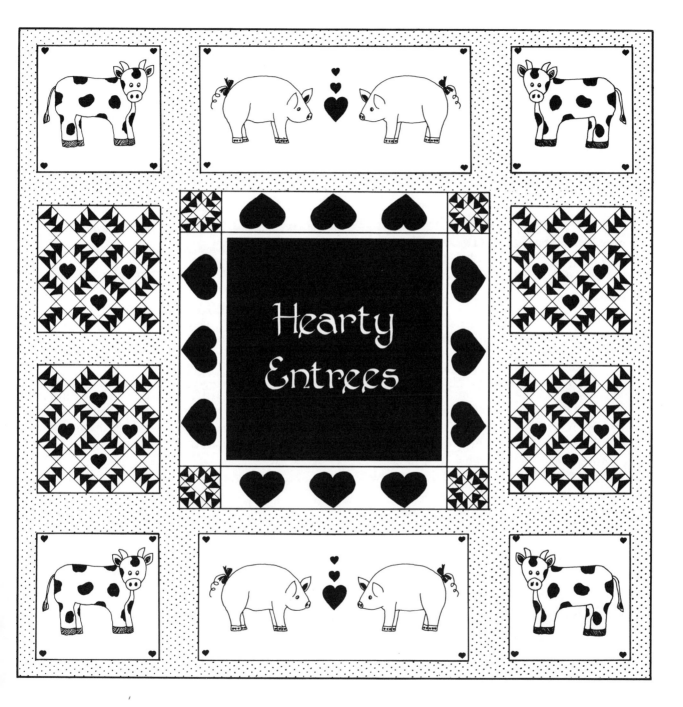

Hearty Entrees

GCI RACLETTE

Serves 4

2 tablespoons olive oil

1 large onion, thinly sliced

1 tablespoon white vinegar

4 small, thin slices smoked ham,
sautéed until browned on both sides

8 small red new potatoes, boiled
in their jackets, sliced ¼-inch thick

3 cups (12 ounces) grated Raclette cheese
(a Swiss melting cheese—look for it at gourmet
shops; if unavailable, substitute Munster or Tilsit)

4 cornichons, cut into fans, for garnish

Preheat oven to 375 degrees.

Heat olive oil over medium heat in medium sauté pan. Sauté onions until soft, about 8 minutes. Stir in vinegar and set aside.

For each serving, lay one slice of ham on bottom of individual ovenproof ramekin or gratin dish. Spread with ¼ of onion mixture. Top with 2 sliced potatoes, then with ¾ cup grated Raclette.

Bake ramekins at 375 degrees until cheese is melted and bubbly, but not really browned. Serve garnished with cornichon fans.

Cook's Note: I recently had Raclette in Switzerland and one serving included 8 medium-sized potatoes. I could barely get up from the table!

■

GRANT CORNER INN RAREBIT

Serves 4

1 cup half and half

¾ cup grated sharp Cheddar cheese

¾ cup grated Swiss cheese

½ teaspoon dry mustard

1 teaspoon Worcestershire sauce

2 egg yolks, beaten

4 ½-inch slices fresh tomato

butter for sautéing

8 slices wheat bread, toasted and halved
diagonally

paprika for garnish

In a small heavy saucepan heat half and half to just below boiling. Gradually add grated cheeses, stirring well to melt and incorporate after each addition. Stir in Worcestershire sauce and mustard. Pour ½ cup cheese mixture into egg yolks, beating constantly with a fork. Pour back into saucepan. Stir over medium heat until mixture thickens and smoothes. Cover and set aside.

Sauté tomato slices in butter until warmed.

Arrange toast points on 4 heated plates; top with tomato slices. Pour cheese sauce over and sprinkle with paprika.

Variation: Add slice of ham and/or a poached egg on top of tomato slice and top with sauce.

■

FALL HARVEST BREAKFAST

Serves 4

1 large butternut squash

8 mushrooms, sliced

2 tart cooking apples, peeled and sliced
(Granny Smiths are good)

1 stick butter, melted and divided

½ pound bulk sausage

½ teaspoon ground sage

¼ cup packed light brown sugar

¼ teaspoon cinnamon

pinch of salt

4 eggs, fried sunnyside up

fresh sage leaves for garnish

Preheat oven to 350 degrees.

Butter 4 ovenproof ramekins. Cut squash in half lengthwise and scoop out seeds. Place squash cut-side-down in 9-inch square baking pan. Fill pan half full of boiling water; bake squash at 350 degrees for about 45 minutes, or until easily pierced with fork.

While squash is baking, sauté mushrooms and apples in ½ stick butter. Add sausage and sage; sauté until sausage is browned, then drain off grease. Set aside.

Scoop cooked squash out of skins into medium bowl. Mash squash with remaining ½ stick butter, brown sugar, cinnamon and salt.

Spread squash mixture in ramekins; layer with sausage mixture and top with fried eggs. Garnish with sage leaves.

■

ARTICHOKE FRITELLAS

Makes 4 fritters

2 6-ounce jars marinated artichoke hearts, drained well, then squeezed in paper towels

1 egg yolk, beaten

4 tablespoons all-purpose flour

½ teaspoon baking powder

2 tablespoons raw grated onion

2 tablespoons finely chopped parsley

¼ teaspoon thyme

½ teaspoon salt

pinch cayenne pepper

flour for dredging

vegetable oil for sautéing

Remoulade Sauce for dipping

Preheat oil to 370 degrees in deep fat fryer.

Cut each artichoke heart in half. Place in small bowl and stir in egg yolk, flour, baking powder, onion, parsley and spices. Drop by ⅓-cupfuls onto flat dish covered with flour. Handling gently, coat both sides of each fritter with flour while at the same time flattening mixture into patty. Chill on plate in refrigerator at least 30 minutes.

Working with one fritter at a time, gently pick up on wide spatula and slide into hot oil. Brown on both sides, turning often to brown evenly. Serve with Remoulade Sauce. *(continued)*

REMOULADE SAUCE

Makes about 2 cups

2 egg yolks

¼ cup vegetable oil

½ cup chopped celery

½ cup chopped green onions

¼ cup chopped parsley

1 tablespoon horseradish

¼ lemon, seeded and sliced

2 cloves garlic, peeled

1 teaspoon salt

2 teaspoons paprika

2 tablespoons tomato puree

2 tablespoons Dijon mustard

1 tablespoon Worcestershire sauce

1 tablespoon vinegar

1 bay leaf

1 tablespoon Louisiana hot sauce

Combine all ingredients in blender. Blend on high speed until ingredients are pureed, scraping down sides of container several times.

∎

ARTICHOKE GERPITTO

Serves 6

Filling:

½ stick butter

½ pound mushrooms, sliced

1 can (15 ounces) artichoke hearts, drained

½ teaspoon chervil

salt and pepper to taste

8 slices bacon, fried crisp and crumbled

6 eggs, separated

⅓ cup all-purpose flour

½ cup hot water

3 tablespoons butter, melted

salt and pepper to taste

1 tablespoon chopped cilantro

Preheat well-seasoned waffle iron.

Make the filling: in medium sauté pan melt butter over medium-high heat. Add mushrooms and sauté, stirring, one minute. Add artichoke hearts and chervil, stirring just until hearts are heated through. Remove from heat and stir in salt, pepper and bacon crumbles. Set aside.

Make the gerpitto: in medium bowl beat egg yolks until thick and lemon-colored; set aside. In small bowl whisk together flour, water, butter, salt and pepper. Beat until smooth, then add to egg yolks.

Beat egg whites until stiff but not dry; fold into egg yolk mixture along with cilantro.

Pour a scant half-cupful into prepared waffle iron and bake for about 1 minute. Repeat for other 5 waffles.

Divide filling among gerpittos and fold each diagonally to form triangle-shaped pocket. Serve hot with Cheddar Sauce.

CHEDDAR SAUCE

Makes about 3 cups

½ stick butter

¼ cup all-purpose flour

2 cups milk

2 cups (½ pound) grated medium-sharp Cheddar cheese

salt, pepper and dry mustard to taste

In medium saucepan melt butter over medium heat; add flour and cook 4 minutes, stirring occasionally. Gradually add milk, stirring to smooth. When thickened, add cheese by handfuls, stirring to melt each addition. Season to taste with salt, pepper and mustard.

Cook's Note: "Gerpitto" (pronounced gĕr/pḗ/tō) is my word for this delicious and fun dish to honor both its creators, Geri Romero and Penny Tubbs.

■

BREAKFAST HOT BROWN

Serves 4

Mornay Sauce:

4 tablespoons flour

½ stick butter

¼ cup chicken broth

¾ cup half and half

¾ cup water

2 egg yolks, beaten

½ cup shredded Fontina cheese

¼ cup grated Parmesan cheese

salt and white pepper to taste

4 slices wheat bread,
toasted and halved diagonally

4 thin slices turkey breast, plain or smoked

4 soft-poached eggs

8 slices bacon, fried crisp

4 slices fresh tomato

additional Parmesan cheese for garnish

Preheat oven broiler. Butter 4 oval gratin dishes.

In medium saucepan heat flour and butter until bubbly. Stir in broth, half and half and water, stirring constantly, and cook on low heat another 2 minutes. Stir about ½ cup of the hot sauce into egg yolks. Pour that mixture back into saucepan; cook another 3 minutes. Gradually add Fontina, stirring to melt after each addition. Stir in Parmesan and correct seasonings. Cover and keep warm.

Arrange 2 toast halves in a gratin dish. On top place a slice of turkey, then a poached egg, then an "X" of 2 bacon slices, then a tomato slice. Spoon Mornay Sauce over all to cover; sprinkle with Parmesan. Repeat with other 3 gratin dishes. Broil 4-6 minutes, or until tops of casseroles are browned and bubbly.

■

BROCCOLI-HAM TIMBALE RING

Serves 4

2 teaspoons butter

4 scallions, finely sliced

1 cup diced smoked ham

½ cup small broccoli florets,
steamed just until bright green

2 tablespoons finely chopped parsley

¼ cup tomato sauce

1¼ cups milk

4 eggs, lightly beaten

salt and pepper to taste

Creole Sauce for topping

Preheat oven to 325 degrees. Generously grease 8-inch ring mold.

In medium sauté pan melt butter. Sauté scallions 1 minute; add ham and broccoli and cook, stirring, just until heated through. Stir in parsley. Turn mixture into colander to drain.

In small bowl beat together tomato sauce, milk, eggs, salt and pepper.

Evenly line bottom of ring mold with broccoli-ham mixture. Pour egg-milk mixture over. Set mold in 2-inch deep baking pan; fill pan with water to within 1 inch of top of mold.

Bake at 325 degrees 50-55 minutes, or until knife inserted at center of custard comes out uncoated. Remove from water bath; allow to set 3 minutes, then unmold onto serving plate. Fill ring with Creole Sauce; cut into 4 portions at table.

CREOLE SAUCE

1 15-ounce can Italian plum tomatoes,
drained and chopped

2 tablespoons olive or vegetable oil

1 medium onion, coarsely chopped

½ green pepper, coarsely chopped

½ cup celery, finely chopped

salt and pepper to taste

Combine all ingredients in medium saucepan and simmer, covered for 45 minutes. Uncover and cook over medium heat another 10 minutes, or until sauce is thickened.

■

PIMENTO SHRIMP TIMBALES

Serves 4

1 tablespoon butter

1 shallot, minced

8-ounce package peeled frozen small cooked shrimp, thawed and drained

3 tablespoons julienne pimento, drained

¼ teaspoon chervil

½ teaspoon salt

1¼ cups milk

¼ cup whipping cream

4 eggs, lightly beaten

Lemon-Chive Sauce

Preheat oven to 325 degrees. Generously grease 4 large custard cups or 4 individual ovenproof ramekins.

In medium sauté pan melt butter over medium heat. Add shallot and sauté 1 minute. Add shrimp, pimento and chervil and sauté just until heated through. Set aside to drain in colander.

In small bowl beat together salt, milk, cream and eggs. Divide shrimp mixture among custard cups. Divide milk-egg mixture among cups. Place cups in 2-inch deep baking pan; fill pan with water to within 1 inch of top of cups.

Bake at 325 degrees 20-30 minutes, or until knife inserted at center of timbale comes out uncoated. Remove from water bath and allow to set 3 minutes, then unmold onto serving plates; top with Lemon-Chive Sauce.

LEMON-CHIVE SAUCE

4 egg yolks

1½ tablespoons lemon juice

¼ teaspoon salt

pinch white pepper

4 tablespoons cream

1 tablespoon chopped chives

Whisk yolks in double boiler over barely simmering water until thickened. Beat in lemon juice, salt, pepper and cream and continue whisking until sauce thickens again. (It should well coat the back of a spoon.) Add chives. Serve warm.

■

RATATOUILLE CREPE CUPS

Serves 4

¼ Cup good quality olive oil

1 clove garlic, minced

1 medium onion, sliced

1 red bell pepper, chopped into 1-inch pieces

1 summer squash, chopped into ¾-inch pieces

1 medium zucchini, chopped into ¾-inch pieces

¼ pound mushrooms, halved

1 small eggplant, cut into ¾-inch cubes

3 large ripe tomatoes, chopped into 1-inch cubes

½ teaspoon thyme

1 teaspoon basil

1 tablespoon red wine vinegar

salt and pepper to taste

4 Basic Crepes (see page 130)

1 cup (¼ pound) grated Mozzarella cheese

2 tablespoons grated Parmesan cheese

Generously butter 4 small ovenproof bowls.

In medium sauté pan heat olive oil over medium-high heat; add garlic and onion and sauté until transparent about 3 minutes. Add red pepper, squashes, mushrooms and eggplant. Cook, stirring frequently, about 8 minutes; add tomatoes. Cook another 4-5 minutes. Add thyme, basil, vinegar, salt and pepper; cover, turn heat to low, and simmer 30 minutes, or until flavors have blended. Remove from heat and set aside. Preheat oven to 375 degrees.

Fit cooled crepes into prepared bowls, forming cups. Bake at 375 degrees until browned and crisp, about 10-12 minutes. Remove from bowls and set on baking sheet.

Divide ratatouille among crepe cups; sprinkle with grated Mozzarella, then Parmesan. Bake at 375 degrees for 5 minutes, or until cheese is melted. Serve immediately.

■

RICH MUSHROOM CREPES

Serves 4

1 stick butter, divided

1 pound mushrooms, thickly sliced

1 shallot, minced

¼ cup all-purpose flour

1 cup rich beef stock or canned beef broth

2 tablespoons brandy

1 cup half and half

½ teaspoon marjoram

½ teaspoon thyme

salt and white pepper to taste

8 Basic Crepes (see page 130)

mushroom caps and watercress sprigs for garnish

In large sauté pan melt ½ stick butter over high heat; add mushrooms and shallots and saute until limp; drain and keep warm.

In medium saucepan melt remaining ½ stick butter over medium heat; add flour and cook, stirring occasionally, 4 minutes. Gradually add beef stock, brandy and half and half, whisking until sauce is smooth and thick. Season to taste with herbs, salt and pepper.

Stir 1¼ cups sauce into mushrooms. Divide filling among crepes and roll allowing 2 to each serving plate. Top with remaining sauce and garnish with mushroom caps and watercress sprigs.

■

GREEN CHILE CREPES

Serves 6

½ pound lean ground beef

½ medium onion, coarsely chopped

¼ cup diced celery

1 clove garlic, minced

1 tomato, diced

1 cup chicken broth

½ pound peeled, chopped mild green chiles (or 4 small cans chopped green chiles, drained)

¼ cup cold water

1 tablespoon cornstarch

2 tablespoons finely chopped cilantro

basil, oregano, salt and pepper to taste

12 eggs, scrambled

6 Basic Crepes (see page 130) or Wheat Germ Crepes (see page 130)

1 cup (¼ pound) mixed grated Monterey and Colby cheeses

cilantro sprigs for garnish

In medium saute pan brown ground beef and drain off grease. Add onion, celery, garlic and tomato and cook, stirring, 10 minutes. Add broth and chiles; bring mixture to a boil. Stir together water and cornstarch and add to boil-ing mixture, stirring until thickened. Add spices and cook another 15 minutes.

Divide scrambled eggs among crepes and roll, placing 1 filled crepe on each ovenproof serving plate. Cover each with green chile, sprinkle with cheese and broil until cheese melts. Garnish with cilantro sprigs.

■

NORMANDY CREPES

Serves 4

2 chicken breasts

2 tablespoons butter

½ red apple, coarsely chopped

1 small onion, minced

½ teaspoon salt

1 tablespoon finely chopped parsley

pinch thyme

⅔ cup apple cider

1 teaspoon Calvados or brandy

1 cup half and half

1 ½ tablespoons cornstarch

8 Basic Crepes (see page 130) or Wheat Germ Crepes (see page 130)

watercress and apple slices

dipped in lemon juice for garnish

In medium saucepan bring 1½ quarts salted water to a boil; add chicken breasts, cover and turn off heat. Let breasts poach 45 minutes.

In medium saucepan melt butter; add apple and onion and sauté 6 minutes. *(continued)*

Add salt, parsley and thyme and bring to a boil. Add cider, cover and simmer over low heat 10 minutes.

Mix half and half into cornstarch and add to apple mixture; bring to a boil, stirring constantly. Add Calvados or brandy and cook another minute or so.

Bone breasts and very coarsely chop. Divide sauce in half; add chicken to half. Divide chicken mixture among crepes; place 2 on each plate and divide remaining sauce among plates to top crepes.

Serve garnished with watercress and apple slices.

■

CURRIED CRAB CUPS

Serves 4

½ stick butter

½ medium onion, finely chopped

1 clove garlic, crushed

2 tablespoons curry powder

¼ cup all-purpose flour

2 cups half and half

2 cups cooked chunk crabmeat, picked over for shells

½ cup sliced ripe black olives

salt and pepper to taste

2 tablespoons sherry

2 ripe peaches, peeled and halved, or 4 canned peach halves

flour for dusting

butter for sautéing

4 Basic Crepes (see page 130)

fresh cilantro sprigs and whole black olives for garnish

Generously grease 4 small ovenproof bowls.

In medium saucepan melt butter over medium heat. Add onion and garlic and sauté until transparent. Add curry powder and cook, stirring, 3 minutes; add flour and cook, stirring occasionally, another 3 minutes. Remove garlic.

Gradually whisk in half and half, stirring until thickened. Add crabmeat, olives, salt, pepper and sherry. Cover and keep warm. Preheat oven to 375 degrees.

Dust peaches with flour and sauté in butter until browned.

Fit crepes into prepared bowls to form tulip-shaped cups. Bake at 375 degrees for 10-12 minutes, or until browned and crisp. Cool 5 minutes, then slip cups out of bowls onto serving plates.

Fit one peach half into each crepe cup, then divide crab curry among cups. (Filling will overflow cups.) Garnish with cilantro sprigs and black olives.

■

MUSHROOM PÂTÉ PUFFS

Makes 8 puffs

¾ pound large fresh mushrooms

½ stick unsalted butter

1 4½-ounce can deviled ham

1 ½ teaspoons Dijon mustard

⅔ recipe Puff Pastry the Easy Way
(see page 191)

1 egg beaten with 1 tablespoon
milk for glaze

Preheat oven to 425 degrees.

Remove mushroom stems and reserve for another use. Sauté mushroom caps in butter until lightly browned; set aside. In small bowl mix deviled ham and mustard. Stuff mushroom caps with ham mixture.

Divide puff pastry in two; roll one half into 12 x 12-inch square. Cut into 4 smaller squares. Divide mushrooms in half; place 6-7 mushrooms at center of each pastry. Bring corners of each pastry together to enclose filling completely, pinching seams to seal. Repeat with other half of dough and mushrooms. Refrigerate 30 minutes.

Brush each pastry with egg glaze and bake on ungreased baking sheet at 425 degrees for 15-18 minutes, or until golden brown.

∎

HAM GRUYERÈ TURNOVERS

Makes 8 turnovers

1 pound Puff Pastry the Easy Way
(see page 191)

2 tablespoons Dijon mustard

2 ounces lean Danish ham, chopped

4 ounces Emmenthaler
or Gruyère cheese, grated

Preheat oven to 425 degrees.

Divide puff pastry in half. Working with one half of dough, rollout to 12 x 12-inch square. Cut into four 6 x 6-inch squares. Spread ¾ teaspoon Dijon to within ½ inch of edges of each square. Divide half the ham among the four; sprinkle on half the cheese. Brush edges with water; fold pastry to form triangle. Using the tines of a fork, crimp edges firmly. Repeat process with other half of dough. Refrigerate 30 minutes on ungreased baking sheet.

Brush pastries with egg glaze and bake at 425 degrees for 20-25 minutes, until pastries are golden brown and puffed. Serve warm.

∎

GREEK SPINACH STRUDEL

Serves 6

2 10-ounce packages frozen spinach

1 stick unsalted butter, melted and divided

½ cup scallions, finely chopped

8 ounces ricotta cheese

8 ounces feta cheese,
finely crumbled in processor

½ teaspoon dill weed

1 teaspoon oregano

½ teaspoon salt, or to taste

½ teaspoon pepper

5 sheets Greek filo dough,
thawed according to directions on package
(available in grocery freezer case)

Avgolemono Sauce

Make the filling: cook spinach according to directions on package. Drain, then squeeze out excess liquid. Set aside in medium mixing bowl.

Into small sauté pan pour 1 tablespoon butter. Add scallions and sauté until transparent. Pour into spinach; add ricotta, feta, dill, oregano, salt and pepper; mix well.

Assemble the pastry: spread a damp kitchen towel on work surface. Lay one sheet of filo dough on towel; brush with some of remaining melted butter. Carefully lay another filo sheet on the first, lining up the edges. Again brush with butter. Repeat the layering/buttering process 3 more times; you'll wind up with a stack of 5 layers of pastry.

Spoon spinach filling along one long side of pastry; roll up jellyroll fashion, using towel to help roll. Transfer strudel to ungreased baking sheet. Make 5 evenly-spaced diagonal slashes across pastry with a sharp knife. Brush pastry with butter.

Bake at 375 degrees for 30-35 minutes, or until golden brown. Cut through strudel at slashes to separate servings. Serve with Avgolemono Sauce.

AVGOLEMONO SAUCE

Makes 1 cup

2 tablespoons unsalted butter

1 teaspoon all-purpose flour

2 egg yolks, lightly beaten

1 teaspoon finely chopped parsley

¾ cup half and half

1½ tablespoons lemon juice

salt and white pepper to taste

In small heavy saucepan combine butter, flour, yolks and parsley. Cook over very low heat, stirring constantly, until ingredients are blended. Gradually add the half and half, stirring and cooking until sauce thickens. Add lemon juice, salt and pepper.

■

SHRIMP-STUFFED BRIOCHE

Makes 10

Brioche Pastry:

1 package active dry yeast

½ cup warm (110-115 degrees) water

1 tablespoon sugar

2 tablespoons nonfat dry milk

1 teaspoon salt

2-2¼ cups all-purpose flour, divided

1 stick butter

3 eggs

Glaze:

1 egg yolk beaten with 1 tablespoon milk

In bowl of a heavy-duty electric mixer combine yeast, water and sugar. Let stand 10 minutes, or until mixture looks slightly foamy. Add milk, salt and one cup of flour. Beat on medium-high speed for several minutes, or until mixture looks spidery. Add butter and beat for 2 more minutes. Turn mixer down to medium speed; alternately add eggs and rest of flour, ½ cup at a time, allowing time between each addition for dough to incorporate ingredient and scraping bowl frequently. Once all ingredients have been added, beat dough on medium speed for about 10 more minutes. Dough will be very sticky and elastic; when done, most of dough will be sticking to beater.

Scrape dough into mixing bowl and cover with plastic wrap; let sit in a warm spot until doubled, about 1½-2 hours.

Punch down dough, re-cover and refrigerate at least 4 hours, preferably overnight. Remove from refrigerator and, using buttered hands, form dough into long, narrow roll. Cut dough into ten pieces.

Grease well 10 cups of a 12-cup muffin tin. Taking one piece of dough, begin to pull out a part of dough about the size of a large marble. Continue pulling almost to the point where the smaller piece (which will become the topknot) separates from the body of the brioche. Twisting

the topknot and using fingers to form a depression below, seat the smaller piece on top of, and slightly inside of, body of brioche. Repeat with all dough pieces. Let brioche sit in a warm spot until doubled.

Preheat oven to 400 degrees. Brush brioche with egg glaze and bake at 400 degrees for about 18-20 minutes, or until golden brown. Slice off topknot and hollow out brioche a bit, pinching out bits of baked dough with fingers. Fill with Tarragon Sherry Shrimp and replace topknot.

TARRAGON SHERRY SHRIMP

1 pound raw medium shrimp

½ lemon

sprig parsley

6 peppercorns

1½ sticks unsalted butter, divided

2 scallions, finely chopped

¾ cup all-purpose flour

1 cup milk

2 cups half and half

2 tablespoons sherry

1 teaspoon tarragon

salt, paprika, and white pepper to taste

Shell and devein shrimp; set aside. Put shells and tails in small saucepan, add 2 cups water, lemon, parsley and peppercorns. Cover and bring to a boil; simmer 30 minutes. Strain 1 cup of stock into small bowl and reserve.

In medium saucepan melt all but 2 tablespoons

(continued)

butter. Add scallions and sauté until transparent. Add flour, stirring to blend; cook 3 minutes on low heat. Gradually add milk, then half and half and reserved shrimp stock, stirring to incorporate. Add sherry. Cover and set aside.

In medium sauté pan melt remaining 2 tablespoons butter. Add shrimp and sauté until they curl and appear opaque, no more than 5 minutes. Add tarragon. Combine shrimp and sauce, adjust seasoning and spoon into hollowed-out brioche.

■

SEAFOOD ETOUFÉE PROFITEROLES

Serves 6

Pastry:

1 cup water

1 stick butter

1 cup flour

4 eggs

Seafood Etoufée:

¼ cup plus 2 teaspoons vegetable oil

1 teaspoon Tabasco sauce

½ cup all-purpose flour

¾ teaspoon salt

½ teaspoon cayenne

¼ teaspoon pepper

½ teaspoon basil

pinch thyme

2 cups bottled clam juice, divided

1 stick plus 2 tablespoons butter, divided

1 pound scallops or peeled, deveined shrimp, or a combination

½ cup finely sliced scallions

paprika for sprinkling

Preheat oven to 425 degrees. Line a baking sheet with parchment or brown Kraft paper. (You can cut paper bags to fit.)

Make the pastry: in medium saucepan bring water and butter to a rolling boil; dump in flour all at once, stirring vigorously with a wooden spoon until mixture pulls away from sides of pan and forms a smooth ball. Remove from heat, cool 5 minutes, then beat in eggs one at a time.

Spoon the mixture by the half cup into mounds on paper-lined sheet. Bake at 425 degrees 30-35 minutes, or until puffed and golden brown. Prick with an ice pick, turn off oven and return to oven for 5 minutes to dry interiors a bit. Remove and set aside.

Make the etoufée: in medium cast iron or other very heavy skillet, heat oil on high heat until it smokes, about 4 minutes. Gradually whisk in flour, stirring to smooth. Whisking constantly, continue cooking oil-flour roux another 3 to 5 minutes, or until it has turned a dark reddish-brown. (Be sure and avoid scorching roux.) Remove from heat and stir in Tabasco, salt, cayenne, pepper, basil and thyme, whisking mixture continually until cooled, about 6 minutes.

In small saucepan bring 1 cup clam juice to a boil; gradually whisk in roux, making sure it is thoroughly combined. Reduce heat to medium-low and cook, stirring 3 minutes. Cover and set aside.

In a medium saucepan melt 5 tablespoons butter over medium heat. Stir in seafood and scallions and sauté, stirring 1 minute. Add remaining 5 tablespoons butter, roux mixture and remaining

1 cup clam juice, shaking pan over heat to incorporate butter. Stir well.

Slice tops off profiteroles and pinch out any uncooked dough. Fill with seafood mixture and replace tops; dust with paprika.

■

CRAB BRUNCH SQUARES WITH RED PEPPER CREAM SAUCE

Serves 10 generously

4 eggs

2 ⅔ cups milk

¾ teaspoon Dijon mustard

6 ounces Brie, rind removed, cut in ¼-inch cubes

½ cup sliced black olives

1 small onion, finely chopped

2 tablespoons parsley, finely chopped

1 teaspoon Worcestershire sauce

3½ cups cooked rice

1 pound fresh frozen or canned lump crabmeat, picked through for shells

paprika

Preheat oven to 325 degrees. In mixing bowl beat eggs, milk and mustard until blended.

Stir in remaining ingredients, except for paprika, and pour into greased 9 x 13-inch baking pan. Bake at 325 degrees for 40-45 minutes, or until knife inserted at center comes out clean. Serve with Red Pepper Cream Sauce.

RED PEPPER CREAM SAUCE

Makes about 2 cups

4 tablespoons unsalted butter

1 large ripe red pepper, seeded and cut in ¼-inch dice

¼ cup thinly sliced green onion

¼ cup all-purpose flour

¼ teaspoon salt

¼ teaspoon white pepper

1¾ cups milk

3 teaspoons lemon juice

fresh snipped chives for garnish

Melt butter in small heavy saucepan. Sauté red pepper and green onion for 2 minutes; add flour and sauté on low heat 3 minutes. Blend in salt and pepper, then gradually whisk in milk and lemon juice. Cook for one minute, then transfer to blender container. Blend on high 2 minutes, or until pepper and onion are pureed. Spoon over brunch squares and garnish with chives.

■

PAN-FRIED TROUT WITH PECAN SAUCE

Serves 4

4 4-5 ounce fresh trout filets

¼ cup all-purpose flour

2 tablespoons pecans, finely ground in processor

¾ teaspoon salt

¼ teaspoon white pepper

pinch cayenne pepper

½ stick unsalted butter

2 tablespoons vegetable oil

Pecan Sauce for topping

large pecan halves for garnish

Rinse trout filets and dry well on paper towels.

Combine flour, ground pecans, salt, pepper and cayenne in cake pan. Dredge filets in flour mixture.

In large saucepan melt butter with oil over medium-high heat. Sauté filets 2 to 3 minutes on each side, or until golden brown, turning once. Drain on paper towels.

Immediately transfer filets to serving plate and top each with a generous 2 tablespoons Pecan Sauce. Sprinkle with pecan halves and serve at once.

PECAN SAUCE

½ stick unsalted butter, softened

2 shallots, coarsely chopped

1 small clove garlic, minced

½ cup pecans, toasted in a 350 degree oven 7-8 minutes

1 teaspoon fresh lemon juice

pinch lemon rind

½ teaspoon Louisiana-style bottled hot sauce

Combine all ingredients in blender and blend on high until smooth, about 2 minutes, scraping down sides of container occasionally.

∎

TURKEY ROULADE

Serves 6

½ stick butter

½ cup flour

½ teaspoon salt

¼ teaspoon white pepper

2 cups milk

1 cup (4 ounces) shredded Fontina cheese

5 eggs, separated

2 tablespoons butter

4 shallots, minced

handful mushrooms, sliced

1 cup cooked spinach, chopped

1 cup minced roast turkey

¼ teaspoon nutmeg

6 ounces cream cheese

salt and pepper

Grease a 10½ x 15½-inch jellyroll pan. Line with waxed paper and grease the paper. Dust with flour. Set aside. Preheat oven to 400 degrees.

In medium saucepan melt butter; stir in flour and cook over medium heat, stirring occasionally. Add salt and pepper. Gradually whisk in milk, regulating so mixture thickens with each addition; stir in cheese.

Beat egg yolks in small bowl; beating a little of hot mixture, then beat yolks into hot mixture over medium-low heat; cook 1 minute, whisking. Cool.

Beat egg whites until stiff but not dry; stir one-third of whites into cheese sauce; fold in remaining whites.

Pour mixture into prepared pan and spread evenly. Bake at 400 degrees 25-30 minutes, or until puffed and brown. Meantime, prepare filling.

In medium sauté pan melt butter. Sauté shallots and mushrooms 4 minutes. Add spinach, turkey and seasonings; beat in cream cheese.

When souffle is baked immediately invert onto a clean tea towel; remove waxed paper. Spread with filling and roll up jellyroll style from a long side, using towel to help roll.

Immediately slice into 6 portions and serve.

■

SAVORY HAM LOAF WITH CREAMED EGGS

Serves 8

1 pound ham, coarsely ground in processor

½ pound fresh lean pork, coarsely ground in processor

2 teaspoons Dijon mustard

1 tablespoon brown sugar

2 eggs

1 small onion, finely chopped

¾ cup fresh bread crumbs

½ cup tomato sauce

½ teaspoon pepper

Creamed Eggs

Preheat oven to 350 degrees.

Thoroughly mix all ingredients, using hands or large spoon. Press into greased medium (8½ x 4-inch) loaf pan. Place pan in shallow pan; fill outer pan with water reaching up 1 inch of side of loaf pan.

Bake at 350 degrees for 1 hour. Drain off any accumulated grease; let loaf sit in pan ½ hour before unmolding. Cut into 1-inch slices and serve hot with Creamed Eggs; garnish with sprinkle of paprika.

CREAMED EGGS

2 cups Basic White Sauce (see page 39)

1 teaspoon Dijon mustard

¼ teaspoon cayenne

½ teaspoon paprika

6 hard-cooked eggs, shelled

paprika for garnish

Season hot white sauce with Dijon, cayenne and paprika. Slice eggs into sauce and stir gently to combine.

■

SAN FRANCISCO SPECIAL

Serves 6-8

1 medium white onion, finely chopped

2 garlic cloves, minced

½ stick butter, melted

1 pound ground beef

1 medium tomato, finely chopped

2 cups cooked, chopped spinach, well-drained

½ teaspoon oregano

½ teaspoon basil

salt and pepper to taste

9 eggs, beaten

In heavy frying pan sauté onions and garlic in butter until transparent. Add ground beef and brown. Add tomatoes and spinach, stirring, and cook another 10 minutes. Drain well. Stir in spices and eggs, using spatula to move mixture around until eggs are cooked.

Serve immediately; sliced tomatoes make a nice accompaniment.

Cook's Note: This hearty breakfast dish was a favorite of ours when we lived in San Francisco. It is often called "Joe's Special," after Joe DiMaggio.

■

CORNED BEEF HASH & EGGS

Serves 6

3 tablespoons oil

½ cup chopped zucchini

1 large onion, chopped

½ green pepper, chopped

¼ cup finely chopped parsley

½ red pepper, chopped

¼ teaspoon thyme

salt and pepper to taste

2 cups chopped corned beef

1½ cups chopped boiled potatoes

6 eggs

chopped parsley for garnish

Preheat oven to 325 degrees.

Heat oil in skillet on high until it sizzles. Add zucchini, onion, pepper and potatoes, stirring until vegetables begin to brown. Turn heat down to low. Add corned beef, thyme, salt and pepper, spreading out mixture and flattening it. Cook very slowly until browned on the bottom. Stir to incorporate browned bits, add parsley, then spread hash in buttered 9 x 13-inch casserole, flattening top. Make six indentations on top of hash with large spoon. Very carefully break an egg into each indentation. Cover with foil and bake at 325 degrees until egg whites have set, about 25 minutes. Garnish with chopped parsley.

■

LAMB ARTICHOKE HASH

Serves 12

6-pound leg of lamb

3 cups water, divided

3 tablespoons Worcestershire sauce

3 tablespoons olive oil

juice of 1 lemon

1 garlic clove

3 cups new potatoes in jackets, cooked and cubed

2 cups mushrooms, sliced

2 cups artichoke hearts, chopped and drained

¼ cup olive oil

1 small onion, minced

2 cloves garlic, minced

½ teaspoon basil leaves

½ teaspoon salt

12 soft-cooked poached eggs

mint sprigs for garnish

To cook leg of lamb preheat oven to 300 degrees. Cut garlic clove into pieces. Make ½-inch cuts into lamb and insert garlic pieces. Place lamb in roasting pan. Pour in 1 cup of the water. Pour Worcestershire and lemon juice over lamb; then brush on olive oil. Roast in 300 degree oven for 1 hour. Reduce the temperature to 160 degrees, add 2 more cups of water, cover tightly and cook for 8-10 hours.

During the last part of the cooking time, prepare the remaining ingredients. Sauté the onion and garlic until transparent, and add potatoes and mushrooms. When potatoes begin to brown, add artichokes, basil and salt. Cube leg of lamb (no gristle allowed!) and add to mixture. Sauté for a couple of minutes, mixing ingredients well. Serve in ramekins, topped with poached eggs. Garnish with mint sprigs and hide the catsup!

Cook's Memory: The "slow-roasting" method of cooking the lamb was taught to me by my mother, who was a great fan of Adelle Davis (Let's Cook it Right). Adelle Davis' belief in the slow-cooking process to enhance flavor and preserve nutrients deserves applause. All meats cooked this way are amazingly tender, juicy and flavorful. The first hour at 300 degrees destroys surface bacteria. The oven is then set to the internal temperature of the meat when it is done. Leg of lamb is generally served with an internal temperature between 155-160 degrees. Because slow-roasting meat needs no attention, the method is ideal to use overnight while sleeping or in the daytime while working.

■

G.W.

GREEN CHILE CHICKEN HASH

Serves 6

4 chicken breast halves, skinned

garlic salt and onion salt

2 ounces chorizo sausage

5 tablespoons butter, divided

1 large onion, chopped in ½-inch dice

½ jalapeño, seeded and finely chopped

1 ½ tablespoons cilantro, finely chopped

1 tablespoon chives, chopped

½ cup fresh coarse bread crumbs

2 teaspoons grated lemon rind

⅔ cup chopped mild green chiles

1 cup thick white sauce, made with 3
tablespoons butter, 3 tablespoons flour,
¼ teaspoon thyme, ¼ teaspoon paprika,
pinch cayenne,
salt and pepper to taste

Preheat oven to 425 degrees.

Place chicken on ungreased baking sheet; sprinkle with garlic salt and onion salt. Bake at 425 degrees for 40 minutes, or until breasts are browned. Bone chicken, chop meat coarsely, cover and set aside.

Fry chorizo in 3-quart saucepan. Drain well and remove from pan. Melt 3 tablespoons butter in same pan and saute onion and jalapeño until transparent. Add chopped chicken, cilantro, chives, bread crumbs, lemon rind, green chiles and white sauce. Stir to blend well, then correct seasonings.

Melt remaining butter in 12-inch skillet; when sizzling, add hash, flattening with spatula. Cook over medium-low heat about 25 minutes, or until underside is crisp and browned. Serve browned-side-up with Bacon Parmesan Popovers (see page 205).

■

NEW MEXICAN SOUFFLE ROLL

Serves 6

1 tablespoon olive oil

2 large onions, halved and thinly sliced

1 bunch scallions, finely chopped,
green tops included

1 clove garlic, minced

6 roasted, peeled and chopped fresh mild
green chiles, or 1 7-ounce can diced
green chiles, drained

½ cup all-purpose flour

2 cups milk

½ teaspoon salt

½ teaspoon cumin

¼ teaspoon pepper

4 eggs, separated

1 cup (4 ounces) shredded Monterey jack cheese

Avocado Sour Cream Sauce for topping

ripe olives for garnish

In medium sauté pan heat oil over medium heat. Add onions, scallions and garlic and saute stirring constantly until onion is limp. Stir in chile and set aside.

Preheat oven to 325 degrees. Line a jellyroll pan with foil and butter foil. Dust with flour shaking out excess and set aside.

Into medium saucepan sift flour. Gradually whisk in milk, stirring until smooth. Stir in salt, cumin and pepper. Cook over medium heat, stirring until thick. In small bowl beat egg yolks; stir in several spoonfuls of hot mixture, then pour yolks into saucepan. Add cheese and cook, stirring constantly for 1 minute. Set aside.

Beat egg whites until foamy; stir in sugar, then beat until whites are stiff, but not dry; gently fold whites into cooked flour-milk mixture. Pour into prepared pan, spreading evenly. Bake at 325 degrees 40-45 minutes, or until lightly browned and puffy.

Turn souffle out onto waxed paper; carefully peel off foil. Spread onion mixture over souffle; using waxed paper as a helper, roll souffle into a tight cylinder. Slice into 6 pieces and serve topped with Avocado Sour Cream Sauce and garnish with ripe olives.

AVOCADO SOUR CREAM SAUCE

1 ripe avocado

2 tablespoons lime juice

1 tablespoon grated onion

1 clove garlic, minced

½ cup sour cream

pinch cumin

salt and pepper to taste

Mash avocado with remaining ingredients; sauce will be chunky.

∎

BREAKFAST CHILE RELLENOS

Makes 6 rellenos

Picadillo Filling:

½ pound very lean ground beef

1 clove garlic, minced

⅓ cup tomato sauce

2 tablespoons raisins

3 tablespoons sherry

1 teaspoon cinnamon

¼ teaspoon ground cloves

2 teaspoons sugar

1 tablespoon red wine vinegar

¾ teaspoon salt

¼ cup slivered toasted almonds

6 roasted, peeled long green chiles

1½ cups milk

¼ cup all-purpose flour

6 eggs

½ teaspoon salt

¼ teaspoon white pepper

2 cups (½ pound) grated mild Cheddar

Preheat oven to 350 degrees. Generously grease 6 oval gratin dishes.

In medium skillet brown ground beef with garlic. Add tomato sauce, raisins, sherry, cinnamon, cloves, sugar, vinegar, ¾ teaspoon salt and almonds. Cook uncovered over medium heat for about 20 minutes, or until most of the liquid has evaporated. Cool. Stuff each chile with as much of the mixture as it will hold. *(continued)*

In medium bowl slowly combine milk and flour, whisking to keep mixture smooth. Add eggs, salt and pepper. Put one chile in each gratin dish and cover with custard mixture. Sprinkle with cheese. Bake uncovered at 350 degrees for about 35-40 minutes, until puffed and lightly browned. Serve with Chile Pod Red Chile.

CHILE POD RED CHILE
Makes about 2 cups

10 dried red chile pods, each 6-7 inches long

1½ cups water

3 cloves garlic

1½ teaspoons salt

Shake most of seeds out of chiles. In medium saucepan bring chiles and water to a boil. Cover and simmer 15 minutes, adding garlic for last 5 minutes.

In electric blender puree chiles and water (some small pieces of skin will remain). Add salt. Pour back into saucepan and simmer on low heat, covered, for about 15 minutes. Adjust salt.

■

BLACK BEAN CHALUPAS
Serves 6

1 cup dried black (turtle) beans

2 slices bacon, optional

½ green pepper, finely chopped

3 cloves garlic, minced

1 medium onion, chopped

2 tablespoons each finely chopped cilantro and parsley

2 bay leaves

1½ tablespoons Louisiana-style bottled hot sauce

¼ teaspoon thyme

salt and pepper to taste

6 blue or yellow corn tortillas, fried into "nests" with special tortilla basket maker, or fried crisp and flat

Guacamole

Red Chile Sauce

1 ½ cups (6 ounces) grated Monterey jack cheese

Pat's Chunky Salsa

(see page 94) for topping

Soak black beans in water to cover overnight. Drain, rinse and cook in enough water to cover beans by one inch for 1½-2½ hours, or until almost tender, adding water as needed,

Add bacon, if desired, along with green pepper, garlic, onion, cilantro, parsley, bay leaves, hot sauce, thyme, salt and pepper. Cook another 45 minutes, or until beans begin to get mushy. Remove bay leaves.

Preheat oven broiler. Mash beans well; spoon into fried tortilla nests or onto hot fried tortillas. Layer with guacamole, red chile and Jack cheese. Run under broiler until cheese is melted and bubbly.

Serve hot; pass Pat's Chunky Salsa separately.

GUACAMOLE
2 ripe avocados (preferably the black-skinned Haas variety)

1 tablespoon lime juice

1 clove garlic, minced

1 small onion, chopped

1 teaspoon finely chopped cilantro

1 jalapeño, seeded and minced

½ ripe tomato, diced

salt and pepper to taste

Scoop avocado out of skins; mash in non-metallic bowl with lime juice, cilantro, garlic, onion and jalapeño. Gently fold in tomato; season to taste with salt and pepper.

RED CHILE SAUCE

Makes about 3 cups

1 pound lean ground beef

1 medium onion, coarsely chopped

2 cloves garlic, minced

¼ cup ground red chile
(not commercial chile powder)

1½ cups water

pinch ground cumin

In medium sauté pan brown ground beef with onion and garlic; drain off grease. Stir in red chile; cook over medium heat 4 minutes. Add water and cumin; bring to a boil, then turn heat to low and simmer 10-15 minutes.

■

TAMALE CORNCAKES

Serves 6

1 cup boiling water

1 cup yellow cornmeal

1 cup milk

½ cup vegetable oil

1 egg, beaten

1 cup all-purpose flour

1 teaspoon cumin

1 teaspoon salt

1 teaspoon chile powder

2¼ teaspoons baking powder

1 8-ounce can corn, drained

12 ripe olives, sliced

Topping Condiments:

1 cup shredded Cheddar cheese

1 chopped ripe tomato

chopped green onion

Pat's Chunky Salsa (see page 94)

sour cream

Preheat well-seasoned griddle.

In medium mixing bowl pour boiling water over cornmeal, stirring well; cool 10 minutes. Add milk, oil and egg, stirring to combine. Sift into liquids the flour, cumin, salt, chile powder and baking powder; stir well. Stir in corn and olives.

Spoon about 4 tablespoons batter onto griddle for each corncake, spreading if needed to form 5-inch cake. Bake until golden brown on both sides, flipping once. Serve 3 to a person, passing toppings at table.

PAULINE'S NO-BIG-DEAL TAMALES

Serves 15-20

8 pounds chuck roast

5 cloves garlic

1 large white onion, sliced

½ cup vegetable oil

¼ cup all-purpose flour

8 pounds masa

3 pounds lard

5 teaspoons salt

5 teaspoons baking powder

15 red chiles, dried

6 cups water

2 pounds husks, washed, soaked and dried

Cover meat with water adding garlic and onion. Simmer covered for 2½ hours or until very tender. Cool and shred beef. Fry shredded beef in oil; add flour and one cup of beef stock from pot.

Beat lard with salt and baking powder until light and fluffy. Add this mixture and one more cup of beef stock to the masa. Beat well, until very light and fluffy. Drop a spoonful of dough into cold water. If it floats to the top, it is ready. If it does not, beat more.

To prepare red chile sauce, boil dry chiles in 6 cups water about 20 minutes. Cool. Put in blender and puree. Strain through a sieve and pour onto meat, mixing well.

To assemble tamales, spread masa mixture on husks, then chile and meat. Fold. Put them into a Dutch oven with a rack across bottom. Add water to bottom. Simmer on top of stove about 1¼ hours, making sure there is always water at the bottom, but that it never touches husks.

Cook's Memory: Pauline cooked for my mother's family when my mother was a teenager, and then she came to take care of our family from the time I was a little girl. She is my "other" mother. She calls her tamales "no big deal" because they are "no big deal" to her!

■

GRILLED MARINATED CHICKEN BREAST WITH CILANTRO CREAM AND RUBY RED GRAPEFRUIT AVOCADO SALSA

Serves 6

CHICKEN

6 boneless skinless chicken breasts

4 tablespoons fresh cilantro, chopped

2 gloves garlic, minced

¼ cup olive oil

juice of 1 lemon

½ teaspoon salt

½ teaspoon white pepper

SALSA

Makes approximately 2½ cups

4 fresh ruby red grapefruit

1 green onion, finely chopped

5 tablespoons fresh cilantro, chopped

2-3 small Serrano peppers, seeded and minced

3 avocados (firm not overripe), chopped in small cubes

2 tablespoons red wine vinegar

juice of ½ lemon

½ teaspoon cayenne

½ teaspoon garlic salt

CILANTRO CREAM

Makes approximately 2 cups

4 tablespoons butter

4 tablespoons all-purpose flour

2 cups milk

juice of 1 lemon

4 tablespoons chopped fresh cilantro

1 teaspoon salt

1 teaspoon white pepper

Marinate chicken with cilantro, garlic, olive oil, lemon, salt and pepper. Cover and refrigerate several hours or overnight.

Make Salsa: Use a very sharp knife to neatly peel grapefruit. Cut down to the flesh leaving no pith. Cut out sections between membranes and then cut sections into smaller pieces. Add onions, cilantro, peppers, avocados, vinegar, lemon, cayenne and garlic salt. Toss lightly. (This does not keep more than a few hours.)

Prepare Cilantro Cream: In saucepan melt butter over medium high heat. Whisk in flour making a roux. Slowly add milk whisking constantly to avoid lumps. Stir until thickened. Add lemon juice, cilantro, salt and pepper. Cook over low heat stirring constantly for about 4 minutes.

Grill chicken on barbeque (medium heat) or broil brushing with marinade and turning occasionally for about 15 minutes until tender and cooked through. Serve with cilantro cream and salsa.

■

PORK BLACK BEAN SOFT TACOS WITH BARBEQUE SAUCE AND APPLE JICAMA SALSA

Serves 6

PORK BLACK BEAN SOFT TACOS

2 pounds pork loin, thinly sliced

¾ cup fresh orange juice

1 red onion, thinly sliced

2 tablespoons chile oil

2 tablespoons balsamic vinegar

1 tablespoon soy sauce

¼ cup cilantro, chopped

1 teaspoon salt

1 teaspoon pepper

4 tablespoons olive oil

2 cups black beans, cooked

12 soft 6" flour tortillas

BARBEQUE SAUCE

Makes approximately 2 cups

4 tablespoons olive oil

½ cup minced white onion

2 cloves garlic, minced

1 15-ounce can tomato sauce

1 6-ounce can tomato paste

3 tablespoons distilled white vinegar

1 tablespoon Liquid Smoke

½ cup brown sugar

1 jalapeno pepper, minced

1 serrano pepper, minced

salt and pepper to taste

APPLE JICAMA SALSA

Makes approximately 3 cups

1 jicama, peeled and finely chopped

3 fresh apples: 1 Granny Smith, 2 Red Delicious, finely chopped

¼ cup fresh cilantro, chopped

1 jalapeno pepper, finely chopped (include the seeds if you like hot)

1 tablespoon red wine vinegar

juice of 1 fresh lime

Slice pork loin into thin strips. Marinate pork overnight or for several hours in orange juice, onion, chile oil, balsamic vinegar, soy sauce, cilantro, salt and pepper.

Prepare Barbeque Sauce: In fry pan, sauté onion and garlic in olive oil. Stir in tomato sauce, paste, vinegar and Liquid Smoke. Add brown sugar, peppers, salt and pepper. Stir and simmer over low heat for about 30 minutes.

Prepare Apple Jicama Salsa: Mix all ingredients in bowl. Stir well. Cover and refrigerate.

Saute pork in large fry pan in 4 tablespoons olive oil. Brown on all sides over medium heat, 10-15 minutes. Lower heat and simmer about 20 minutes. Add black beans, stir and cook another 4 minutes.

Warm tortillas. Spread each tortilla with Barbeque Sauce and fill with pork mixture. Serve with Apple Jicama Salsa.

■

NEW MEXICO CHRISTMAS STEW

Serves 8

4 pounds boned chicken

4 tablespoons flour

½ cup olive oil

1 large white onion, sliced

1 cup chopped green chile, roasted and peeled

1 15-ounce can garbanzo beans

1 cup chicken broth

1 pound Italian pear tomatoes, quartered

2 6-ounce cans tomato paste

1 clove garlic, minced

1 bunch cilantro, chopped

1 teaspoon oregano

salt and pepper to taste

1 green pepper, chopped

Sauté onions in olive oil. Sauté lightly floured chicken in olive oil. Add all ingredients to 6 quart crock pot and cook on high for 1 hour. Reduce heat to low and cook for 5 hours.

Cook's Note: "Christmas" in New Mexico indicates not only a holiday but also the inclusion of both red and green chiles in one dish! This is a delightful winter brunch stew served with Blue Corn Honey Sesame Corn Muffins. (Page 149).

■

STUFFED TURKEY BURGERS

Serves 4

1½ pounds ground turkey

1 apple, Pippin or Granny Smith, chopped (leave skin on)

1/8 pound smoked Jarlsberg cheese, grated

¼ cup pinon nuts

2 tablespoons butter

½ teaspoon salt

½ teaspoon pepper

Preheat oven to 350 degrees. Sauté apples and pinons in butter until slightly browned. Add salt and pepper to ground turkey. Form turkey into four patties. Make a cavity in the patties and add apples, nuts and cheese and seal in with ground meat. Bake in greased baking dish for about one hour.

■

MARINATED LAMB AND POLENTA WITH YOGURT MINT SAUCE

Serves 6

POLENTA

1 cup yellow cornmeal

1 teaspoon salt

1 teaspoon sugar

butter for sautéing

In medium saucepan, bring 2¾ cups water to a boil. In small mixing bowl combine cornmeal with 1 cup cold water; add salt and sugar. Add cornmeal to boiling water a spoonful at a time, stirring constantly. When cornmeal is thick, cover and cook over very low heat without stirring for 10 minutes. Scrape into 2 miniature loaf pans and chill for several hours.

Unmold the 2 loaves and slice into ½ inch slices. Sauté slowly in butter until lightly browned.

To assemble, heat olive oil and sauté lamb slices with red pepper and juices. Place hot polenta slices on plate brushing with pepper jelly. Arrange several lamb slices with peppers over polenta. Garnish with fresh cilantro and serve with Yogurt Mint Sauce.

YOGURT MINT SAUCE

1 pound lowfat yogurt

½ fresh small lime, squeezed

2 tablespoons fresh mint, chopped

4 tablespoons fresh cilantro, chopped

2 tablespoons green onion, chopped

¼ teaspoon salt

1 small fresh jalapeno, chopped

Whisk ingredients together. Cover and refrigerate for 1 hour before serving.

■

GRILLED SALMON STEAKS ON BLACK BEAN PASTE WITH RED CHILE DRIZZLE AND MANGO SALSA

Serves 6

6 salmon steaks

Grill salmon steaks, brushing with lemon juice and melted butter until cooked through. Serve on bed of Black Bean Paste with Red Chile Drizzle and Mango Salsa.

BLACK BEAN PASTE

2 16-ounce bags black beans

2 tablespoons dark molasses

½ teaspoon salt

1 bunch green onions, chopped

4 tablespoons bacon grease

1 teaspoon minced fresh garlic

2 tablespoons butter

Soak beans overnight with enough water to cover 3 inches. Boil until tender, drain and mash.

Sauté onion and garlic in butter. In saucepan, heat molasses, onion-garlic mix, bacon grease and salt. Add beans and mix well. Heat over low heat, stirring until liquid reduces and beans thicken (about 10 minutes).

RED CHILE DRIZZLE

¾ cup beef broth

½ cup red chile powder

½ cup bacon grease

1 teaspoon salt

½ teaspoon white pepper

2 cloves garlic, minced

Mix ingredients in saucepan. Heat, stirring constantly until liquid reduces. (Add hot water to thin.) Put in squeeze bottle for drizzling.

MANGO SALSA

2 ripe mangos

4 green onions

½ red onion

½ red pepper

½ green pepper

1/3 cup chopped cilantro

1 clove garlic, minced

2 tablespoons balsamic vinegar

juice of 1 lime

1 tablespoons butter

Chop onions and peppers. Sauté with garlic in butter, just slightly keeping color and crispness. Let cool. Chop mango. In bowl, mix all ingredients.

■

GRANT CORNER INN CRABCAKES

Serves 8

2 tablespoons butter

1 red onion, diced fine

½ red pepper, chopped

1 teaspoon chopped fresh oregano

1 tablespoon chopped fresh cilantro

¼ teaspoon ground dried red chile

2 tablespoons flour

½ cup dried breadcrumbs

1 cup heavy cream

2 eggs, beaten

1 tablespoon mayonnaise

2 pounds blue lump crabmeat

½ cup flour for dredging

In saucepan sauté onion, red pepper, oregano, cilantro and red chile until onion is translucent. Add flour and cream and simmer for about 4 minutes. Set aside and cool. In medium bowl mix all ingredients except crab. Cool completely in refrigerator before adding crab. Mix thoroughly and chill a bit more before making patties. Roll patties in flour and sauté in butter.

Serve with Lemon Chive Sauce (page 67). Add a touch of cayenne.

■

SOUTHWESTERN MOUSSAKA

Serves 6

1 pound cooked leg of lamb

5 tablespoons olive oil

1 large white onion, sliced thin

1 red pepper, sliced

1 Hatch chile, chopped

1 large eggplant

1 cup cooked tomatoes, drained well

1 cup Monterey Jack cheese, grated

1 tablespoon chopped fresh cilantro

1 teaspoon salt

1 teaspoon white pepper

4 eggs, slightly beaten

Banana Melon Salsa

Preheat oven to 350 degrees. Saute onion, pepper and chile in olive oil. Beginning with the eggplant, arrange all ingredients except the eggs in layers in a 2-quart casserole. Season all layers with cilantro, salt and pepper. Pour in beaten eggs and bake for approximately 1 hour.

BANANA MELON SALSA

Makes about 4 cups

3 bananas, firm, not overripe, peeled and chopped fine

1 cantaloupe, peeled, seeded and chopped

juice of 1 lemon

3 tablespoons fresh mint, chopped

1 jalapeno, finely chopped

Mix ingredients in bowl to blend. Serve immediately. This salsa does not keep more than a few hours.

■

CORNISH GAME HENS WITH SPICY SAUSAGE STUFFING AND RED CHILE PECAN SAUCE

Serves 6

6 Rock Cornish hens, thawed and cleaned

¼ cup chopped onion

1 teaspoon minced garlic

2 cups orange juice

STUFFING

1 pound ground spicy sausage

¾ stick butter (6 tablespoons)

1 white onion, chopped

6 slices day-old bread, cubed

2 tablespoons minced fresh parsley

1 teaspoon dried sage

1 teaspoon dried thyme

½ cup chopped apple

½ cup chopped pear

½ cup chopped seedless grapes

¾ stick butter, melted

3 tablespoons Worcestershire Sauce

Marinate hens in orange juice, onion and garlic for 1 hour, reserving marinade.

For stuffing, cook ground sausage until browned. Drain grease and set aside. Melt butter in saucepan over low heat. Add onion and sauté until golden. In mixing bowl combine bread sausage and seasonings. Pour in butter and onions. Mix well with large wooden spoon. Stir in fruit.

Preheat oven to 425 degrees. Stuff each hen. Arrange hens in roasting pan. Melt butter in small saucepan, adding Worcestershire Sauce and reserved marinade. Baste hens with this mixture. Roast for 10 minutes and reduce oven temperature to 250 degrees. Continue cooking, basting frequently, for about 1 hour 15 minutes.

Serve hens with Red Chile Pecan Sauce and Pat's Cranberry Salsa.

RED CHILE PECAN SAUCE

5 Ancho chiles

5 Hatch chiles

2 cups chicken broth

4 tablespoons peanut oil

4 tablespoons olive oil

4 teaspoons white wine vinegar

3 tablespoons maple syrup

2/3 cup orange juice

1 cup toasted pecans, chopped

3 cloves garlic, minced

1 ½ teaspoon salt

Shake most of the seeds out of the chiles. In medium saucepan bring chiles and chicken broth to a boil. Cover and simmer 15 minutes, adding garlic for last 5 minutes.

In electric blender puree chiles and water (some small pieces of skin will remain). Add salt. Pour back into saucepan and simmer on low heat, covered for about 15 minutes.

Add oils, vinegar, maple syrup, orange juice and pecans to blender. Puree sauce until smooth.

PAT'S CRANBERRY SALSA

1 cup fresh cumquats, chopped

2 cups dried cranberries, chopped

½ cup balsamic vinegar

3 green onions, chopped

1 white onion, chopped

1 bunch cilantro, chopped

Stir all ingredients together. Refrigerate for 1 hour.

■

Asides

PAT'S CHUNKY SALSA

Makes about 4 cups

2 large firm tomatoes, coarsely chopped

⅔ cup roasted, peeled, chopped green chiles, or 2 cans chopped green chiles, drained

½ cup canned tomato sauce

1 small onion, finely chopped

3 tablespoons finely chopped cilantro

2 tablespoons finely chopped parsley

2 teaspoons red wine vinegar

1 teaspoon fresh lemon or lime juice

1 small hot dried chile, crushed

Mix all ingredients in medium porcelain or glazed earthenware bowl; let stand at room temperature 2 hours to blend flavors.

■

FRIED APPLE RINGS WITH CHEESE

Serves 4

2 medium red cooking apples
(like Roman Beauties or MacIntosh)

2 tablespoons butter

2 tablespoons brown sugar

½ cup grated sharp Cheddar cheese

Core apples, but don't peel them. Slice into ¼-inch rings.

Melt butter in medium sauté pan and sauté apples 2 minutes on each side. Add brown sugar and continue cooking rings until sugar carmelizes.

Remove from pan and sprinkle with grated cheese.

■

SAUTÉED GREEN TOMATO SLICES

Serves 8

1 stick butter, softened

2 tablespoons dried basil

2 tablespoons minced fresh parsley

2 cloves garlic, minced

2 tablespoons grated Parmesan cheese

½ teaspoon salt

¼ teaspoon rosemary

2 medium green or greenish-red tomatoes, sliced ¼-inch thick

½ stick butter plus ¼ cup olive oil
for sautéing

Mash butter with basil, parsley, garlic, salt, Parmesan and rosemary. Top each tomato slice with generous spoonful of herbed butter.

Heat butter and oil in large sauté pan over medium heat. Sauté tomato slices butter-side-up for 6 minutes, or until slices are tender and butter has partially melted.

Cook's Memory: Thanks to the Considines for introducing me (at an early age) to their own sautéed garden green tomatoes.

■

PAT'S SWEET TOMATO SLICES

Serves 4

2 medium almost-ripe tomatoes

¼ cup fresh lemon juice

½ cup sugar

½ teaspoon cinnamon

butter for sautéing

parsley for garnish

Cut ends of unpeeled tomatoes; core a bit if needed. Cut tomatoes into ⅓-inch slices. Lay slices in flat ceramic or glass dish and pour lemon juice over; let stand 5 minutes, turning once.

Pour sugar into small brown paper bag; add cinnamon. Taking 2 slices at a time, shake in sugar-cinnamon mixture until well coated. Sauté in butter until golden brown. Drain on paper towels.

Place 2 slices on each plate; garnish with parsley.

■

PAT'S STAR POTATOES

Serves 6

1 dozen small red new potatoes,
1½-2 inches in diameter

½ cup butter, melted

¼ teaspoon cayenne

salt and pepper to taste

2 tablespoons finely chopped cilantro or parsley

1 cup chilled sour cream

Put unpeeled potatoes in medium saucepan, adding cold water to just cover tops of potatoes.

Salt the water, then bring potatoes to a boil. Cover and boil 10-15 minutes, until potatoes are almost, but not quite, tender.

Preheat oven on "Broil" setting.

Drain potatoes and let cool 1 hour. Cut each in half, using a small, sharp knife. Make four cuts on flat surfaces of potato halves, scoring each no deeper than ¹⁄₁₆ inch. Cut surface should look like this:

Combine melted butter and cayenne; season with salt and pepper. Brush starred tops of potatoes with mixture. Sprinkle with cilantro or parsley.

Broil potatoes cut-side-up about 6 inches from heat for about 5 minutes, or until tops are golden brown. Using a pastry bag fitted with a ¼-inch star tip, pipe a star of sour cream onto each potato. Dollops with a spoon are fine if you don't want to fool with a pastry bag early in the morning.

■

DOUG'S PARMESAN POTATOES

Serves 6

12 small (2"-diameter) new red potatoes

1 stick butter, melted

2 tablespoons grated Parmesan cheese

1 tablespoon finely chopped parsley

½ teaspoon paprika

Preheat oven to 400 degrees. Grease a 9 x 12-inch baking pan.

In large covered saucepan boil potatoes in their jackets until almost done but still crisp at centers. With sharp knife make small parallel cuts ¼"-⅛" apart almost through each potato. Place cut-sides-up in pan. Drizzle with butter, then sprinkle on Parmesan, parsley and paprika.

Bake potatoes at 400 degrees for 30 minutes, then broil them 5 minutes, or until golden brown.

Cook's Memory: Doug is Bumpy's God-Daddy, and he is famous in San Francisco for his very "elegante" dinner parties. His entertaining style, like this recipe, is simple and easy, so Doug can sip vodka with his dinner guests.

CARAWAY POTATO CAKES

Serves 4

2 large baking potatoes, peeled and quartered

1 small onion, finely chopped

½ stick butter

1 tablespoon grated Parmesan cheese

1 teaspoon caraway seed, crushed a bit

½ teaspoon nutmeg

milk for thinning mashed potatoes

salt and pepper to taste

oil for sautéing

In medium saucepan bring potatoes to a boil in enough salted water to cover. Cover, lower temperature and boil potatoes until tender, 15 to 20 minutes; drain.

In medium sauté pan sauté onion in butter until tender. Add to potatoes, along with Parmesan, caraway and nutmeg. Mash potatoes, adding milk as needed to keep mixture moist but still fairly stiff. Season to taste with salt and pepper; chill for ½ hour.

Form mixture into patties, using about ¼ cupful for each. Fry in hot oil 3-4 minutes on each side, until golden brown. Drain on paper towels.

■

SKILLET COUNTRY POTATOES

Serves 6

12 red new potatoes, 2-3 inches in diameter

1 cup virgin olive oil

1 clove garlic, chopped

1 bunch green onions, chopped,
including some green tops

6 mushrooms, sliced

½ green pepper, sliced thin

2 tablespoons cilantro, chopped

Boil unpeeled potatoes in salted water until almost, but not quite, tender—about 15 minutes. Drain, then cut lengthwise into 6 wedges. Set aside.

In large, heavy skillet heat olive oil; sauté garlic and green onion for 3 minutes, stirring, then add mushrooms and green pepper. Sauté another 5 minutes, then add potatoes. On medium-high heat, brown vegetable mixture 15-20 minutes, flipping with a spatula to incorporate browned parts. Season to taste with salt and pepper; garnish with cilantro.

∎

SPICY PAN POTATOES

Cook 12 new potatoes as above, peeling them after boiling. Chop into ½-inch cubes and sauté in butter, sprinkling with cayenne, salt and pepper to taste.

∎

SAVORY POTATO PANCAKES

Serves 6

3 large potatoes, peeled

2 tablespoons finely grated onion

2 eggs

1 teaspoon salt

pepper and freshly grated nutmeg to taste

⅓ cup flour

oil and butter for frying

sour cream and applesauce for garnish

Grate potatoes by hand or in processor, pressing out excess moisture between two paper towels. Stir in onion, eggs, salt, pepper, nutmeg and flour. Heat thin layer of oil and butter in heavy, large skillet. Drop potato mixture by heaping tablespoonsful into fat, flattening each mound with a spatula. Fry pancakes about 4 minutes on each side, until uniformly crisp and golden brown. Drain on paper towels. Serve hot with applesauce and sour cream.

∎

GREEK HASH BROWN PATTIES

Serves 6

4 medium waxy red potatoes
(not baking potatoes)

1 tablespoon butter

1 medium onion, cut into ¼-inch dice

½ green pepper, cut into ¼-inch dice

½ medium tomato, seeded, cut into ¼-inch dice

2 teaspoons Cavender's Greek seasoning

salt and pepper to taste

¼ cup flour

1 teaspoon salt

2 tablespoons parsley, finely chopped

½ teaspoon paprika

1 3-ounce package cream cheese, softened

3 tablespoons sour cream

1 tablespoon milk

1 egg, beaten

butter and oil for sautéing

finely chopped red pepper
and parsley for garnish

Boil potatoes in salted water to cover until almost tender, but still firm. Drain and rinse with cool water, then let cool for one hour. Peel and shred, then set aside.

In large skillet melt 1 tablespoon butter over medium-high heat. Sauté onion and pepper for 2 minutes, then add tomatoes and continue sautéing for another minute. Add Greek seasoning, salt and pepper to taste. Set aside.

In a mixing bowl blend flour, 1 teaspoon salt,

parsley and paprika. Gradually blend in cream cheese, sour cream, then milk, then egg. Gently fold in vegetable mixture, then potatoes.

Heat ¼ cup butter and ¼ cup oil in heavy skillet. Spoon about a quarter cup of the potato mixture for each patty into the skillet and cook until golden brown and crisp on one side—flip and brown other side. Drain on paper towels and serve on a heated platter, sprinkled with finely chopped red pepper and parsley.

Cook's Note: For a main dish meal, spread hash brown mixture in a baking pan; make several "wells" in mixture with back of spoon. Break an egg into each well; bake at 400 degrees 10-15 minutes, or until egg whites are set.

■

G.W.

CHEESY BULGARIAN POTATOES AND SAUSAGE

Serves 8

3 cups cottage cheese

2 sticks butter, melted

2 teaspoons salt, divided

1 teaspoon pepper

6 large Idaho potatoes, peeled and thinly sliced

1 pound hot bulk breakfast sausage, cooked and drained

4 eggs

2 cups sour cream

1 tablespoon chives, fresh or frozen

Preheat oven to 375 degrees. Generously grease a 9 x 13-inch baking dish.

Mix cottage cheese, butter, 1½ teaspoons salt and pepper; stir in onion.

Layer casserole with potato slices, sausage and cheese mixture, ending with a cheese layer. Bake at 375 degrees for 30 minutes.

Beat eggs with sour cream and chives; spread over casserole. Bake another 35-45 minutes, or until topping is puffed and golden brown and potatoes test tender with a fork.

■

POPPY SEED-WILD RICE PATTIES

Serves 4

¼ cup wild rice

1 cup water

2 teaspoons salt

2 small baking pototoes, peeled and boiled until tender

2 egg yolks

1 tablespoon sour cream

4 slices bacon, diced

4 scallions, finely sliced

1 tablespoon minced parsley

pinch marjoram

1 tablespoon poppy seed

pinch nutmeg

⅔ cup fine fresh bread crumbs

butter for sautéing

In small saucepan bring wild rice, water and salt to a boil. Lower heat and simmer, covered, 50 minutes. Drain, rinse and set aside.

Mash potatoes with egg yolks and sour cream. Set aside.

In medium sauté pan fry bacon until crisp; add scallion, parsley and marjoram and sauté 3 minutes. Cool.

Mix potatoes, rice and bacon mixture. Season to taste with salt and pepper. Stir in poppy seed, nutmeg and bread crumbs and refrigerate until firm.

Form mixture into patties and sauté in butter over medium heat until golden brown, 4 minutes on each side, turning once.

■

FAVORITE SPOONBREAD

Serves 6

2 cups milk, scalded and hot

1 cup cornmeal, preferably
stone- or water-ground

1 tablespoon butter

1 teaspoon salt

2 eggs, separated

1 cup milk

Preheat oven to 400 degrees. Generously grease a 1½-quart casserole dish.

Pour scalded milk gradually over cornmeal in medium saucepan over medium-high heat, stirring constantly to prevent lumping and sticking. Boil 5 minutes, then remove from heat. Add butter, salt and egg yolks which have been beaten with milk.

Beat egg whites; fold into cornmeal mixture. Pour into prepared dish and bake at 400 degrees for 20-25 minutes, or until top is lightly browned. Serve immediately with lots of butter.

∎

SANTA FE SPOONBREAD

Serves 12

1 cup yellow cornmeal

2 teaspoons salt, divided

1 teaspoon soda, divided

1½ cups milk, divided

⅔ cup vegetable oil, divided

4 eggs, beaten, divided

1 cup blue cornmeal

1 16-ounce can creamed corn

2 4-ounce cans chopped green chiles

12 ounces (3 cups) grated
Monterey jack cheese

Preheat oven to 350 degrees.

In medium mixing bowl combine yellow cornmeal with one teaspoon salt and ½ teaspoon soda. Add ¾ cup milk and ⅓ cup vegetable oil, then beat in 2 eggs. In another bowl repeat steps, this time using blue cornmeal. To yellow cornmeal mixture, add creamed corn.

Pour blue cornmeal into greased 9 x 13-inch baking pan. Sprinkle with chiles, then with cheese. Pour on the yellow cornmeal mixture. Bake at 350 degrees for 45 minutes, until slightly puffed and brown.

∎

NEW MEXICO CHILE-CHEESE GRITS

Serves 12

5¾ cups water

1⅓ cups quick-cooking grits

1 stick butter, melted

1 pound (4 cups) grated medium-sharp
Cheddar cheese

3 eggs

¾ cup chopped mild green chiles

2 cloves garlic, minced

2 teaspoons salt

2 teaspoons Tabasco sauce

½ teaspoon paprika

Generously grease a 3-quart casserole dish.

Bring water to a boil in large (3-quart) saucepan.

Gradually stir in grits, making sure water is kept at a boil throughout. Cook grits 5-7 minutes; cover and remove from heat.

In medium mixing bowl combine butter, cheese, eggs, chiles, garlic, salt and Tabasco. Stir in grits. Pour into prepared casserole dish. Sprinkle with paprika.

Bake at 325 degrees for 30-40 minutes, or until puffed and lightly browned.

■

GARLIC GRITS CASSEROLE

Serves 10

5 cups water

1½ teaspoons salt

1½ cups quick grits

2 6-ounce rolls
garlic cheese spread, chunked

1½ sticks butter

4 eggs, beaten

½ cup milk

¼ teaspoon white pepper

½ teaspoon paprika, divided

Preheat oven to 350 degrees. Grease a 3-quart casserole dish.

In large saucepan bring water and salt to a boil; stir in grits gradually. Reduce heat and cook 3 minutes, stirring constantly. Add cheese and butter, stirring until melted and incorporated.

Add eggs, milk, pepper and ¼ teaspoon paprika. Pour into prepared dish and sprinkle with remaining paprika.

Bake at 350 degrees for 1 hour, or until puffed and golden.

■

CHILE-CHEESE RICE

Serves 8

1 bunch scallions, most of green tops removed, finely chopped

1 jalapeño chile, finely chopped, optional

½ stick butter

3 cups cooked rice

1¼ teaspoons salt

1½ cups sour cream

2 cups (8 ounces) cubed Monterey jack cheese

2 4-ounce cans chopped green chiles, drained

½ cup (2 ounces) grated mild Cheddar cheese

Preheat oven to 350 degrees. Generously butter a 2-quart casserole dish.

In small sauté pan sauté scallions and jalapeño in butter until translucent. Stir into cooked rice; add salt, sour cream, cubed Monterey jack and green chiles. Pour into prepared casserole dish; sprinkle with Cheddar.

Bake at 350 degrees for 30 minutes, or until cheese topping is melted and casserole is bubbly.

Cook's Note: For an even spicier side dish, use 2 chopped fresh jalapeños along with the mild chiles.

■

SURULLITOS DE MAIZ

Makes about 40 cornmeal fingers

2 cups water

1¼ teaspoons salt

1½ cups yellow cornmeal

1 cup grated Parmesan cheese

oil for deep fat frying

Heat oil in deep fat fryer to 375 degrees.

In medium saucepan, bring water and salt to a boil. Gradually add cornmeal, stirring mixture constantly with a wooden spoon. Cook over medium heat until mixture thickens and pulls away from bottom and sides of pan. Remove from heat and thoroughly mix in cheese; chill until cooled.

For each finger, take a generous tablespoonful of cornmeal mixture and shape by hand into a cigarlike log about 3 inches long. Deep-fry in preheated oil for 2-3 minutes, or until golden brown. Drain on paper towels and serve hot with Adobo Dipping Sauce.

ADOBO DIPPING SAUCE

2 cups homemade or commercial mayonnaise

½ cup chile sauce or ketchup

2 shallots, finely minced

2 tablespoons capers, finely minced

1 small sweet pickle, minced

2 tablespoons finely minced parsley

1 teaspoon Adobo seasoning (a Puerto Rican spice mix; if unavailable, substitute ½ teaspoon

garlic powder, ¼ teaspoon black pepper and ¼ teaspoon ground oregano)

salt, pepper and cayenne pepper to taste

Combine all ingredients well; chill before serving.

■

BACON TWISTS

Serves 4

8 slices bacon (thick-sliced)

Preheat oven to 350 degrees.

Cut each slice in half. Spiral twist and arrange on a baking sheet. Bake for approximately 20 minutes or until crisp. Drain grease and pat with paper towels.

■

SAUSAGE PINWHEELS

Serves 9

1 teaspoon baking soda

1½ cups buttermilk

4 cups all-purpose flour

4 teaspoons baking powder

1 teaspoon salt

¾ cup shortening

¾ stick butter, melted

1¼ pounds hot bulk sausage (Italian or breakfast)

2½ cups chopped mild green chiles

In small bowl sprinkle soda over buttermilk and stir; set aside.

Into medium mixing bowl sift flour, baking powder and salt; cut in shortening using fingers or pastry blender. Stirring dry ingredients with fork, add buttermilk and melted butter. Turn out onto floured surface and knead 6 times. Wrap with plastic wrap and chill 40 minutes.

Meantime, thoroughly mix sausage meat and green chiles. Preheat oven to 400 degrees.

Turn chilled dough out onto very well-floured surface and roll into 12 x 18-inch rectangle. Carefully spread with sausage mixture.

Working carefully, and using a pastry scraper if necessary, roll dough jellyroll fashion, starting with long side. Pinch seam to seal; transfer to floured baking sheet and place in freezer for 30 minutes.

Remove roll from freezer and cut into 1-inch slices. Bake at 400 degrees on ungreased baking sheets for about 20 minutes, or until golden brown.

■

PAT'S REFRIED BEANS

Serves 6

1 pound dried pinto beans

1 pound lean ground beef

2 cloves garlic, minced

1 egg

¼ cup oyster sauce (available in Oriental groceries and large supermarkets)

1 tablespoon tomato paste

1½ teaspoons Worcestershire sauce

1½ teaspoons salt

¼ cup bacon grease

1 large onion, coarsely chopped

½ teaspoon Adobo seasoning (a Puerto Rican spice mixture)

1 small jalapeño pepper, minced

Soak the beans in water overnight. At the same time prepare the beef; combine beef, garlic, egg, oyster sauce, tomato paste and Worcestershire, kneading to mix thoroughly. Press into bowl; use large enough bowl to hold mixture, wrap with plastic wrap and chill overnight.

Next day, cook beans until tender, adding salt last half hour of cooking. At the same time, cook beef in medium sauté pan; drain off grease.

When beans are cooked, drain off cooking liquid, reserving one cup. Heat bacon grease over medium-high heat. In large sauté pan sauté onion 4 minutes, then add beans. Mash with potato masher until a chunky puree forms. Stir in Adobo seasoning and jalapeño and cook, stirring, over low heat ½ hour.

Stir in beef and continue cooking mixture another 45 minutes, covered, over very low heat.

■

CAMELBACK INN
SWEET POTATO CROQUETTES
WITH
MAPLE HONEY SAUCE

Serves 4 to 6

2 cups sweet potatoes, pureed

3 cups breadcrumbs (divided)

½ cup flour

⅓ cup brown sugar

3 tablespoons butter

1 teaspoon nutmeg

1 teaspoon cinnamon

1 teaspoon white pepper

1 teaspoon salt

1 egg yolk

2 tablespoons sherry

2 eggs lightly beaten

¾ cup toasted crushed pecans

Add butter, 1½ cups breadcrumbs, flour, brown sugar, spices, egg yolk and sherry to sweet potatoes. Beat until light. Refrigerate several hours.

Shape into round flat patties ½" thick x 2". Fry in deep fat over medium heat until golden brown on both sides. Drain and serve hot with Maple Honey Sauce.

MAPLE HONEY SAUCE

Makes 2 ¼ cups

2 cups honey

¾ cup maple syrup

½ cup fresh orange juice

4 teaspoons grated orange rind

2 teaspoons ground chile powder

Whisk together ingredients in saucepan and simmer over medium heat. Serve warm.

Cook's Memory: These croquettes evoke such a sweet memory of growing up at Camelback Inn. This recipe came from my aunt Helen Donnelly..

■

CORN MEDLEY

Serves 6 to 8

1 10 ounce package frozen corn or 1 cup fresh corn

1 red pepper, chopped

1 pound broccoli, washed and chopped

¼ cup butter

½ teaspoon Italian seasonings

1 teaspoon cilantro, chopped

Sauté pepper and broccoli together in fry pan. Cook corn according to package directions. Add drained corn to broccoli mixture. Serve hot.

Cook's Note: This is delicious mixed into scrambled eggs.

■

RICE MEDLEY WITH CHORIZO

Serves 6

2 tablespoons olive oil

1 cup chopped white onion

2 cloves garlic, chopped

1 red bell pepper, chopped

6-ounce packages long grain rice and wild rice mix

2 teaspoons chile powder

1 15-ounce can tomato sauce

1 bunch fresh cilantro, chopped

3 cups chicken broth, heated

1 tablespoon olive oil

1/3 pound chorizo

1/2 cup roasted piñon nuts

chick peas drained

large pitted green olives stuffed with pimentos, drained

In saucepan, heat oil over medium heat. Sauté onion and garlic until translucent. Add the red pepper and sauté 5 minutes. Add rice and chile powder and stir well. Mix in tomato sauce, cilantro and broth. Bring mixture to boil. Cover and reduce heat. Simmer about 25 minutes until rice is tender and liquid is absorbed. While rice is cooking, in sauté pan heat 1 tablespoon oil over medium heat. Remove casing of chorizo and sauté about 10 minutes until browned and cooked through. Drain. Fluff rice when done. Stir in cooked chorizo, piñons, chick peas and olives. Blend well and serve hot.

■

BEAN RAGOÛT

Serves 4

1 cup cooked black beans

1 cup cooked white beans

1/2 cup cooked kidney beans

1/2 yellow onion, chopped fine

2 cloves garlic, minced

1/2 green pepper, chopped fine

1/2 tablespoon fresh basil

1/2 tablespoon fresh parsley, chopped

1/2 tablespoon fresh oregano, chopped

1/2 tablespoon fresh chives, chopped

1/4 cup water

4 tablespoons butter

salt and pepper to taste

Sauté onion, garlic and green pepper in 2 tablespoons of butter. Set aside. In medium saucepan, place the beans, basil, parsley, oregano, chives and water. Simmer the ingredients for 5 minutes, or until they are heated. Add sautéed vegetables and rest of butter and stir in. Season the ragout with salt and pepper.

Cook's Note: We serve this bean ragout with any kind of burrito or enchilada.

■

BEST BLACK BEANS

Serves 6

2 cups black beans, sorted and cleaned

1 tablespoon olive oil

1 jalapeno, chopped

1 medium red onion, chopped

2 cloves garlic, minced

5 green chile peppers, mild, roasted, peeled, seeded and chopped

1 small tomato, chopped

1 small bunch fresh cilantro, finely chopped

1 tablespoon molasses

1 tablespoon brown sugar

1 teaspoon chile powder

1 teaspoon ground cumin

1 tablespoon fresh lime juice

salt and pepper to taste

In stockpot, cover black beans with water. Bring them to a boil and simmer for 2 hours, or until tender. Skim off the foam from the top. Drain beans and set aside.

In sauté pan, heat oil on medium heat until hot. Add jalapeno, onion and garlic and sauté until onions are translucent. Add the green chile and continue to sauté 2-3 minutes. Add this mixture to beans in stockpot and stir. Add remaining ingredients, stir and simmer for 15 minutes. Serve beans hot.

■

SHIRLEY'S SQUASH

Serves 8 to 10

4-5 yellow crookneck squash, sliced

2 white onions, chopped

4 cups water

½ cup butter

1 cup grated Cheddar cheese

2 eggs slightly beaten

½ cup sour cream

1 can cream of chicken soup

salt and pepper to taste

1 cup corn bread croutons

Preheat oven to 325 degrees. Boil squash and onions together. Cook until tender. Drain. Mash and add butter, eggs, sour cream, soup and salt and pepper. Grease glass baking dish. Line with corn bread croutons and pour in squash mixture. Bake for approximately ½ hour until bubbly.

Cook's Note: My dear friend Shirley Tart shared this delicious recipe with me. This, served with a fresh green salad, also make a lovely main course.

■

STUFFED BABY ARTICHOKES

Serves 6

6 baby artichokes (if you cannot find baby artichokes, the large ones are wonderful too – just double the stuffing recipe)

1 clove garlic

3 tablespoons olive oil

5 cloves garlic

1 large Portebello mushroom

½ red pepper

3 tablespoons fresh cilantro

3 sun dried tomatoes

6 Kalamata olives, pitted

3 tablespoons olive oil

2 tablespoon balsamic vinegar

2 cups breadcrumbs

Herbed Mayonnaise

With scissors, snip spiny ends of all artichoke leaves. Cut off stem and cut top of choke about ½ inch down. Rub artichokes with olive oil. In pot cover with water and add garlic clove. Simmer (adding more water if necessary) for approximately 45 minutes, until tender and leaves will pull off. Set aside.

When artichokes have cooled enough, take out the very center leaves and the stringy spiny section right above the heart. (In the large artichokes, use a spoon to clean it out well.) Put all the remaining ingredients except bread crumbs in the blender. Blend just until pulverized with tiny lumps. Put mixture in bowl and blend in breadcrumbs. Fully stuff each artichoke cavity.

Serve with Herbal Mayonnaise on the side. Artichokes can be served hot or cold.

HERBED MAYONNAISE

Makes approximately 2 cups

2 cups mayonnaise

2 tablespoons lemon juice

1 tablespoon parsley, chopped

1 tablespoon fresh basil, chopped

1 tablespoon fresh oregano, chopped

Blend all ingredients together.

■

PINEAPPLE, CORN, CUCUMBER SALAD

Makes approximate 1 quart

1 fresh pineapple, grilled and chopped medium

1 red pepper, grilled and diced medium

1 yellow bell pepper, grilled and diced medium

1 1/2 cup corn, grilled

1 cucumber, peeled, chopped

1 red onion, grilled, chopped

1 jalapeño, grilled, seeded, chopped

1 teaspoon cilantro, chopped

1 lime, squeezed

1/4 cup balsamic vinegar

1/4 cup olive oil

salt and pepper to taste

In large bowl, mix all ingredients and chill for hour before serving.

■

GEORGIA O'KEEFFE SALAD

Serves 6 to 8

2 pounds fresh garden baby greens

1 medium red onion, sliced thin

1 red delicious apple, sliced thin

1 orange peeled and sliced

1/4 cup toasted pinons

fresh garden edible flowers

(pansies, nasturtiums, etc.) for garnish

Toss greens with other ingredients and drizzle with Spicy Vinaigrette.

SPICY VINAIGRETTE

Makes approximately 4 cups

1 1/4 cups sugar

2 teaspoons dry mustard

2 teaspoons ground chile powder

2 teaspoons celery seed

1/2 teaspoon salt

2/3 cup strained honey

3/4 cup vinegar

2 tablespoons fresh lemon juice

2 teaspoons grated onion

2 cups olive oil

Mix dry ingredients; add honey, vinegar, lemon juice and onion. Pour oil into mixture slowly and whisk.

Cook's Note: This salad illustrates the essence of the artist's work - nature's freshness and simplicity. Arrange the salad as Georgia O'Keeffe would have – be creative!

■

PEAR LEEK SALAD

Serves 8

2 cups baby greens

4 red Bartlett pears, sliced (do not peel, color is pretty with greens!)

2 fresh leeks, cleaned and chopped

1 cup toasted chopped walnuts

Combine ingredients in salad bowl. Toss with Herb Balsamic Vinaigrette.

HERB BALSAMIC VINAIGRETTE

Makes approximately 1 ½ cups

1 tablespoon cilantro, minced

pinch cayenne

1 tablespoon fresh basil, minced

2 tablespoons red bell pepper, minced

1 clove garlic, minced

¼ teaspoon dry mustard

⅓ cup balsamic vinegar

1 cup olive oil

salt and pepper to taste

■

CITRUS SPINACH SALAD

Serves 6

1 pound fresh spinach

½ pound mixed baby salad greens

3 oranges, skinned and sectioned

2 grapefruit, skinned and sectioned

1 red onion, finely sliced in rings

4 ounces blue cheese, crumbled

1 cup walnuts, toasted and chopped

Wash spinach leaves and baby greens. Dry. Toss together. Put greens on plates. Arrange orange and grapefruit sections and onion slices topping with walnuts and blue cheese.

Serve with Orange Vinaigrette and garnish with purple edible pansies.

ORANGE VINAIGRETTE

Makes 1 cup

1 teaspoon dry mustard

¼ teaspoon finely chopped fresh garlic

½ teaspoon white pepper

1 tablespoon fresh lemon juice

1 tablespoon red wine vinegar

½ cup fresh orange juice

½ cup canola oil

1 egg

Whisk all ingredients together.

■

MARINATED GARDEN SALAD

Serves 6 to 8

½ cup sugar

⅔ cup red wine vinegar

⅓ cup olive oil

1 teaspoon salt

¼ teaspoon pepper

⅓ cup crumbled bacon

½ cup chopped green pepper

½ cup chopped green onion

3 cups cooked sliced zucchini, drained

3 cups cooked sliced yellow squash, drained

1 cup medium size ripe olives pitted

1 jar marinated artichokes and dressing
(Cara Mia)

Pour sugar into vinegar, add oil and spices an mix. Pour over vegetables in bowl and sprinkle bacon over. Cover and refrigerate overnight.

■

ARTICHOKE-CORN SALSA

Makes 10 cups

2 cups cooked, chopped artichoke hearts
(marinated in vinegar and oil)

2 cups cooked roasted corn

1 cup black beans, cooked

1 cup red, yellow and green peppers, cooked
and chopped

Blend with 4 cups of Roasted Roma Tomato Salsa (page 56).

■

JALAPEÑO CORN MASHED POTATOES

Serves 6

4 3-ounce packages cream cheese

¼ cup milk

5 tablespoons butter

5 cups mashed potatoes

4 jalapeños, chopped and seeded

1 ½ cups cooked corn, drained

2 teaspoons salt

2 teaspoons white pepper

Preheat oven to 350 degrees. Cook cream cheese, milk and butter over low heat until butter and cream cheese melt. Stir this mixture into mashed potatoes. Add jalapeños, corn, salt and pepper. Mix well and bake in a 9 x 12-inch greased glass baking dish. Bake about 3 minutes.

■

Pancakes & Waffles

CRUNCHY APPLE WALNUT FRENCH TOAST

Serves 4

4 thick (1½-inch) slices soft "Italian" bread

½ Cup Applesauce (see page 31) or
sauteed apples

8 eggs

1 teaspoon vanilla

½ cup milk

pinch salt

½ cup finely chopped walnuts

¾ cup sugar

1 teaspoon cinnamon

butter for sautéing

thin apple slices dipped in
lemon juice for garnish

warmed maple syrup for topping

Make "pockets" in bread slices by cutting into each about halfway, then moving blade down and around inside rest of slice. Stuff each with 2 tablespoons applesauce; press edges together to close.

Beat eggs with vanilla, milk and salt. Soak stuffed bread in eggs to coat both sides, turning once.

Mix walnuts, sugar and cinnamon in low, wide bowl; roll each bread slice in nut-sugar mixture to coat. Chill 10 minutes.

Melt butter in large sauté pan over medium heat. Sauté slices until golden brown and crispy on both sides, turning once.

Garnish with apple slices and serve with warmed maple syrup.

Cook's Note: I love this recipe made with fresh banana filling, covered with ground peanuts.

■

DEEP-FRIED FRENCH TOAST WITH BOURBON VANILLA SAUCE

Serves 4

2 eggs, beaten

½ cup milk

1 tablespoon vanilla

1 teaspoon cinnamon

4 thick (1-inch) slices cinnamon-raisin bread

vegetable oil for deep fat frying

Bourbon Vanilla Sauce for topping

Preheat oil in deep fryer to 375 degrees.

In low, wide baking dish beat eggs with milk, vanilla and cinnamon. Soak bread in egg-milk mixture until totally absorbed.

Using wide spatula, slip bread slices into hot oil, frying one at a time until deep golden brown. Keep each piece warm in a 200 degree oven while you finish frying. Drain well on paper towels.

Serve warm with Bourbon Vanilla Sauce.

BOURBON VANILLA SAUCE

¼ cup sugar

¼ cup packed light brown sugar

1 tablespoon cornstarch

¼ teaspoon salt

1 cup boiling water

3 tablespoons butter

1 teaspoon vanilla

2 teaspoons bourbon

In medium saucepan combine sugars, cornstarch and salt. Gradually add boiling water, stirring constantly. Bring to a boil and boil 1 minute; remove from heat and stir in butter, vanilla and bourbon. Serve warm.

■

VOGELHAI

Serves 6

6 eggs

½ cup milk

8 1-inch slices good, stale French bread, cubed

6 tablespoons butter, divided

1 medium leek, sliced
(white and light green parts only)

1 cup (4 ounces) grated Gruyère cheese

1 cup apricot preserves

In small mixing bowl beat eggs with milk. Soak bread cubes in custard mixture, turning to coat evenly.

In medium sauté pan melt 3 tablespoons butter. Sauté leeks in butter until soft, about 6 minutes. Remove from pan, add remaining 3 tablespoons butter and sauté bread cubes as you would French toast, turning to lightly brown all sides. Toss with leeks.

Divide cubes among 6 warmed plates. Top immediately with Gruyère and serve with a generous spoonful of apricot preserves.

Cook's Note: This Swiss breakfast recipe may sound a bit strange, but the mixture of sweet and savory is quite delicious.

■

STUFFED FRENCH TOAST

Serves 4

4 ounces cream cheese, softened

¼ cup ricotta cheese

8 slices whole wheat bread, crusts removed

3 tablespoons blueberry preserves

10 eggs, beaten

¼ cup whipping cream

1 tablespoon vanilla

butter for sautéing

warmed maple syrup and fresh
blueberries for topping

In small bowl beat cream cheese with ricotta until smooth. Divide cheese among 4 pieces of bread, spreading to edges. Dot each cheese-topped slice with blueberry preserves, then top each with another slice of bread. Cut "sandwiches" in half diagonally.

Beat eggs with whipping cream and vanilla in low, wide baking dish. Soak sandwiches in egg mixture, turning once.

Heat butter in large sauté pan over medium heat. Sauté French toast until golden brown on both sides, turning once.

Serve with warmed maple syrup and fresh blueberries.

Cook's Memory: I entered this recipe in the Las Vegas, Nevada 1984 Daily Sun Recipe Contest (Eggs & Cheese Category). Ray and Kay Crossman from Omaha were staying at the Inn for the days before the contest finals.

At breakfast the morning I left for Las Vegas, the Crossmans enthusiastically shouted their well-rehearsed cheer: "Who's the best in Eggs and Cheese? Loueeeese! Loueeeese!!" With guests like that, I didn't even mind not winning in Las Vegas!

■

BILL MANNING'S SPECIAL FRENCH TOAST

Note: Bill's specialty is prepared exactly like regular Stuffed French Toast except for this filling variation:

4 ounces cream cheese

¼ cup smooth peanut butter

1 banana, sliced, tossed with 1 tablespoon
lemon juice

Cook's Note: Bill Manning is like me—he has a constant craving for the flavor combination of bananas and peanut butter (at boarding school I introduced my fellow dormmates to the "delicious duo"). Bill, like Mac Cunningham, Bob Mundy and a few others, has crossed the boundary separating "guest" from "family member". In other words, except for paying his bill when he leaves, he's a part of our extended family.

When the dining room fills up, we don't hesitate to ask Bill to join us in the kitchen and sit on Bumpy's stool as he enjoys breakfast. And if the waitresses need the stool for reaching the high cupboards, he stands. That's why Bill gets his very own recipe!

■

PLUM COTTAGE CHEESE PANCAKES

Serves 6

6 eggs

2½ cups cottage cheese

¼ cup vegetable oil

½ cup all-purpose flour

½ teaspoon salt

1 tablespoon sugar

3 fresh purple plums, coarsely chopped

3 sliced plums and warmed
maple syrup for topping

Preheat well-oiled griddle or large non-stick sauté pan.

In large mixing bowl beat eggs with cottage cheese; add remaining ingredients in order, beating well after each addition.

Pour batter onto griddle by the half-cupful; bake until golden brown on both sides, carefully turning once.

Garnish each serving with sliced plums and serve with warmed maple syrup.

Cook's Note: These are the "favorite" at the Inn. Because of the many eggs and little flour, they are exceptionally light and not filling like most traditional pancakes. They are also delicious with peaches, apples and cherries.

■

WHEAT BUTTERMILK PANCAKES WITH RHUBARB SAUCE

Serves 4

2 eggs

¼ cup mild honey

½ stick butter, melted

2 cups buttermilk
(or use milk and sift 6 tablespoons dry
buttermilk powder with dry ingredients)

1 cup all-purpose flour

2¼ teaspoons baking powder

1 teaspoon salt

1 cup whole wheat flour

2 tablespoons wheat germ

Rhubarb Sauce for topping

Preheat well-greased, seasoned griddle or large skillet.

In medium mixing bowl beat eggs with honey, butter and buttermilk; set aside.

In medium bowl sift flour, baking powder and salt; stir in whole wheat flour and wheat germ.

Stir dry ingredients into buttermilk mixture until blended. Drop by ¼-cupfuls onto prepared griddle. Bake until golden brown on both sides, flipping once. Serve with Rhubarb Sauce.

RHUBARB SAUCE

¾ pound fresh or frozen rhubarb,
chopped into 1-inch pieces

3 tablespoons honey

3 tablespoons sugar

½ cup water

1 tablespoon cornstarch

In medium saucepan bring rhubarb, honey and sugar to a boil. Mix water and cornstarch and stir into rhubarb. Bring back to boil and cook, stirring, 1 minute. Serve warm.

■

SOUR MILK PANCAKES WITH PEACHY SAUCE

Serves 4

1 tablespoon vinegar

1 cup milk

1 cup minus 2 tablespoons all-purpose flour

2 teaspoons sugar

½ teaspoon salt

¾ teaspoon baking powder

½ teaspoon soda

1 egg

2 tablespoons butter, melted

Peachy Sauce for topping

Grease and preheat griddle.

In small bowl stir together vinegar and milk; let stand 10 minutes to clabber.

Into small mixing bowl sift flour, sugar, salt, baking powder and soda; set aside.

Beat egg and butter into soured milk; stir into dry ingredients.

Bake on prepared griddle until golden brown on both sides, flipping once. Serve with Peachy Sauce.

PEACHY SAUCE

Makes 1 cup

2 medium peaches, peeled, pitted and sliced

1 tablespoon sugar

pinch each cloves, nutmeg and cinnamon

2 teaspoons cornstarch

⅓ cup cold water

1 teaspoon brandy, optional

In medium saucepan combine peaches and sugar. Cook over medium heat, stirring until peaches are tender. Add spices. Combine cornstarch and water and stir into peaches; bring to a boil, then remove from heat and stir in brandy, if desired. Serve warm.

■

ORANGE GRANOLA PANCAKES

Serves 4

1¼ cups all-purpose flour

2½ teaspoons baking powder

¾ teaspoon salt

1½ tablespoons sugar

2 eggs

1¼ cups milk

3 tablespoons butter, melted

1 cup Granola (see page 26)

grated rind of 2 oranges

Preheat oiled griddle or large nonstick sauté pan.

Into medium mixing bowl sift flour, baking powder, salt and sugar; set aside.

Beat eggs with milk in small mixing bowl. Stir into dry ingredients, blending only until moistened. Add butter, granola and orange rind. Bake pancakes on preheated griddle until golden brown on both sides, flipping once.

Serve with sauce made by warming 1 cup orange juice with 1 cup packed light brown sugar.

■

PUMPKIN RAISIN PANCAKES

Serves 6

1½ cups all-purpose flour

3½ teaspoons baking powder

1 teaspoon cinnamon

1 teaspoon salt

1 teaspoon nutmeg

1 teaspoon allspice

1¼ cups canned or fresh pureed pumpkin

3 eggs, beaten slightly

1 cup sugar

2 cups milk

¾ cup vegetable oil

1 teaspoon vanilla

1 cup raisins

Preheat griddle or large skillet.

Into medium mixing bowl sift flour, baking powder, cinnamon, salt, nutmeg and allspice. Add pumpkin to eggs, beating thoroughly to blend. Stir in sugar, milk, oil and vanilla. Add dry ingredients to this mixture, stirring well. Mix in raisins.

Ladle batter onto hot griddle by cupfuls. Bake until golden brown on both sides. Serve at once with warmed maple syrup.

■

RAISIN-RICE GRIDDLE CAKES

Serves 4

1 cup milk

1 cup cooked rice

½ teaspoon vanilla

½ teaspoon salt

2 eggs, separated

1 tablespoon melted butter

½ teaspoon cinnamon

⅞ cup all-purpose flour

¼ cup raisins

Orange Marmalade Sauce for topping

Heat well-seasoned, greased griddle or large skillet.

In medium mixing bowl beat together milk, rice, vanilla, salt, egg yolks, butter and cinnamon. Sift flour over mixture and stir well to combine; stir in raisins. Beat egg whites until stiff. Fold into batter.

Bake by ¼-cupfuls on prepared griddle until lacy brown on both sides, turning once. Serve hot with Orange Marmalade Sauce.

ORANGE MARMALADE SAUCE

½ cup good quality orange marmalade

½ stick butter, melted

½ cup freshly-squeezed orange juice

In small saucepan warm marmalade just until liquefied; stir in butter and orange juice. Serve slightly warm.

■

OATMEAL PANCAKES WITH BRANDIED CIDER SAUCE

Serves 4

1 cup milk

½ cup quick-cooking oats

2 tablespoons butter, melted

1 egg

½ cup plus 2 tablespoons all-purpose flour

2 teaspoons baking powder

2 tablespoons sugar

½ teaspoon salt

Brandied Cider Sauce for topping

Preheat well-seasoned griddle or large skillet.

Heat milk to scalding and pour over oats in medium mixing bowl; stir and let stand 10 minutes. Then blend in butter and egg.

Into small bowl sift flour, baking powder, sugar and salt. Stir dry ingredients into oatmeal mixture. Drop by ¼-cupfuls onto prepared griddle. Bake until golden brown on both sides, turning once. Serve with Brandied Cider Sauce.

BRANDIED CIDER SAUCE

1 cup apple cider, divided

½ cup sugar

1 teaspoon lemon juice

1 cinnamon stick

2 cloves

4 teaspoons cornstarch

2 teaspoons brandy

In small saucepan heat ¾ cup cider, sugar, lemon juice, cinnamon stick and cloves to a boil; lower heat and simmer 10 minutes.

Mix remaining ¼ cup cider with cornstarch and stir into sauce; bring to a boil and cook, stirring, 1 minute; remove from heat and stir in brandy.

■

APPLE CORNMEAL PANCAKES

Serves 4

Corncakes:

1½ cups boiling water

1 cup yellow or white cornmeal

1 teaspoon salt

2 eggs

¼ cup honey

⅔ cup milk

½ stick butter, melted

1¼ cups all-purpose flour

1 tablespoon baking powder

Topping:

½ stick butter

1 large red cooking apple (Roman Beauty is nice), unpeeled, sliced thinly

2 tablespoons brown sugar

1 teaspoon cinnamon

warmed maple syrup for topping

Preheat well-seasoned griddle or large skillet.

In small bowl pour boiling water over cornmeal and salt; stir to blend, then set aside to soak 5 minutes.

In medium mixing bowl beat together eggs, honey, milk and butter. Stir in cornmeal.

Into small bowl sift flour and baking powder. Stir into liquids; set aside while you make the topping.

Melt butter in medium sauté pan; add apple slices and sauté, flipping slices occasionally, until tender. Add sugar and cinnamon and stir until melted.

Drop corncake batter by ½-cupfuls onto prepared griddle. Bake until golden brown on both sides, turning once.

Serve 4 to a person; top each stack with 4-5 overlapping slices of apple and drizzle with maple syrup.

■

SWEDISH PANCAKES WITH CINNAMON HONEY BUTTER

Serves 4

4 slices bacon, fried crisp and crumbled, ¼ cup drippings reserved

6 eggs

2 cups milk

1 cup sifted all-purpose flour

2 tablespoons sugar

¾ teaspoon salt

½ cup grated Gruyère cheese

Cinnamon Honey Butter for topping

Preheat oven to 375 degrees. Sprinkle bacon and pour ¼ cup bacon drippings into 9-inch cast-iron skillet. Transfer skillet to oven to heat while you prepare batter.

Put eggs into blender container with milk and

blend on medium speed 1 minute. Gradually add flour, sugar and salt, blending another 30 seconds after all ingredients are added.

Remove skillet from oven and pour in batter, sprinkle with cheese and quickly return to oven. Bake at 375 degrees for 30 minutes, or until golden brown and puffy. Cut into quarters and serve immediately, topped with spoonfuls of Cinnamon Honey Butter. *(continued)*

CINNAMON HONEY BUTTER

1 stick butter

¼ cup mild honey

1 teaspoon cinnamon

Beat butter on medium-high speed of heavy duty mixer until softened. Gradually add honey, scraping down sides frequently. Add cinnamon and beat until mixture is light and fluffy.

■

POLENTA BREAKFAST

Serves 4

1 cup yellow cornmeal

1 teaspoon salt

1 teaspoon sugar

butter for sautéing

8 links breakfast sausage, fried crisp

maple syrup for topping

In medium saucepan bring 2 ¾ cups water to a boil. In small mixing bowl combine cornmeal with 1 cup cold water; add salt and sugar. Add cornmeal to boiling water a spoonful at a time, stirring constantly. When cornmeal is thick, cover and cook over very low heat without stirring for 10 minutes. Scrape into a buttered medium loaf pan, cool; then chill for several hours.

Unmold cornmeal mixture. Slice loaf into 8 slices. Sauté slowly in butter until browned and crispy, turning once. For each serving, layer 2 sausage links between two slices of polenta and pour warmed maple syrup over.

■

CATHY'S FINNISH PEAR PANCAKES

Serves 8-10

5 eggs

1½ cups milk

½ teaspoon salt

4 tablespoons sugar

2 cups sifted all-purpose flour

4 ripe pears, peeled, cored and thinly sliced

2 tablespoons lemon juice

2 sticks butter, melted

1 cup packed light brown sugar

2 tablespoons cinnamon

sweetened whipped cream and cinnamon for garnish

Preheat oven to 400 degrees. Butter two 9-inch glass pie pans.

In medium mixing bowl beat eggs slightly; add milk, salt and sugar. Sift in flour, mixing well. Let mixture stand while you prepare pear mixture.

Arrange pears in fan shape in pans and sprinkle with lemon juice. Mix butter, sugar and cinnamon; spread mixture over pears. Pour batter over pears.

Bake at 400 degrees for 30 minutes, or until golden brown. Cut each into 4-5 wedges and serve with dollops of whipped cream and a dusting of cinnamon.

Cook's Memory: Cathy Wright visited the Inn a month before we opened. During the stay, she made these wonderful pancakes.

■

BANANA DUTCH BABIES

Serves 4

½ stick unsalted butter

4 eggs

1 cup milk

1 cup all-purpose flour

powdered sugar and Banana Topping

Preheat oven to 425 degrees.

Place butter in large cast-iron skillet and put into oven to heat. While butter is melting, prepare batter.

Beat eggs on high speed of mixer or blender for 1 minute. Slowly add milk, then flour, beating another 30 seconds after all ingredients are in.

Remove skillet from oven. Swirl butter around to coat sides, then quickly pour in batter. Return to oven and bake at 425 degrees for 25-30 minutes, or until pancake is well-browned and puffy. Sprinkle with powdered sugar and spoon on Banana Topping. Cut into quarters for serving.

BANANA TOPPING

4 large, ripe bananas, peeled

2½ teaspoons cinnamon

¼ teaspoon nutmeg

¼ cup fresh lemon juice

2 tablespoons banana liqueur

Chop bananas; toss with spices and lemon juice, then gently fold in liqueur.

Cook's Note: At the Inn we have 6"-skillets for individual Dutch Babies. These puffed pancakes make a real spectacle, especially topped with whipped cream. For the most sensational results, serve "post haste" from oven to table.

■

APRICOT WHEAT GERM WAFFLES

Serves 8

5 eggs

3 cups milk

1 cup apricot nectar

1½ cups vegetable oil

1 tablespoon vanilla

3 cups all-purpose flour

1 teaspoon salt

4 teaspoons baking powder

½ teaspoon nutmeg

2 tablespoons sugar

1 cup whole wheat flour

½ cup wheat germ

1 cup chopped fresh or canned apricots

sliced fresh apricots and
warmed maple syrup for topping

Preheat well-greased waffle iron.

In large mixing bowl beat eggs with milk, nectar, oil and vanilla; set aside.

Into medium bowl sift flour, salt, baking powder, nutmeg and sugar. Stir in wheat flour and wheat germ. Stir dry ingredients into liquids until just blended; fold in apricots.

Bake in waffle iron until golden brown. Serve at once, garnished with sliced apricots and topped with warmed maple syrup.

■

LEMON WAFFLES

Serves 4 to 5

4 eggs, separated

3 tablespoons sugar

½ teaspoon salt

1 cup milk

2 teaspoons fresh lemon juice

2 tablespoons grated lemon rind

½ stick butter, melted and cooled

1 cup all-purpose flour

Lemon Cream for topping

Preheat greased waffle iron.

In medium mixing bowl beat egg whites until stiff but not dry and set aside.

In medium mixing bowl beat egg yolks with sugar and salt. Blend in milk, lemon juice, rind and butter, beating well. Sift in flour and fold in egg whites.

Bake in prepared waffle iron until golden brown. Serve right away with Lemon Cream.

LEMON CREAM

5 eggs yolks

½ cup sugar

1 cup milk, scalded

5 tablespoons fresh lemon juice

½ cup heavy cream, whipped

Combine eggs yolks and sugar in top saucepan of double boiler; beat until thick and lemon-colored. Blend in milk and set over simmering water. Cook, stirring constantly, until custard thickens and coats a spoon, about 8 minutes.

Transfer custard to medium glass or porcelain bowl. Stir in lemon juice; chill at least 3 hours.

Just before serving, fold in whipped cream.

■

ORANGE-PECAN WAFFLES

Serves 4

2 cups all-purpose flour

2 teaspoons baking powder

1 teaspoon baking soda

½ teaspoon salt

1 tablespoon wheat germ

2 eggs

juice and grated rind of 2 oranges

1½ cups milk

6 tablespoons butter, melted

¼ cup chopped pecans

warmed maple syrup for topping

Preheat a well-greased waffle iron.

Into medium mixing bowl sift flour, baking powder, soda and salt; stir in wheat germ.

In small mixing bowl whisk eggs with orange juice, rind, milk and butter. Stir into dry ingredients; fold in pecans.

Bake in prepared waffle iron until golden brown on both sides. Serve hot with maple syrup.

■

ANNE'S BLUE CORN WAFFLES

Makes 6-8 waffles

1 cup sifted cake flour

3 tablespoons sugar

1 tablespoon baking powder

½ teaspoon salt

¾ cup blue cornmeal

2 eggs, separated

1¼ cups buttermilk

5 tablespoons butter, melted and cooled

Honey-Orange Sauce

Sift flour, sugar, baking powder and salt; stir in blue cornmeal and set aside.

Beat egg yolks until thick and lemon-colored. Beat in buttermilk and melted butter. Add to dry ingredients and stir just until blended.

Beat egg whites until stiff, not dry, peaks form. Stir ⅓ of whites into batter: gently fold in the rest.

Bake in a waffle iron and serve immediately with Honey-Orange Sauce.

HONEY-ORANGE SAUCE

Makes about 2½ cups

2 cups honey

4 teaspoons grated orange rind

½ cup freshly-squeezed orange juice

4 teaspoons Grand Marnier or Triple Sec

Warm honey in saucepan; add remaining ingredients and stir until combined.

■

CHERRY-ALMOND BUTTER WAFFLE SANDWICHES

Makes 4 sandwiches

1 cup whole almonds

2 teaspoons vegetable oil

¼ teaspoon salt

8 large slices commercial "wheat" bread (not whole wheat)

½ cup good quality cherry preserves

melted butter

Roast almonds at 350 degrees for about 10 minutes, or until they start to darken. Put almonds in food processor outfitted with steel knife; process until coarsely ground. Slowly add oil through feed tube, scraping down sides frequently and processing until almonds are consistency of coarse peanut butter. Add salt.

Preheat waffle iron.

Cut crusts off wheat bread. Spread each slice thinly with almond butter; spoon about 2 tablespoons preserves onto the centers of four of the slices. Top with other slices, almond-butter-side down. Brush each sandwich generously with butter on both sides.

Place one sandwich on hot waffle iron so that one corner is at top. Carefully close iron, being careful not to press down.

Grill sandwich for about 1 minute, or until golden brown. Repeat with other sandwiches.

Cook's Note: This sandwich is especially good served with hot, crispy bacon on the side; try it for Sunday night supper.

■

SOUR CREAM COCOANUT WAFFLES

Serves 4

¼ cup canned cream of cocoanut
(available in liquor stores and
large supermarkets)

¾ cup sour cream

½ cup milk

1 tablespoon butter, melted

1½ cups all-purpose flour

1 tablespoon baking powder

1 tablespoon sugar

½ teaspoon salt

¾ cup moist shredded cocoanut, divided

Tropical Sauce for topping

Preheat greased waffle iron.

In medium mixing bowl beat cream of cocoanut with sour cream, milk and butter; set aside. Into small bowl stir flour, baking powder, sugar and salt.

Mix dry ingredients into liquids; stir in ½ cup of the cocoanut.

Pour batter by the ½-cupful onto prepared iron. Sprinkle each with 1 tablespoon of remaining cocoanut. Bake until golden brown and crisp; serve with Tropical Sauce.

TROPICAL SAUCE

Serves 4

1½ cups coarsely chopped fresh pineapple

⅓ cup powdered sugar

5 tablespoons half and half

1 tablespoon canned cream of cocoanut

2 teaspoons cornstarch

3 tablespoons cold water

1 tablespoon chopped dried papaya, optional

In medium saucepan bring pineapple, powdered sugar, half and half and cream of cocoanut to a boil. Mix cornstarch with water and add, stirring, to boiling mixture. Cook, stirring, until thickened. Add papaya, if desired.

■

BELGIAN WAFFLES
WITH CRÈME FRAÎCHE

Serves 4

½ cup warm (110-115 degrees) water

1 package active dry yeast

2 cups lukewarm milk

1 stick unsalted butter, melted

1 teaspoon salt

1 tablespoon sugar

2 cups all-purpose flour

2 eggs, slightly beaten

1 teaspoon vanilla

pinch baking soda

Crème Fraîche for topping

1½ cups sliced fresh
strawberries for topping

The night before you want to serve the waffles, stir together in large mixing bowl water and yeast. Allow to stand 10 minutes, then stir in milk, butter, salt and sugar. With wooden spoon, beat in flour. Wrap bowl tightly with plastic wrap and let stand overnight on counter top—do not refrigerate.

Next morning, preheat well-greased waffle iron. Stir in eggs, vanilla and soda; beat well.

Bake on prepared waffle iron until golden brown. Serve at once topped with Crème Fraîche and strawberries.

CRÈME FRAÎCHE

1 cup whipping cream

1 teaspoon buttermilk

Stir together cream and buttermilk; pour into jar with lid. Cap and let sit on kitchen counter 1-3 days, until consistency is like sour cream. Whisk a bit to loosen, if desired.

■

GINGERBREAD WAFFLES

Serves 4

1 stick butter

1 cup packed dark brown sugar

½ cup light molasses

½ cup mild honey

4 eggs, separated

1½ cups milk

½ cup sour cream

4 cups all-purpose flour

2½ teaspoons baking powder

2 teaspoons cinnamon

1½ teaspoons ginger

½ teaspoon cloves

¾ teaspoon salt

1 cup heavy cream, whipped

honey for drizzling

chopped candied ginger for sprinkling

Preheat greased waffle iron.

In large mixing bowl cream butter and sugar; when creamy, beat in molasses, honey, egg yolks, milk and sour cream. Set aside.

Into medium bowl stir flour, baking powder, spices and salt; set aside. In medium bowl beat egg whites until stiff, but not dry, peaks form.

Stir flour mixture into liquids; fold in whites.

Bake waffles in prepared iron until deep golden brown. Serve topped with a dollop of whipped cream, a drizzle of honey and a sprinkling of candied ginger.

Cook's Note: These waffles will seem a bit on the soft side when they first come off the iron, but will crisp-up once they stand a minute.

■

CHOCOLATE WAFFLES

Serves 6

6 eggs, separated

6 tablespoons sugar

$\frac{2}{3}$ cup all-purpose flour

$\frac{1}{2}$ cup Nestle's Quik instant cocoa mix

2 teaspoons baking powder

pinch salt

$\frac{1}{2}$ cup milk

$\frac{1}{4}$ cup vegetable oil

Preheat greased waffle iron.

In small mixing bowl beat egg yolks with sugar until smooth and light; set aside.

Into medium mixing bowl sift flour, cocoa mix, baking powder and salt. Stir into egg yolk mixture; add milk and oil and beat to form smooth batter. Beat egg whites until stiff; fold into batter.

Bake in prepared waffle iron until golden brown and serve with Fresh Cherry Sauce.

FRESH CHERRY SAUCE

2 cups pitted fresh Bing cherries

$\frac{1}{4}$ cup sugar

1 cup water

2 tablespoons cornstarch

small amount of cold water

Add cherries to water in medium sized saucepan. Let cherries cook on medium heat until soft. Add sugar. Soften cornstarch in small amount of cold water and add. Let boil, stirring constantly.

Cook's Memory: These waffles are reminiscent of the wonderful chocolate waffles served at Camelback's luncheon buffet. They were a childhood dream, topped with rich vanilla ice cream and Mother's hot fudge sauce!

■

BLACK FOREST CREPES

Serves 4

1 pound frozen tart cherries, or
15-ounce can tart cherries, drained

$\frac{3}{4}$ cup sugar

$\frac{1}{2}$ teaspoon almond extract

1 tablespoon cornstarch

2 tablespoons cold water

8 Basic Crepes (see page 130)

$\frac{1}{2}$ cup sour cream or Crème Fraîche
(see page 127)

shaved chocolate for garnish

Not-too-sweet Chocolate Sauce

In medium saucepan combine cherries, sugar and almond extract. Bring to boil; mix cornstarch and water and stir in, whisking constantly until mixture thickens; cover and cool to lukewarm.

Divide mixture among crepes; for each serving place 2 crepes on dessert plates which have been thinly coated with chocolate sauce (about 2 tablespoons per plate). Garnish with generous dollops of sour cream and shaved chocolate.

NOT-TOO-SWEET CHOCOLATE SAUCE

1 square (1 ounce) semi-sweet chocolate, chopped

3 tablespoons sugar

3 tablespoons hot cream

½ teaspoon vanilla

pinch salt

Combine all ingredients in blender; blend on high speed until smooth.

■

BLUEBERRY BLINTZES

Serves 4

8 ounces cream cheese, softened

4 ounces ricotta cheese

½ cup sugar

12 Basic Crepes (see page 130)

sour cream and Blueberry Sauce for garnish

In medium bowl beat together cream cheese, ricotta and sugar until smooth.

To assemble each blintz, place about 2 tablespoons cheese filling at center of crepe. Fold sides over filling, then fold bottom and top toward center; place flap-side-down on a platter.

Melt ½ stick butter in large sauté pan and sauté 6 blintzes; blintzes should be golden brown on both sides. Repeat with remaining butter and blintzes. Serve hot with Blueberry Sauce.

BLUEBERRY SAUCE

2 cups blueberries, fresh or frozen

¼ cup sugar

1 ½ cups cold water

2 tablespoons cornstarch

Bring blueberries and sugar to a boil in medium saucepan. Mix cold water and cornstarch; stir into blueberries. Bring back to a boil, stirring constantly until thickened.

■

BASIC CREPES

Makes about 30

4 eggs

¼ teaspoon salt

2 cups all-purpose flour

2 cups milk

⅓ cup butter, melted

melted butter or oil

In medium mixing bowl blend eggs and salt. Gradually beat in flour alternately with milk, using whisk or hand mixer, until mixture is smooth. Beat in melted butter.

Refrigerate batter for at least one hour.

Brush crepe pan with melted butter or oil, then heat over medium-high heat. Holding pan over heat at an angle with right hand, quickly pour in 2-3 tablespoons of batter. Immediately swing pan so batter covers bottom of pan in very thin layer. Return to burner, cook over medium-high heat until bottom is lightly browned. Carefully flip the crepe over using fingers or spatula. Brown second side a few seconds. Remove crepe, stack on plate or tray, covering with damp tea towel.

Freeze what you don't need, wrapping tightly in plastic wrap, then foil.

■

WHEAT GERM WHOLE WHEAT CREPES

Makes about 1½ dozen

2 eggs

½ cup all-purpose flour

¼ cup whole wheat flour

¼ teaspoon salt

½ cup wheat germ

1¼ cups milk

Combine all ingredients in medium mixing bowl and beat with hand mixer or whisk until smooth. Let rest at least one hour, then proceed as with Basic Crepes recipe. These also freeze well.

■

B & B ORANGE POPPY SEED PANCAKES

Serves 4

1¼ cups flour

1½ teaspoon baking powder

¾ teaspoon salt

1½ tablespoons sugar

2 eggs

1¼ cups milk

3 tablespoons melted butter

1 tablespoon B & B liqueur

1 cup poppy seeds

grated rind of 2 oranges

Preheat oiled griddle. Into medium mixing bowl, sift flour, baking powder, salt and sugar; set aside.

Beat eggs with milk in small mixing bowl, stir into dry ingredients, blending until moistened. Add butter, B & B and orange rind. Stir in poppy seeds.

Bake pancakes on preheated griddle flipping once until golden on both sides. Serve with B & B Orange Sauce.

B & B ORANGE SAUCE

1 cup orange juice

1 cup light brown sugar

3 tablespoons B & B

2 tablespoons orange rind

Warm ingredients together in a small saucepan.

■

GINGER PANCAKES

Serves 4

1½ cups flour

1 teaspoon baking soda

1 teaspoon ginger

1 teaspoon nutmeg

1 teaspoon mace

3 tablespoons melted butter

1¼ cups buttermilk

2 eggs, slightly beaten

Preheat griddle. Combine flour, baking soda, ginger, nutmeg and mace. Add butter, buttermilk and eggs. Stir until moistened. Batter will be slightly lumpy. Bake until golden on both sides, turning once. Sprinkle with powdered sugar and serve with maple syrup or warm fruit sauce (apples or peaches are good!).

■

FRENCH PANCAKES

Serves 6

1 ½ cups flour

2 teaspoons baking powder

½ teaspoon salt

5 tablespoons powdered sugar

4 eggs

1 ½ cups milk

½ cup water

2 teaspoons vanilla

FILLING

2 cups chopped sautéed apples and peaches

1 cup sour cream, room temperature

1 ½ cups brown sugar

Preheat griddle. Sift together flour, salt, baking powder and powered sugar. Beat eggs and add milk, water and vanilla to eggs. Beat all together. Add liquid ingredients to dry ingredients. Mix lightly. The mixture will be lumpy. Pour onto hot griddle. Pancakes should be thin. Roll pancakes around filling ingredients. Sprinkle with powdered sugar. Serve with Honey Rum Syrup.

HONEY RUM SYRUP

Serves 8

2 cups honey

2 cups maple syrup

2 tablespoons butter

2 tablespoons rum

Mix ingredients in saucepan. Stir over low heat until well blended. Serve hot.

■

PEANUT BUTTER PANCAKES

Serves 4

1 cup flour

1 teaspoon baking powder

½ teaspoon baking soda

½ teaspoon salt

1 ¼ cups milk

3 tablespoons crunchy peanut butter

Into small bowl, sift flour, salt, baking powder and soda. Make a well in the center and add the eggs. Beat well. Add oil and milk slowly. Add peanut butter. Beat until smooth.

Drop onto prepared griddle and bake until brown on both sides. Serve hot with Lucy's Strawberry Jam (page 212).

Cooks Note: These pancakes are also delicious with honey rum syrup and sliced sautéed bananas.

■

ROBERT'S BLUE CORN PANCAKES

Serves 4

2 cups blue corn flour

1 teaspoon salt

¼ cup all-purpose flour

½ teaspoon baking powder

¼ teaspoon baking soda

2 eggs

¼ cup brown sugar

1 cup milk

½ stick butter, melted

Preheat well seasoned griddle.

In medium bowl, sift all dry ingredients. In small bowl, mix together eggs, brown sugar, milk and butter. Add wet ingredients slowly to dry ingredients and mix thoroughly. Drop batter by ¼ cupfuls onto hot griddle. Bake until golden brown on both sides.

Cook's Note: Delicious with dollop of vanilla yogurt and strawberry preserve heated with butter.

■

Muffins

PEAR MUFFINS

Makes 18 muffins

3 cups all-purpose flour

½ teaspoon salt

1 tablespoon baking powder

⅛ teaspoon baking soda

1 stick unsalted butter

1¼ cups sugar

2 eggs

¼ cup fresh lemon juice

¾ cup pear nectar

1½ teaspoons vanilla

2 pears, peeled, cored and coarsely chopped

3 tablespoons sugar for topping

Preheat oven to 400 degrees.

Into small mixing bowl sift flour, salt, baking powder and soda; set aside. In medium mixing bowl, cream butter with sugar until light and fluffy. Beat in eggs. Stir flour mixture into creamed ingredients. Add lemon juice, pear nectar and vanilla, stirring just until combined. Fold in pears. Spoon batter into paper-lined muffin tins. Sprinkle with sugar.

Bake at 400 degrees for 20 minutes, or until muffin tops are light brown in spots and spring back when touched.

■

GRANT CORNER INN BLUEBERRY MUFFINS

Makes 20 muffins

1 stick butter

1 cup sugar

2 eggs

1 cup sour cream

1 teaspoon vanilla

2 cups all-purpose flour

1 teaspoon baking powder

1 teaspoon baking soda

2 teaspoons cinnamon

1 bag (1 pound) frozen blueberries, unthawed, or 1 pound fresh blueberries (when available)

Preheat oven to 375 degrees.

In medium mixing bowl cream butter and sugar until light and fluffy. Add eggs, sour cream and vanilla, beating well to incorporate; set aside. Into medium mixing bowl sift flour, baking powder, soda and cinnamon. Stir flour mixture into creamed mixture until just blended; fold in blueberries.

Bake at 375 degrees in greased or paper-lined tins for 20 minutes, or until tops are golden brown. Cool muffins in tins 10 minutes before removing.

■

GRANT CORNER INN ORANGE MUFFINS

Makes 1 dozen muffins

Muffin Batter:

2 sticks (1 cup) unsalted butter

1 cup sugar

2 eggs

1 teaspoon soda

1 cup buttermilk

2 cups all-purpose flour

grated rind of 2 oranges

½ cup raisins

Glaze:

1 cup brown sugar

juice of 2 oranges

Preheat oven to 400 degrees.

In medium mixing bowl cream butter with sugar until light and fluffy. Beat in eggs. Set aside. In small bowl, mix soda and buttermilk. Add buttermilk alternately with flour to creamed ingredients. Stir in rind and raisins. Fill paper-lined muffin cups ⅔ full.

Bake at 400 degrees for 15-20 minutes, or until golden brown. Mix glaze ingredients, pour over muffins and immediately remove from the tins. Serve warm.

■

LEMON YOGURT MUFFINS

Makes about 2 dozen muffins

2 cups sugar

3¼ cups all-purpose flour

¼ cup toasted wheat germ

1½ tablespoons baking powder

3 sticks unsalted butter, melted

1½ cups plain yogurt

½ cup milk

¼ cup fresh lemon juice

2 tablespoons grated lemon rind

5 eggs

1 cup (about 8) egg whites

Glaze:

¼ cup fresh lemon juice

¾ cup sugar

Preheat oven to 350 degrees.

In large mixing bowl stir together sugar, flour, wheat germ and baking powder. Set aside. In medium bowl, beat butter, yogurt, milk, lemon juice, rind and whole eggs. Stir into dry ingredients. Beat egg whites until soft peaks form. Fold into batter. Fill paper-lined muffin cups ¾ full.

Bake at 350 degrees until very lightly browned, about 15-20 minutes. Brush with combined glaze ingredients and immediately turn out of pans.

Cook's Note: Another favorite at Grant Corner Inn; these muffins are tender, tangy and carry the nutritional bonus of wheat germ.

■

BANANA WALNUT MUFFINS

Makes 24 muffins

2 cups all-purpose flour

1 tablespoon baking powder

¼ teaspoon soda

1 teaspoon salt

½ teaspoon cinnamon

½ teaspoon nutmeg

3 tablespoons buttermilk powder

1 stick butter

2 tablespoons oil

1 cup packed light brown sugar

½ cup sugar

2 eggs

1½ cups mashed ripe banana

⅓ cup milk

½ cup walnuts, chopped

Preheat oven to 350 degrees.

Into large mixing bowl sift dry ingredients. Set aside.

In medium mixing bowl cream butter, oil and sugars. Add eggs, beating thoroughly. Mix in banana and milk.

Add wet mixture to dry one, stirring just until blended. With last few strokes, mix in nuts. Fill paper-lined muffin cups ⅔ full; bake at 350 degrees for 20 minutes, or until tops spring back when lightly touched.

■

APPLESAUCE DATE MUFFINS

Makes 12 muffins

1¾ cups all-purpose flour

½ cup sugar

2 teaspoons baking powder

½ teaspoon salt

½ teaspoon cinnamon

¾ stick (6 tablespoons) butter

½ cup milk

½ cup applesauce

1 egg

1 cup dates, very coarsely chopped

Preheat oven to 375 degrees.

Into medium mixing bowl sift flour, sugar, baking powder, salt and cinnamon. With pastry blender cut butter into flour until mixture resembles coarse crumbs; set aside.

In small bowl beat milk with applesauce and egg. Stir into dry ingredients only until moistened; mixture will be lumpy. Gently stir in dates.

Fill paper-lined muffin cups ¾ full. Bake at 375 degrees 25-30 minutes, or until browned.

■

DOUBLE APPLE MUFFINS

Makes 24 muffins

2 ¾ cups all-purpose flour

3 teaspoons baking powder

¼ teaspoon baking soda

1 teaspoon salt

½ teaspoon cinnamon

¼ teaspoon mace

¼ teaspoon allspice

1 stick butter

1 cup packed brown sugar

½ cup sugar

2 tablespoons vegetable oil

2 eggs

1 cup applesauce

½ cup buttermilk

1 apple, peeled, cored and finely chopped

½ cup walnuts, chopped

Preheat oven to 350 degrees.

Into large mixing bowl sift flour, baking powder, soda, salt and spices. Set aside.

In medium mixing bowl cream butter and sugars until light and fluffy. Add oil, then eggs, beating thoroughly. Mix in applesauce and buttermilk.

Add liquids to sifted flour mixture, stirring just until blended. With last few strokes mix in apple and walnuts. Fill paper-lined muffin cups only ⅔ full. Bake at 350 degrees for 20 minutes, or until tops spring back when lightly touched.

■

FRENCH APPLE BUTTER MUFFINS

Makes 10 muffins

Muffin Batter:

¾ stick (6 tablespoons) unsalted butter

½ cup sugar

1 egg

½ cup milk

1½ cups all-purpose flour

2½ teaspoons baking powder

¼ teaspoon salt

½ teaspoon nutmeg

about ¼ cup good-quality apple butter

Topping:

1 stick butter, melted

½ cup sugar

1 teaspoon cinnamon

Preheat oven to 350 degrees.

In medium mixing bowl cream butter and sugar. Beat in egg and milk. Sift flour, baking powder, salt and nutmeg into creamed mixture and stir until blended. Divide batter in half; divide one half among 10 muffin tins lined with paper muffin cups. Make depression in batter in each cup; fill with a generous teaspoon of apple butter. Divide second half of batter among cups, spreading to cover apple butter.

Bake at 350 degrees 20-25 minutes, or until golden brown. Let cool 5 minutes. Dip tops of muffins in butter and roll in sugar mixed with cinnamon.

Cook's Note: These muffins freeze beautifully.

■

GRANT CORNER INN CARROT MUFFINS

Makes 36 muffins

4 cups all-purpose flour

1 cup packed light brown sugar

1½ cups sugar

4 teaspoons baking soda

4 teaspoons cinnamon

1 teaspoon mace

1 teaspoon salt

1 pound carrots, peeled and grated

1 cup golden raisins

1 can (15 ounces) crushed pineapple

6 eggs, beaten

1 cup vegetable oil

4 teaspoons vanilla

Preheat oven to 350 degrees.

Into large mixing bowl sift flour, sugars, baking soda, cinnamon, mace and salt. Add carrots and raisins, tossing to coat and separate; set aside. In medium mixing bowl combine pineapple, eggs, oil and vanilla. Pour into dry ingredients, stirring well to blend.

Pour batter into muffin cups which have been well-greased or lined with papers, filling ¾ full. Bake at 350 degrees for 30 minutes, or until tops spring back when touched. Let muffins cool for at least 10 minutes before removing from pans.

Cook's Note: The favorite muffin here! These freeze beautifully—taste almost like tiny carrot cakes. Frost them with cream cheese icing and you have carrot cupcakes!

■

MOTHER'S OFTEN BRAN MUFFINS

Makes 2 dozen muffins

1 cup buttermilk

1 teaspoon soda dissolved in ¼ cup hot water

1 egg, beaten

½ cup light molasses

½ cup lemon marmalade

1 cup sifted all-purpose flour

¼ teaspoon salt

2 cups bran

1 cup raisins

Preheat oven to 375 degrees.

In small bowl combine buttermilk, soda, water, egg, molasses and marmalade, beating well; set aside.

Into medium mixing bowl sift flour and salt; stir in bran and raisins. Gradually beat in liquids.

Fill paper-lined muffin cups ⅔ full. Bake at 375 degrees for 20 minutes, or until tops spring back when touched.

Cook's Memory: My own mother's recipes are sadly missing from this cookbook. Mother was tremendously creative in the kitchen, and she loved to originate new recipes for Camelback Inn. Because of illness, she was unable to complete a monumental cookbook, a compilation of friends' recipes. Most of her own recipes were held in her head. I hold strong a memory of her talents, something that has motivated me through many projects.

■

TANGERINE BRAN MUFFINS

Makes 12

1 cup Kellogg's All-Bran cereal

1 cup milk

2 tablespoons grated tangerine rind

3 tablespoons tangerine juice

1 egg

¼ cup vegetable oil

¼ cup sugar

1¼ cups all-purpose flour

1 tablespoon baking powder

¼ teaspoon soda

½ teaspoon salt

1 tangerine, peeled and sectioned

Glaze:

2 tablespoons sugar

2 tablespoons tangerine juice

Preheat oven to 400 degrees.

In medium mixing bowl soak cereal in milk 5 minutes. Add rind, juice, egg and oil; beat well and set aside. Into small bowl sift sugar, flour, baking powder, soda and salt. Add to bran mixture. Spoon into paper-lined muffin cups, each should be ⅔ full. Top each muffin with a tangerine section.

Bake at 400 degrees for 20 minutes. Cool slightly and brush with glaze.

∎

BRAN MARMALADE MUFFINS

Makes 3 dozen

1½ cups all-purpose flour

1½ teaspoons salt

1 tablespoon soda

4½ cups Kellogg's All-Bran cereal

1½ cups whole wheat flour

3 eggs

2 cups milk

1 cup plain yogurt

1¼ cups sour cream

1½ cups honey

6 tablespoons butter, melted

½ cup orange marmalade

1 cup raisins

Preheat oven to 400 degrees.

Into medium mixing bowl sift dry ingredients; stir in cereal and whole wheat flour. Set aside. In another medium bowl beat eggs with milk. Whisk in yogurt, sour cream, honey, butter and marmalade. Stir wet mixture into flour-bran mixture until just blended. Add raisins. Fill paper-lined muffin cups ¾ full. Bake at 400 degrees 18-20 minutes or until tops are browned and shiny.

Cook's Note: We think these are among the best muffins we serve—hearty, yet still light, with a decided orange tang.

∎

PEANUT BUTTER BRAN MUFFINS

Makes 12 muffins

1 cup all-purpose flour

⅓ cup packed light brown sugar

2 teaspoons baking powder

½ teaspoon salt

¼ teaspoon baking soda

1 egg, beaten

1 cup sour cream

3 tablespoons vegetable oil

1 cup 100% bran cereal

½ cup chunky peanut butter

2 tablespoons honey

Preheat oven to 400 degrees. Line muffins tins with paper muffin cups.

In medium bowl combine flour, sugar, baking powder, salt and baking soda; set aside. In small bowl mix egg, sour cream and oil; stir in bran cereal and let stand 5 minutes. Add peanut butter and honey, stirring to mix thoroughly. Stir liquid mixture into flour until just blended; do not overmix.

Fill muffin cups ⅔ full. Bake at 400 degrees for 20-25 minutes, or until tops spring back when lightly touched.

∎

COCOANUT TEA CAKES

Makes 24 muffins

3½ cups all-purpose flour

2 cups sugar

1½ tablespoons baking powder

3 sticks butter, melted

2 cups milk, room temperature

2 tablespoons cream of cocoanut

5 eggs, room temperature

1 cup egg whites (about 5)

3 cups sweetened flaked
or shredded cocoanut

Preheat oven to 375 degrees.

Into medium mixing bowl sift flour, sugar, and baking powder; mix in cocoanut and set aside. In another bowl whisk butter, milk, cream of cocoanut, and whole eggs; set aside.

In small bowl beat egg whites until stiff but not dry.

Pour butter mixture into flour mixture. Stir well to blend. Fold in beaten egg whites. Fill paper-lined muffin cups ⅔ full. Bake at 375 degrees for 15-20 minutes, or until golden brown.

Cook's Note: Cocoanut Tea Cakes are very special; light, rich, almost cake-like in their tenderness.

∎

GINGERBREAD MUFFINS

Makes 16 muffins

½ cup light molasses

½ cup mild honey

¾ stick (6 tablespoons) butter

½ cup buttermilk

1 egg, slightly beaten

2 cups all-purpose flour

1½ teaspoons soda

¼ teaspoon ground cloves

¼ teaspoon nutmeg

1½ teaspoons ground ginger

½ teaspoon salt

1 cup raisins

Preheat oven to 325 degrees.

In small saucepan heat molasses, honey and butter just enough to melt butter. Beat in buttermilk and egg; set aside.

Into medium mixing bowl sift flour, soda, cloves, nutmeg, ginger and salt. Stir in liquid ingredients, mixing only until blended. Fold in raisins.

Fill paper-lined muffin cups ¾ full. Bake at 325 degrees for about 25 minutes, or until tops are lightly browned.

■

OATMEAL MAPLE MUFFINS

Makes 18 muffins

Muffin Batter:

1½ cups boiling water

1 cup quick oats

1 stick butter, softened

¾ cup packed brown sugar

2 egg yolks

1½ cups all-purpose flour

½ teaspoon baking powder

½ teaspoon baking soda

1 tablespoon cinnamon

Glaze:

¾ cup sifted powdered sugar

¼ cup maple syrup, warmed

Preheat oven to 350 degrees.

Pour boiling water over oats and stir to mix. Set aside to cool. In medium mixing bowl cream butter and brown sugar. Add egg yolks and oatmeal mixture and beat at medium speed for 2 minutes.

Sift dry ingredients into a small mixing bowl, then add to creamed mixture, mixing just until dry ingredients are moistened. Fill paper-lined muffin cups ¾ full; bake at 350 degrees for 25 minutes or until tops are slightly browned.

While muffins are baking, beat glaze ingredients until smooth. Brush hot muffins with glaze and immediately remove from tins. Serve warm.

■

MAPLE SPICE MUFFINS

Makes about 2 dozen muffins

1¼ cups all-purpose flour

1½ cups whole wheat flour

½ cup quick oats

1 teaspoon baking soda

2 teaspoons baking powder

2 teaspoons cinnamon

½ teaspoon ground cloves

2 eggs

1 cup plain yogurt

1 cup maple syrup

½ cup packed brown sugar

½ cup vegetable oil

1 cup walnuts, chopped

1 banana, mashed

additional maple syrup for topping

Preheat oven to 400 degrees.

Into small mixing bowl sift flours, oats, baking soda, baking powder and spices. Set aside. In medium mixing bowl combine eggs, yogurt, maple syrup, brown sugar and oil; beat thoroughly. Stir in dry ingredients, nuts and banana.

Fill paper-lined muffin cups ¾ full. Bake at 400 degrees for 20 minutes, or until tops spring back when touched. Drizzle maple syrup over muffins and serve warm.

■

CHOCOLATE ORANGE MUFFINS

Makes 2 dozen muffins

2 sticks unsalted butter, room temperature

2 cups sugar

grated rind of 4 oranges

4 eggs

1 cup sour cream

1 cup freshly-squeezed orange juice

4 cups all-purpose flour

1 teaspoon salt

1½ teaspoons baking powder

¾ teaspoon baking soda

6 ounces bittersweet chocolate, chopped

Preheat oven to 375 degrees.

In large mixing bowl, cream butter with sugar. Beat in orange rind and eggs. Add sour cream and orange juice; set aside.

Into small mixing bowl sift flour, salt, baking powder and soda. Gently stir into creamed ingredients. Fold in chocolate.

Spoon batter into paper-lined muffin tins, filling ¾ full. Bake at 375 degrees for 20-25 minutes, until golden brown and springy.

■

PUMPKIN STREUSEL MUFFINS

Makes 24 muffins

Muffin Batter:

3½ cups all-purpose flour

1 cup packed light brown sugar

1 tablespoon plus 1 teaspoon baking powder

1½ teaspoons cinnamon

1 teaspoon salt

1 teaspoon nutmeg

1¼ cups cooked, pureed pumpkin

2 eggs, beaten

1 cup milk

⅔ cups vegetable oil

6 ounces cream cheese

Topping:

½ cup packed light brown sugar

1 teaspoon cinnamon

2 tablespoons butter, melted

½ cup walnuts, finely chopped

Preheat oven to 375 degrees.

Into medium bowl sift flour, brown sugar, baking powder, cinnamon, salt and nutmeg; set aside. In a second medium mixing bowl whisk pumpkin with eggs; mix in milk and oil. Add flour mixture, stirring until just moistened. Fill paper-lined muffin cups half full.

Divide cream cheese into 24 chunks. Place one chunk on batter in each cup, then top with remaining batter. Mix topping ingredients; sprinkle over tops of muffins.

Bake at 375 degrees for 20-22 minutes, or until lightly browned.

Cook's Note: These are the muffins to make when you want to do something a little special for brunch, especially in the fall.

BLUE CORN MUFFINS

Makes 12 muffins

2 cups finely ground blue cornmeal

⅓ cup all-purpose flour

2 teaspoons baking powder

¼ teaspoon salt

1 cup buttermilk

⅔ cup honey

⅝ cup oil

2 eggs

Preheat oven to 425 degrees.

In medium mixing bowl thoroughly combine dry ingredients. Set aside. In medium bowl whisk together liquid ingredients. Pour liquids into blue cornmeal mixture and stir just until dry ingredients are moistened. Fill paper-lined muffin cups ¾ full and bake at 425 degrees for 15 minutes, or until tops are well-browned.

■

RICE-CORN MUFFINS

Makes 18 muffins

1½ cups boiling water

1½ cups white cornmeal

¾ cup cooked rice

1 cup milk

¾ teaspoon salt

3½ teaspoons baking powder

3 tablespoons butter, softened

2 eggs, separated

Preheat oven to 450 degrees.

In medium mixing bowl, pour boiling water over cornmeal, stirring until thickened. Beat in rice, milk, salt, baking powder, butter and egg yolks.

In small bowl beat egg whites until stiff but not dry. Fold into batter. Spoon into well-greased muffin cups, filling ¾ full.

Bake at 450 degrees 25 minutes, or until well-browned.

■

CHOCOLATE CHERRY MUFFINS

Makes 12 muffins

2 cups all-purpose flour

½ cup sugar

3½ tablespoons unsweetened cocoa

1 tablespoon baking powder

½ teaspoon salt

1 egg

1 cup milk

⅓ cup vegetable oil

2½ cups fresh or frozen
unthawed tart cherries

Preheat oven to 400 degrees.

In large mixing bowl stir together flour, sugar, cocoa, baking powder and salt; set aside. In small bowl mix egg, milk and oil. Make a well in flour mixture and pour in liquids. Stir just until moistened (there may be a few lumps). Fold in cherries; spoon into paper-lined muffin cups.

Bake at 400 degrees for 20-25 minutes, or until golden brown.

■

CHOCOLATE MACAROON MUFFINS

Makes 12 muffins

Muffin Batter:

2 cups all-purpose flour

½ cup sugar

3½ tablespoons unsweetened
Dutch-process cocoa

1 tablespoon baking powder

½ teaspoon salt

1 egg

1 cup milk

⅓ cup oil

Filling:

1¼ cups sweetened flaked cocoanut

½ cup condensed milk

½ teaspoon almond extract

Preheat oven to 400 degrees.

In medium mixing bowl combine flour, sugar, cocoa, baking powder and salt; set aside. In small bowl mix egg, milk and oil. Make a well in flour mixture; pour in milk-egg mixture, stirring until moistened (mixture will be lumpy). Mix together filling ingredients.

Fill paper-lined muffin cups half full of pastry batter. Spoon about 2 teaspoons macaroon filling on top. Top with remaining batter. Bake at 400 degrees for 20-22 minutes, or until lightly browned.

■

CHOCOLATE CHIP MUFFINS

Makes 16 muffins

2½ cups all-purpose flour

1½ teaspoons baking soda

1 teaspoon salt

1 tablespoon vinegar

1 cup milk

1½ sticks butter, softened

¼ cup cream cheese, softened

1 cup packed light brown sugar

1 tablespoon vanilla

3 eggs

2 tablespoons vegetable oil

6 ounces chocolate chips

¾ cup chopped pecans

Preheat oven to 375 degrees.

Into a small bowl sift flour, soda, and salt; set aside. Measure vinegar into 1 cup measure; fill with milk to 1 cup line. Set aside.

Cream butter, cream cheese, and brown sugar; add vanilla, eggs and oil, blending well. Add flour mixture alternately with milk-vinegar mixture. Stir in chocolate chips and nuts.

Fill paper-lined muffin cups ⅔ full. Bake at 375 degrees 15-20 minutes, or until lightly browned.

■

BACON CHEESE MUFFINS

Makes 16

1¾ cups all-purpose flour

1 teaspoon baking powder

½ teaspoon salt

1 tablespoon sugar

½ teaspoon soda

1 cup (4 ounces) grated sharp Cheddar cheese

8 slices bacon, fried crisp and crumbled,
2 tablespoons drippings reserved

1 cup sour cream

1 beaten egg

2 tablespoons milk

2 teaspoons sesame seeds

Preheat oven to 400 degrees.

Into medium mixing bowl sift flour, baking powder, salt, sugar and soda. Stir in Cheddar cheese and bacon; set aside.

In small bowl beat bacon drippings, sour cream, egg and milk until smooth. Stir into dry ingredients just until blended; mixture will be lumpy.

Fill paper-lined muffin cups ¾ full. Sprinkle with sesame seeds. Bake at 400 degrees 20-25 minutes, or until golden brown.

■

JALAPEÑO CHEESE MUFFINS

Makes 16 muffins

2½ cups yellow cornmeal
(preferably stoneground)

½ cup all-purpose flour

2 teaspoons baking powder

½ teaspoon baking soda

1 teaspoon salt

2 eggs

2 cups buttermilk

½ cup vegetable oil

2 fresh jalapeños, seeded and finely chopped

1 cup grated sharp Cheddar cheese

1 cup fresh or frozen corn

Preheat oven to 425 degrees.

In medium mixing bowl combine cornmeal, flour, baking powder, soda and salt, stirring well. Set aside.

In medium bowl beat eggs with buttermilk and oil. Pour into dry ingredients, stirring just to moisten. Stir in jalapeños, cheese and corn. Spoon into paper-lined muffin cups; fill ¾ full.

Bake at 425 degrees for 15-18 minutes, or until lightly browned.

■

POPPY SEED BANANA MUFFINS

Makes approximately 18 muffins

2 cups flour

1 teaspoon baking powder

½ teaspoon baking soda

¼ cup honey

1 egg

¼ oil

1 cup banana, mashed

1 cup yogurt

¼ cup poppy seeds

Beat egg, mix in oil and honey, mashed banana and yogurt. Mix dry ingredients together and add. Stir in poppy seeds.

Bake in paper-lined muffin tins at 350 degrees for approximately 30 minutes.

■

BLUE CORN HONEY SESAME MUFFINS

Makes approximately 18 muffins

1½ cups water

pinch salt

½ cup blue corn meal

½ cup + 2 tablespoons sugar

½ cup milk

2 tablespoons vegetable oil

2 large eggs

1 ¼ cup flour

1 tablespoon baking powder

½ teaspoon salt

Bring water to boil, add pinch of salt and blue corn meal until thick.

In medium bowl mix wet ingredients with cornmeal. Sift dry ingredients together then add to wet ingredients. Bake at 375 degrees for 12 to 15 minutes. When still warm brush with honey and sprinkle with sesame seeds.

■

CRANBERRY PUMPKIN MUFFINS

Makes 3 dozen muffins

3 1/3 cups flour

2 teaspoons baking soda

1 teaspoon baking powder

1 teaspoon salt

2 teaspoons cinnamon

1 teaspoon nutmeg

2 cups pumpkin, pureed

1/2 cup milk

2/3 cup oil

2 cups brown sugar

2 eggs

2 1/2 cups cranberries

Combine dry ingredients. Set aside. Combine pumpkin and milk until blended. Add oil, sugar and eggs and mix well. Add dry ingredients slowly, beating well. Stir cranberries into batter. Fill paper-lined muffin tins 3/4 full. Bake in 350 degree oven approximately 40 minutes.

■

RASPBERRY ALMOND MUFFINS

Makes 1 dozen muffins

2 cups flour

2 teaspoons baking powder

1/2 teaspoon salt

2 teaspoons cinnamon

1/4 teaspoon ground cloves

1/2 cup brown sugar

1/4 cup sugar

1/2 cup butter, softened

1 egg beaten

1 teaspoon Amaretto

1 cup milk

3/4 cup almonds, chopped

1/4 cup raspberry jam

1/4 cup almond paste

In large bowl, sift flour, baking powder, salt, cinnamon and cloves. In another bowl, cream sugars with butter. Beat in egg and Amaretto. Stir in milk. Add liquid ingredients slowly to dry ingredients. Stir in butter and almonds.

Spoon 1/2 of batter into greased muffin cups. Add a spoonful of jam and almond paste and top with a spoonful of batter. Bake at 400 degrees for 15 – 20 minutes. Sprinkle with cinnamon and cool before removing from muffin cups.

■

KAHLUA MUFFINS

Makes 1 dozen

1¾ cups flour

½ cup cocoa

2 teaspoons baking powder

3 tablespoons sugar

½ teaspoon salt

1 egg, beaten

¾ cup milk

¼ cup Kahlua

⅓ cup melted butter

½ cup chocolate chips

½ cup mashed bananas

Sift dry ingredients. Combine egg, milk, Kahlua and butter. Pour wet mixture slowly into dry ingredients. Stir in chocolate chips and bananas. Bake about 15 minutes at 375.

TOPPING

¼ cup Kahlua

½ cup powdered sugar

¼ cup hot water

Combine ingredients and drizzle over hot muffins.

■

Yeast Specialties

HERBAL WHITE BREAD

Makes 1 large loaf

1 package active dry yeast

¼ cup warm water (110-115 degrees)

2 cups warm milk

3 tablespoons butter, melted

1 tablespoon salt

2 tablespoons sugar

approximately 5¼ cups all-purpose flour

2 tablespoons dried dill weed, rosemary, basil or thyme, or any combination thereof

In a large mixing bowl dissolve yeast in warm water, letting stand until foamy. Stir in warm milk, then add butter, salt and sugar, blending well. Stir in 3 cups of flour, one cup at a time, along with herbs. Beat 50 strokes. Add another cup of flour; beat until smooth. Work in a fifth cup of flour with hands. Turn dough out onto floured surface and knead 10 minutes, adding flour as needed to keep dough from sticking.

Oil a medium mixing bowl. Turn dough into bowl, cover and let rise until doubled, about one hour. Punch down dough, knead to smooth, then shape into loaf. Put in greased 9 x 5-inch loaf pan, cover and let rise until doubled. Bake at 375 degrees for about 30 minutes, or until top is golden brown and loaf sounds hollow when tapped. Brush with melted butter if desired and let cool before slicing.

■

VANILLA-GLAZED RAISIN BREAD

Makes 1 large loaf

Dough:

1 package active dry yeast

½ cup warm (110-115 degrees) water

1 teaspoon honey

½ stick unsalted butter

3 tablespoons sugar

1¼ teaspoons salt

1 cup milk, scalded

about 4 cups all-purpose flour

1 egg beaten

Filling:

¼ cup packed light brown sugar

2 teaspoons grated orange rind

⅓ cup fine dry bread crumbs

1 teaspoon cardamom

2 teaspoons cinnamon

2 tablespoons unsalted butter

1 cup golden raisins, chopped

1 egg yolk, beaten with 1 teaspoon water

Glaze:

¼ cup powdered sugar, sifted

⅓ cup boiling water

¼ teaspoon vanilla extract

Grease a 9 x 5-inch loaf pan.

Make the dough: in small bowl stir together yeast, warm water and honey; set aside until foamy.

In medium mixing bowl combine butter, sugar and salt. Pour in scalded milk and stir to melt butter. Beat in a half cup of flour, then add yeast.

Gradually stir in another 1½ cups of flour, then beat in egg. Beat in enough of remaining flour to form a stiff dough.

Turn out onto floured surface and knead until smooth and elastic, about 8 minutes. Form into ball, put in greased bowl, cover and let rise in a warm place until doubled.

Punch down dough, then roll out into a 10 x 12-inch rectangle.

Make the filling: in a small bowl mix brown sugar, orange rind, bread crumbs, cardamom, cinnamon and raisins. Rub in butter with the fingers.

Brush pastry rectangle with egg-water glaze, then sprinkle on filling to within ½ inch of edges. Roll up jellyroll fashion, then form into loaf. Fit into prepared pan, cover and let rise again until doubled, about 45 minutes. Preheat oven to 375 degrees.

Bake at 375 degrees for about 45 minutes, until loaf is deep golden brown and sounds hollow when tapped. Let cool 15 minutes, then brush top several times with combined glaze ingredients, letting glaze set for a few minutes between layers. Serve warm.

■

ANADAMA BREAD

Makes 2 medium loaves

2 cups hot (not boiling) water

¼ cup mild honey or light molasses

5-5½ cups all-purpose flour

1 tablespoon salt

2 packages active dry yeast

1 cup yellow cornmeal, preferably stone-or water-ground

½ stick plus 1 tablespoon butter, softened

In small bowl stir together water and honey; set aside.

In large mixing bowl stir together 3 cups flour, salt, yeast and cornmeal; add ½ stick butter. Gradually stir in honey mixture, then beat with wooden spoon 100 strokes. Stir in enough remaining flour to form moderately stiff dough, working flour in with the hands. Turn out onto floured work surface and knead 8 minutes, adding more flour as needed to keep dough from sticking.

Turn into greased bowl, cover and let rise in a warm place until doubled, 45 minutes to 1 hour. Punch down, divide in half and form into loaves. Place in two 8½ x 4-inch loaf pans, cover with waxed paper and let rise again until doubled. Preheat oven to 375 degrees.

Bake loaves at 375 degrees for 45 minutes, turning loaves around midway through baking to brown evenly. Loaves are done when light brown and hollow-sounding when tapped on bottoms.

Brush warm loaves with 1 tablespoon softened butter.

Cook's Note: This bread makes divine toast and interesting French toast.

■

HONEY-WHEAT BREAD

Makes 4 loaves

1 cup warm (110-115 degrees) water

4 packages active dry yeast

¾ cup honey, divided

7 cups all-purpose flour

3½ cups whole wheat flour

1 cup non-fat dry milk

4 teaspoons salt

⅔ cup bulgur wheat

1 stick butter, melted

2 tablespoons vegetable oil

5 eggs, beaten

approximately 1¾ cups warm water

melted butter for brushing baked loaves

In medium mixing bowl combine water, yeast and ¼ cup honey, stirring until yeast dissolves; set aside. In large mixing bowl combine flour, whole wheat flour, milk, salt and bulgur wheat, stirring well. Add yeast mixture, remaining ½ cup honey, butter, oil and eggs, stirring until ingredients are somewhat moistened (mixture will be lumpy). Add water, stirring to partially incorporate. Turn out onto floured surface and knead until mixture feels elastic, about 8 minutes. Turn into large greased bowl, cover and let rise until doubled, about 1 hour. Punch down dough and divide into quarters.

Flatten each quarter into an 8 x 10-inch rectangle. Roll dough jellyroll fashion, starting on long side, pinching edges to seal. Fold ends under middle, again pinching to seal. Fit into four 8½ x 4-inch loaf pans. Cover and let rise in pans until almost doubled, about 45 minutes.

Bake at 375 degrees for 25-30 minutes, or until tops are well-browned and bottoms sound hollow when thumped. Brush with melted butter and cool before slicing.

■

OATMEAL BREAD

Makes 2 large loaves

2 packages active dry yeast

½ cup honey, divided

2¾ cups warm (110-115 degrees) water, divided

1 cup quick-cooking oats

3 cups whole wheat flour

4 cups all-purpose flour

¼ cup packed brown sugar

2 eggs

2 teaspoons salt

Preheat oven to 375 degrees. Grease 2 large loaf pans.

In a small bowl mix yeast with 2 tablespoons honey and ½ cup warm water to proof. Set aside until slightly bubbly.

In another small bowl soak oatmeal in 1 cup warm water. Set aside for 10 minutes.

In large mixing bowl combine dry ingredients, stirring well.

To oatmeal add yeast, brown sugar, eggs and salt, beating well to mix. Add oatmeal mixture to dry ingredients and stir to blend, adding as much of remaining water as needed to form very stiff dough (some flour will remain unmixed at this point). Turn out onto floured surface and knead until dough is elastic, about 9 minutes. Turn into greased bowl, cover and let rise in a warm place until doubled, about one hour. Punch down, divide in half and form into loaves. Let rise in pans, covered, until doubled, about 45 minutes. Bake at 375 degrees for about 30-35 minutes, or until tops are browned and loaves sound hollow when tapped. Let cool before slicing.

■

7-GRAIN LOAF

Makes 2 medium loaves

½ cup bran

½ cup yellow cornmeal, preferably stone-ground

½ cup toasted wheat germ

½ cup rolled oats

½ cup rye flour

2 packages active dry yeast

2 cups warm (110-115 degrees) water

¼ cup light molasses

4 egg yolks

2 teaspoons salt

⅓ cup vegetable oil

1 cup nonfat dry milk

1 cup whole wheat flour

3-3½ cups all-purpose flour

In small bowl stir together bran, cornmeal, wheat germ, rolled oats and rye flour; set aside.

In large mixing bowl stir together yeast, water and molasses; let stand 5 minutes.

Beat in egg yolks, salt, oil and milk, then stir in bran-cornmeal mixture. Stir in whole wheat flour, then as much all-purpose flour as needed to form stiff dough.

Turn out onto floured surface and knead, adding more flour as needed to keep dough from sticking. Turn into greased bowl, cover and let rise until doubled, about 50 minutes to 1 hour.

Punch down dough and cut in half. Form each half into a loaf; place in two 8½ x 4-inch loaf pans. Let rise again until doubled.

Preheat oven to 375 degrees. Slash tops of loaves with razor blade or sharp knife; brush with water and sprinkle with poppy or sesame seeds, if desired. Bake at 375 degrees for 15 minutes, then lower heat to 350 degrees and bake another 25 - 30 minutes.

■

SOURDOUGH WHEAT LOAVES

Makes 2 loaves

Starter Ingredients:
(must be mixed 3 days before
you make the bread)

2 cups warm (110-115 degrees) water

2 packages active dry yeast

½ cup nonfat dry milk

2 cups whole wheat flour

1 cup all-purpose flour

½ cup bulgur wheat

Breadmaking Day Ingredients:

¼ cup honey

1 tablespoon salt

¼ cup shortening, melted and cooled

2½-3 cups all-purpose flour

On 1st day, stir together all starter ingredients in medium mixing bowl. Cover tightly with plastic wrap and put in a warm place to ferment.

On 2nd and 3rd days, stir starter once and replace plastic wrap.

On breadmaking day, grease two 8½ x 4-inch loaf pans. Stir in honey, salt and shortening. Stir in as much flour as possible, then use hands in bowl to knead in most of remaining flour.

Turn out onto floured surface and knead until dough becomes workable and elastic. Put into greased bowl, cover and let rise in a warm place until doubled, about 1½ hours.

Punch down and divide dough in half. Form each half into an oval the length of the pans, then fold it over and pinch seam. Tuck ends under and fit into pans. Cover and let rise again until dough is almost doubled, about 1 hour.

Preheat oven to 375 degrees. With razor blade make several diagonal cuts in tops of loaves. Bake at 375 degrees 45-50 minutes, or until loaves are deep brown and sound hollow when bottoms are tapped.

■

CHEDDAR BREAD

Makes 2 medium loaves

1¾ cups (6½ ounces) grated
extra sharp Cheddar cheese

¾ cup milk

½ teaspoon salt

1½ teaspoons sugar

1 teaspoon Dijon mustard

¾ teaspoon caraway seed, crushed a bit

2 tablespoons butter

1 package active dry yeast

¼ cup warm (110-115 degrees) water

1 egg, beaten

3-3½ cups all-purpose flour.

Grease two 8½ x 4-inch loaf pans.

In small saucepan heat cheese, milk, salt, sugar, mustard, caraway and butter over medium-low heat, stirring, until cheese is almost totally melted. Cool to lukewarm.

In medium mixing bowl stir together yeast and water to dissolve yeast. Add cheese-milk mixture, egg and 2 cups flour; beat until smooth. Add remaining flour and mix.

Turn out onto floured surface and knead until dough is smooth and elastic, 7-8 minutes.

Turn into greased bowl, cover and let rise in a warm spot until doubled, about 45 minutes.

Punch down dough, divide in half, form into loaves and fit into prepared pans. Cover and let rise again until almost doubled, 45 minutes to 1 hour.

Bake at 375 degrees for 30 minutes, or until tops are deep golden brown and bottoms of loaves sound hollow when tapped.

■

HONEY-WHEAT ENGLISH MUFFINS

Makes 16

1 package active dry yeast

⅓ cup warm (110-115 degrees) water

1 cup hot water (not boiling)

3 tablespoons butter, softened

2 tablespoons honey

1½ teaspoons salt

½ cup nonfat dry milk

1 cup whole wheat flour

3-3½ cups all-purpose flour

1 egg, room temperature

2 tablespoons cornmeal
for rolling out dough

In small bowl mix yeast and water, stirring to dissolve; set aside. In large mixing bowl stir together hot water, butter, honey, salt, dry milk, whole wheat flour and 2 cups all-purpose flour. Add yeast mixture. Beat on medium speed of electric mixer 2 minutes; add eggs, beating well.

Stir in remaining flour with wooden spoon, ½ cup at a time, until dough is fairly firm. Turn out onto floured work surface and knead 6 minutes, until dough is smooth and elastic. Turn into greased bowl, cover and let rise until doubled, about 1 hour. Punch down dough and allow to rest 10 minutes.

Sprinkle work surface with cornmeal. Roll out dough ½-inch thick, letting it rest 5 minutes if it resists rolling. Cut out 3½-inch rounds. Sprinkle baking sheet with cornmeal and transfer rounds to it. Cover and let rise again until doubled, about 45 minutes. Preheat well-seasoned griddle on medium-high.

Bake muffins 2 minutes on each side. Lower heat to medium and bake another 6 minutes on each side. Cool on rack before splitting and toasting.

■

JAM AND CHEESE LOAF

Serves 8

Pastry:

½ cup warm (115-120 degrees) water

1 package active dry yeast

1 tablespoon sugar

2 cups sifted all-purpose flour

2½ teaspoons baking powder

¼ teaspoon baking soda

1 teaspoon salt

⅓ cup shortening

1 egg, beaten

Filling:

2 8-ounce packages cream cheese,
softened

½ cup sugar

1 tablespoon lemon juice

Topping:

¼ cup raspberry or apricot jam

Generously grease a 12 x 15½-inch baking sheet.

Make the pastry: in small mixing bowl combine water, yeast and sugar, stirring to dissolve. Set aside.

In medium mixing bowl combine flour, baking powder, soda and salt; cut in shortening. Stir into yeast mixture, then add egg; mix well. Turn out onto floured surface and knead gently 20 times. Put dough at center of prepared baking sheet. Roll out to 9 x 14-inch rectangle.

Make the filling: in small mixing bowl combine cream cheese, sugar and lemon juice, beating until smooth.

Spread mixture lengthwise down center third of rectangle. Make 3-inch cuts one inch apart on both sides toward the middle third. Starting at one end, fold strips over filling at an angle, alternating strips on either side. Cover and chill loaf overnight.

Bake at 350 degrees for 20 minutes. Remove from oven, spoon jam down center of loaf, then bake another 5 minutes. Cool for at least 10 minutes before slicing.

■

CINNAMON TWIST COFFEE CAKE

Makes 2 8-inch twists

Pastry;

1 package active dry yeast

3¼-3¾ cups all-purpose flour

¾ cup half and half

½ stick unsalted butter

3 tablespoons sugar

1 teaspoon salt

2 eggs

Filling:

3 tablespoons butter, softened

½ cup packed light brown sugar

2 teaspoons cinnamon

½ cup chopped pecans

Icing:

1 cup sifted powdered sugar

¼ teaspoon vanilla

1½ tablespoons milk

Grease two 8-inch round cake pans.

Make the pastry: in medium mixing bowl stir together yeast and 1½ cups flour; set aside. In small saucepan heat half and half, butter, sugar and salt until warm (butter may not completely melt). Add to yeast mixture, along with eggs. Beat on low speed of electric mixer about one minute, then beat at medium speed another 3 minutes. Using a wooden spoon, stir in as much of remaining flour as you can.

Turn dough out onto floured surface. Knead in enough of remaining flour to form a moderately stiff dough, working dough about 10 minutes. Turn into greased bowl, cover and let rise in a warm place until doubled. Punch down dough and divide in half. Wrap each half in plastic wrap and let rest 10 minutes.

Working with first half, roll out into a 9 x 20-inch rectangle. Spread with half the butter, then sprinkle with half the combined filling ingredients. Starting at long side, roll up jellyroll fashion, pinching seam to seal.

Slice roll in half lengthwise. Place halves side by side, cut-surfaces-up. Moisten an end of each portion; push those ends together to join the two pieces of dough. Twist pieces together; shape into a ring and fit into a prepared pan. Moisten ends and press to seal.

Repeat process with other half of dough and filling. Preheat oven to 350 degrees.

Cover twists and let rise until nearly doubled. Bake at 350 degrees for about 25 minutes, or until golden brown. Let stand 3 minutes, loosen edges with spatula and transfer to serving plates. Combine icing ingredients, beat until smooth and drizzle over cakes. ■

SWEDISH TEA RING

Serves 10

Pastry:

1 package active dry yeast

¼ cup warm (110-115 degrees) water

2 tablespoons sugar

1 teaspoon salt

½ stick unsalted butter

½ cup milk, scalded and kept hot

1 egg, beaten

2½-3 cups all-purpose flour

Filling:

½ cup pitted prunes

½ cup dried apricots

1 teaspoon grated lemon rind

¼ cup sugar

pinch allspice

6 tablespoons unsalted butter,
softened and divided

Frosting:

1 cup sifted powdered sugar

2 teaspoons lemon juice

1 teaspoon unsalted butter, softened

1-2 teaspoons warm water

Grease a baking sheet.

Make the pastry: in small bowl stir together yeast, warm water and sugar; set aside until foamy. In large bowl combine salt, butter and milk, stirring to partially melt butter. Add yeast and egg. Stir in flour gradually, adding just enough to form stiff dough. Knead on floured surface until smooth and satiny, about 10 minutes. Turn into greased bowl, cover and let rise until doubled.

Make the filling: simmer prunes and apricots in enough water to cover until tender, about 30 minutes. Drain and process fruits in blender or processor until pureed; mix in lemon rind, sugar and allspice.

Punch down dough and roll out to ½-inch thickness on floured surface. Dot with 2 tablespoons of butter. Fold sides over center to make one strip of 3 thicknesses; seal edges. Chill 15 minutes. Roll out into a 9 x 12-inch rectangle.

Repeat buttering, folding, chilling and rolling process 3 times. After the third, spread rectangle with fruit filling. Roll up jellyroll style from a long side. Place on prepared baking sheet and form into a ring, joining ends and sealing. With scissors, make cuts into ring ¾ inch apart to within ½ inch of inside of ring. Turn each slice on its side, cut-side-up. Cover and let rise until doubled, 50-60 minutes. Preheat oven to 350 degrees.

Bake at 350 degrees for 30 minutes, or until golden brown. Cool 20 minutes, then drizzle with combined frosting ingredients. Serve warm.

Cook's Note: If the dough resists rolling, let it rest an extra 5 minutes between roll-outs.

■

GOLDEN APRICOT TWIST

Serves 12

Pastry:

2 tablespoons milk

½ stick butter

¼ cup plus 1 teaspoon sugar, divided

½ teaspoon salt

½ package active dry yeast

2 tablespoons very warm (120 degrees) water

1 egg yolk

1 egg

1 tablespoon grated orange rind

2-2¼ cups all-purpose flour

Filling:

1 (6-ounce) bag dried apricots

½ cup currants

½ cup water

3 tablespoons sugar

2 tablespoons butter, softened

1 egg white

Frosting:

½ cup sifted powdered sugar

2 teaspoons half and half

¼ teaspoon almond extract

Make the pastry: in small saucepan stir together milk, butter, ¼ cup sugar and salt over low heat just until butter melts. Pour into medium mixing bowl and cool slightly.

In small bowl stir together yeast, 1 teaspoon sugar and warm water; stir to dissolve yeast. Let stand 10 minutes.

Into milk mixture stir egg yolk, egg, orange rind and yeast. Beat in 1 cup flour on medium speed of electric mixer until mixture is smooth, about 2 minutes. Stir in enough of remaining flour to form soft dough.

Turn out onto floured surface and knead until smooth and elastic, about 6 minutes. Turn into greased bowl, cover and let rise in a warm place until doubled, about 1 hour and 10 minutes.

Meantime, prepare the filling: in medium saucepan stir together apricots, currants, water and sugar. Bring to a boil; simmer over medium-low heat, stirring often until most of liquid is absorbed. Cool.

Once dough has risen once, punch down; let rest 10 minutes. Roll out on floured surface into 8 x 20-inch rectangle. Spread with softened butter, then with fruit filling. Roll up jellyroll style, starting on a long side; pinch seam to seal.

Shape dough into ring, pinching ends together to seal. Place on greased baking sheet.

With kitchen scissors, make 10 equally spaced cuts into dough, cutting to within ¾ inch of center. Twist each slice, turning each on its side to reveal filling.

Brush with beaten egg white, cover with waxed paper and allow to rise in a warm place until doubled, about 1 hour. Preheat oven to 350 degrees.

Bake at 350 degrees for 25 minutes, or until coffee cake is golden brown. Cool 15 minutes, then frost with combined frosting ingredients.

■

POPPY SEED RING CAKE

Serves 12

Pastry:

1 package active dry yeast

½ cup milk, scalded and cooled to 110-115 degrees

1 stick butter, softened

¼ cup sugar

2 eggs, beaten

½ teaspoon salt

2 tablespoons lemon juice

1½ teaspoons grated lemon rind

2¾-3 cups all-purpose flour, sifted

Filling:

¾ cup poppy seed, whirled in blender to crush

⅔ cup grated apple

¼ cup sugar

2 tablespoons sour cream

¼ teaspoon salt

powdered sugar for dusting

Make pastry: in a small bowl mix yeast with milk to proof; after ten minutes, mixture should look slightly bubbly.

In medium mixing bowl cream butter and sugar. Add eggs, salt, lemon juice and rind. Add 1½ cups flour and beat. Stir in yeast mixture and enough additional flour to make moderately stiff dough. Turn out onto floured surface and knead until smooth, about 7 minutes. Let rest 10 minutes, then roll out into 10 x 12-inch rectangle.

Make the filling: combine all ingredients.

Spread filling on dough to within ¼ inch of all sides. Starting at a long side, roll up jellyroll fashion, pinching seam to seal. Form into a ring, pinching ends together. Lay in greased 10-inch tube pan. Cover and let rise until doubled, about 1½ hours. Bake at 375 degrees for 40-45 minutes, or until golden brown. Turn out of pan and cool. Dust with powdered sugar.

■

"CHEESE DANISH" COFFEE CAKE

Makes 12 servings

Pastry:

1 package active dry yeast

¼ cup warm (110-115 degrees) water

2 tablespoons sugar

1 egg, beaten

2-2¼ cups all-purpose flour

½ teaspoon salt

1½ sticks butter

Filling:

12 ounces cream cheese, softened

½ cup sugar

1 teaspoon lemon juice

powdered sugar for dusting

Make the pastry: in small bowl stir together yeast, water and sugar; let stand until bubbly, about 10 minutes. Add egg; set aside.

Into medium mixing bowl sift flour and salt; with pastry blender cut in butter until mixture resembles coarse meal. Add liquid and mix well.

Divide dough into 2 balls. For each, roll dough

into 8 x 10-inch rectangle; set aside while you prepare filling.

Beat cream cheese with sugar and lemon juice until smooth. Spread half the filling on each rectangle, lengthwise. Fold sides to middle, overlapping flaps a bit. Fold up ends of rectangles about 1½ inches.

Bake immediately at 375 degrees for 25 minutes, or until golden brown. When cool, dust with powdered sugar.

■

CHOCOLATE BABKA

Serves 8

Pastry:

½ tablespoon active dry yeast

¼ cup warm (110-115 degrees) water

2 tablespoons sugar

½ stick butter, softened

2 eggs

1½-1¾ cups all-purpose flour

½ teaspoon salt

melted butter for brushing pastry

Streusel:

⅓ cup sugar

1 cup all-purpose flour

⅓ cup butter, melted

½ cup pecans, finely chopped

2 tablespoons Dutch-process cocoa

1 teaspoon cinnamon

Make the pastry: in medium mixing bowl mix

yeast with warm water and sugar; let sit 10 minutes, or until foamy. Add butter and eggs, then stir in 1 cup flour; beat until smooth. Add salt and enough of remaining flour to make soft dough. Knead until smooth and elastic, about 10 minutes.

Pat dough into ball and turn into greased bowl. Cover and let rise in a warm place until doubled, about 1½ hours.

Punch down dough. Turn out onto floured surface and roll into an 8 x 12-inch rectangle. Mix all ingredients to make streusel. Sprinkle all but ⅔ cup streusel over dough. Roll jellyroll fashion, starting with long side. Pinch seams to seal. Form roll into horseshoe shape on greased baking sheet, flattening slightly. Brush with butter and sprinkle with remainder of streusel, pressing it into dough. Let rise again until almost doubled, about 45 minutes.

Bake at 375 degrees for about 20-25 minutes, or until golden brown. Drizzle with a bit more butter and serve warm.

■

CHOCOLATE BREAD

Makes 2 rings, 12 servings each

Pastry Dough:

1 package active dry yeast

½ cup half and half, warmed

¼ cup warm (110-115 degrees) water

3¼-3½ cups all-purpose flour

½ cup sugar

3 tablespoons unsweetened cocoa

1 teaspoon salt

2 eggs

½ stick butter, melted

¼ cup sour cream

1 teaspoon vanilla

Filling:

⅓ cup sugar

1 teaspoon cinnamon

2 tablespoons butter, softened

¼ cup finely chopped pecans

Glaze:

1 square (1 ounce) unsweetened chocolate

4 tablespoons butter

1 cup powdered sugar

1 teaspoon vanilla

1-2 tablespoons half and half

Make the bread dough: grease two cookie sheets. Dissolve yeast in half and half and water; set aside.

In a large mixing bowl combine 1 cup flour, sugar, cocoa and salt. Add dissolved yeast, eggs, butter, sour cream and vanilla. Beat with electric hand mixer 3 minutes at medium speed. Stir in 1¾-2 cups flour, until dough pulls away from bowl.

Turn out onto floured surface and knead in another ¼-½ cup flour until dough becomes smooth and elastic (about 10 minutes). Put dough in greased bowl, cover with damp towel or plastic wrap and let rise in warm place until doubled.

Punch down dough, divide in half and shape each half into a ball. Allow to rest under plastic wrap for 15 minutes.

On lightly floured surface roll out half of dough to form 9 x 12-inch rectangle.

Make the filling: in small bowl combine sugar and cinnamon. Spread butter over rectangle; sprinkle with sugar-cinnamon mixture and half the pecans. Starting with the long side, roll up jellyroll fashion, pinching seam to seal. Put seam-side-down on prepared cookie sheet. Form into ring, pinching ends together to seal. Repeat with other half of dough.

With scissors, cut from outside edges of rings to within ¾-inch of inside of rings, making cuts about an inch apart. Twist each slice so that cut side faces up. Cover rings and let rise until doubled. Bake at 350 degrees for 20-25 minutes or until golden brown. Cool.

Make the glaze: melt chocolate and butter in double boiler. Beat into other ingredients and spoon over rings. Separate slices when glaze has set.

■

FRESH BLUEBERRY KOLACKY

Makes 24 kolacky

Pastry:

2 packages active dry yeast

1 cup warm milk

1 stick butter, melted

½ cup sugar

3 eggs, beaten

2 teaspoons grated orange rind

½ teaspoon salt

4-4½ cups all-purpose flour

Glaze:

1 egg yolk, beaten with 4 tablespoons
half and half

Filling:

1½ pints fresh blueberries

¼ cup sugar

2 tablespoons lemon juice

1 tablespoon cornstarch

Streusel:

½ cup almonds or hazelnuts, toasted,
then ground in processor

½ cup sugar

½ cup all-purpose flour

1 stick cold butter

Make the pastry: in a large mixing bowl dissolve yeast in milk. Add butter, sugar, eggs, orange rind and salt. Stir in flour gradually until a soft dough forms. Place in greased bowl, cover with plastic wrap and chill until handleable.

Turn dough out onto floured surface and roll into 14 x 18-inch rectangle, letting dough rest 5-10 minutes if it's difficult to roll (dough should be about ½ inch thick). Using edge of a small juice glass, cut into rounds. Reknead, reroll and recut scraps. Arrange rounds on greased cookie sheet 2 inches apart. Let rise until doubled, about 30 minutes.

Make the filling: in medium saucepan bring blueberries and sugar to a low boil. In small bowl mix lemon juice and cornstarch, then stir into blueberries. Let simmer until thickened. Cool slightly.

Make the streusel: blend nuts, sugar and flour. Cut in butter to make coarse crumbs.

Press each pastry round down in the center, leaving a ½-inch margin. Brush with combined glaze ingredients, then fill with about 2 teaspoons blueberry mixture. Sprinkle each pastry with streusel. Bake at 375 degrees about 15 minutes, or until pastries are golden brown.

■

MARTHA'S HOT CROSS BUNS

Makes 24 rolls

Pastry:

2 cups warm milk

2 packages dry yeast

6 whole eggs

3 egg yolks

8 cups all-purpose flour

1 tablespoon salt

1 cup sugar

1 cup butter

1 cup currants

1 tablespoon orange rind

Icing:

1½ cups powdered sugar

1 tablespoon butter

1 tablespoon hot water

½ teaspoon vanilla

Dissolve yeast in warm milk. Add eggs and egg yolks. Add flour and salt. Cream butter and sugar. Add to flour mixture. Add currants and orange rind. Place in buttered bowl. When doubled in bulk make into 1-ounce rolls. Let rolls rise until doubled in size. Bake at 350 degrees for about 15 minutes. Make icing and make a cross on each roll.

Cook's Memory: Martha Caine and Harriet Eleeson came out from North Dakota about the same time in the 60's to be bakers at Camelback. They are both currently still at Marriott's Camelback Inn, still making all those delicious baked goods, and more of them.

■

ALMOND FANS

Makes 12

Pastry:

2 packages active dry yeast

½ cup warm (110-115 degrees) water

½ cup plus 2 tablespoons sugar, divided

½ cup lukewarm sour cream

1 teaspoon salt

2 eggs, beaten

1 stick butter, softened

4½-5 cups all-purpose flour

Filling:

½ cup sugar

2 teaspoons cinnamon

½ stick butter, softened

Frosting:

1½ cups sifted powdered sugar

2 tablespoons butter, softened

1½ tablespoons milk

½ cup toasted sliced almonds

Grease a baking sheet.

Make the pastry: in large mixing bowl combine yeast, water and 2 tablespoons sugar. Let stand 10 minutes, or until slightly bubbly. Mix in sour cream, salt and remaining sugar. Stir in eggs and butter. Gradually add enough flour to make soft dough. Turn out onto floured surface and knead until smooth and satiny, about 8 minutes. Put into greased bowl, cover and let rise in a warm place until doubled, about 45 minutes. Punch down, and let rise again until almost doubled, about 35 minutes.

Turn dough out onto floured surface and roll out into a 6 x 24-inch rectangle.

Spread softened butter on dough, then sprinkle with filling. Roll up jellyroll fashion, starting on long side; pinch seam to seal. Flatten roll slightly, then slice into 12 2-inch slices. With scissors, make 3 cuts into each slice, cutting to within ½ inch of other side. Spread the fans out a bit, then place on a greased baking sheet. Cover sheet and let fans rise until puffed, about 25 minutes. Bake at 375 degrees for 15-20 minutes, or until golden brown.

Make the frosting: beat ingredients until smooth and lump-free. Drizzle cooled pastries with frosting, then immediately sprinkle with toasted almonds.

■

ALMOND HEAVEN

Makes 32 pastries

Pastry:

2 sticks unsalted butter, ice-cold, cut into 1-inch cubes

3 cups all-purpose flour

2 packages active dry yeast

¼ cup warm (110-115 degrees) water

¼ cup plus 1 teaspoon sugar

½ cup evaporated milk

2 eggs, room temperature

1 teaspoon salt

Filling:

1½ sticks unsalted butter

1¼ cups sifted powdered sugar

⅓ cup almond paste (available in gourmet section of many supermarkets)

2 teaspoons vanilla

Make the pastry: place butter and flour in bowl of food processor. Process only until butter is the size of kidney beans, no smaller. Refrigerate while you prepare yeast mixture.

In medium mixing bowl stir together yeast, warm water and 1 teaspoon sugar; allow to stand 10 minutes, or until bubbly. Add remaining ¼ cup sugar, evaporated milk, eggs and salt, beating well. Stir into dry ingredients just until blended; mixture will be very lumpy. Cover and refrigerate 4 hours or overnight.

Make the filling: in processor, beat butter until softened. Add powdered sugar, almond paste and vanilla and process until smooth, scraping down sides often.

Assemble pastries: divide dough in half, keeping half in refrigerator. Roll out other half into an 8 x 16-inch rectangle on lightly floured surface. Spread evenly with ½ the filling. Roll up jellyroll style, starting with long side.

Slice roll into 16 1-inch pieces. Place each piece cut-side-up in a paper cupcake liner and arrange on baking sheet 1 inch apart. Repeat with second half of dough.

Cover pastries and let rise in a warm place until doubled.

Bake at 400 degrees for 12-15 minutes, or until golden brown. Cool 10 minutes before serving.

Cook's Note: The name says it all! These are best served immediately after baking, to savor their delicate almond flavor.

■

APPLE CINNAMON TWISTS

Makes approximately 48

Dough:

4½-5 cups all-purpose flour, divided

1½ teaspoons salt

2 packages active dry yeast

1½ cups milk

½ stick butter

¼ cup honey

2 eggs

1 cup raisins

Filling:

1½ cups sugar

2 teaspoons cinnamon

2 medium apples, peeled, seeded and finely chopped

½ stick butter, melted

1½ cups walnuts, finely chopped

Glaze;

1½ cups powdered sugar

2-4 teaspoons apple juice or water

2 teaspoons milk

½ teaspoon vanilla

Make the dough: generously grease 2 large cookie sheets. In large mixing bowl combine 2 cups flour, salt and yeast; set aside. In small saucepan heat milk, butter and honey until very warm (120-130 degrees). Add warm liquid and eggs to flour mixture. Using electric hand mixer, beat at low speed for 1 minute, then on medium speed for 3 minutes. By hand, stir in raisins and another 2½ cups flour to make stiff dough. Turn out onto floured surface and knead in up to 1 cup more flour, until dough is smooth and elastic, about 10 minutes. Place in greased bowl, cover with plastic wrap and allow to rest 20 minutes.

Make the filling and assemble: in large bowl combine sugar, cinnamon and apples. Let stand until moist.

Punch down dough and cut in half. Roll out one half to 9 x 16-inch rectangle. Brush with melted butter. Spread quarter of apple mixture down center third of rectangle, lengthwise. Sprinkle nuts over apples; fold one dough flap over filling. Sprinkle flap with another quarter apple mixture, then nuts. Fold last dough flap over and pinch to seal on 3 sides. Repeat process with second half of dough.

Slice across rectangles at 1-inch intervals; twist each slice two times in opposite directions. Line up in rows on cookie sheets. Cover and refrigerate 2-24 hours.

When ready to bake, uncover and let twists stand at room temperature for 10 minutes. Bake at 375 degrees for 30-40 minutes or until golden brown, covering with foil if they're browning too quickly. Remove from sheets immediately, lining up on cooling racks.

Make the glaze: combine all glaze ingredients and beat until smooth. Drizzle glaze in zig-zag pattern over twists.

■

OLD-FASHIONED CINNAMON ROLLS

Makes 16 rolls

Pastry:

5 cups all-purpose flour, divided

1½ packages active dry yeast

½ cup sugar

1½ teaspoons salt

¾ cup milk

¾ cup water

1 stick butter

2 eggs

Filling:

½ cup packed light brown sugar

3 tablespoons sugar

1 tablespoon cinnamon

½ stick butter, softened

Grease a 10 x 14-inch baking pan.

Make the pastry: in large mixing bowl combine 2¼ cups flour, yeast, sugar and salt; set aside. In small saucepan heat milk, water and butter until warm (110-115 degrees); butter doesn't need to melt. Stir into flour mixture. Add eggs and stir until moistened. Beat on medium speed of electric mixer for 3 minutes. By hand, gradually stir in enough of remaining flour to make soft dough. Knead until smooth, 5-8 minutes. Turn into greased bowl, cover and let rise until doubled, about one hour.

Make the filling: in small bowl combine brown sugar, sugar and cinnamon.

Punch down dough. On floured surface, roll out into 10 x 12-inch rectangle. Spread with softened butter, then sprinkle with filling. Roll up jellyroll fashion, beginning with a long side; pinch seam to seal. Cut into 16 slices; place each slice cut-side-up in prepared pan, squeezing them in if necessary. Cover and let rise 30 minutes.

Bake at 375 degrees for 20-25 minutes, or until golden brown. Remove from pan and cool. Sprinkle with powdered sugar.

■

ORANGE-RAISIN CINNAMON ROLLS

Makes 32 rolls

Pastry:

3 packages active dry yeast

½ cup plus 1 tablespoon sugar, divided

1 cup warm (110-115 degrees) water

1 stick butter, softened

2 teaspoons salt

3 eggs, beaten

3-4 cups all-purpose flour

Filling:

3 tablespoons butter, softened

⅔ cup sugar

2 teaspoons cinnamon

1 cup raisins, soaked in ¼ cup
Grand Marnier and drained

Icing:

1 cup powdered sugar

1 tablespoon butter, softened

1 teaspoon grated orange rind

1-2 tablespoons
freshly-squeezed orange juice

Make the pastry: dissolve yeast and 1 tablespoon sugar in water; let stand until bubbly. In large mixing bowl cream butter, ½ cup sugar and salt; add eggs. Stir in yeast mixture. Add enough flour (3-3½ cups) to make a non-sticky dough. Turn out onto floured surface and knead up to ½ cup more flour into dough until smooth and elastic, about 10 minutes. Put into greased bowl, cover, and let rise until doubled.

Punch down dough; roll into 18 x 24-inch rectangle; cut in half lengthwise. Spread halves with butter, sprinkle with mixed cinnamon and sugar and dot with raisins. Roll up each rectangle jellyroll fashion from long side, pinching seams to seal.

Cut into 1½-inch slices and place on greased cookie sheets about 2 inches apart. Let rise for 30 minutes. Bake at 350 degrees for 20-30 minutes, or until golden brown. Let cool 15 minutes.

Make the icing: mix all ingredients and drizzle over warm rolls.

■

RUM-BUTTER STICKY BUNS

Makes 20 rolls

Pastry:

1 package active dry yeast

1 cup warm (110-115 degrees) milk

1½ sticks butter, divided

¾ cup sugar, divided

2 eggs

4 cups all-purpose flour

½ cup chopped candied cherries

½ cup mixed candied lemon and orange rind

Sticky Topping:

1 cup packed light brown sugar

1 stick butter, melted

¼ teaspoon cinnamon

¼ teaspoon nutmeg

3 tablespoons dark rum

In small bowl dissolve yeast in milk, adding pinch of sugar to help proofing; let stand until bubbly.

In large mixing bowl soften 1 stick butter, beat in ½ cup sugar, mixing until light and fluffy. Add eggs, then add flour and yeast mixture alternately, stirring well after each addition.

Turn dough onto floured surface and knead until smooth and satiny, about 6 minutes. Place in greased bowl, cover and let rise in a warm place until doubled in bulk.

Turn out onto floured surface. Roll out into 12 x 24-inch rectangle. Melt remaining ½ stick butter; brush on dough. Sprinkle with remaining sugar and candied fruit. Roll up jellyroll fashion. Starting at long side, pinch seam to seal. Cut into 20 slices.

Mix topping ingredients and spread on bottom of 10 x 14-inch baking pan. Top with pastry slices cut-side-up. Cover and let rise until rolls are doubled. Preheat oven to 350 degrees.

Bake buns at 350 degrees for 25-30 minutes, or until golden brown. Immediately invert pan onto baking sheet. Cool slightly before serving.

■

GOOEY PECAN BUNS

Makes 32 small buns

Pastry:

1 package active dry yeast

¼ cup warm (110-115 degrees) water

¼ cup plus 1 tablespoon sugar

½ cup sour cream, heated slightly

½ stick unsalted butter, very soft

1 egg, beaten

1 teaspoon salt

3 cups all-purpose flour

Sticky Base:

1 cup packed light brown sugar

2 tablespoons unsalted butter, melted

1 tablespoon light corn syrup

¼ cup water

Filling:

2 tablespoons unsalted butter, softened

½ cup sugar

2 teaspoons cinnamon

½ cup pecans, chopped

½ cup golden raisins

Make the pastry: mix yeast into warm water, adding 1 tablespoon sugar to help proof. In medium mixing bowl combine sour cream and butter, stirring to melt butter. Add egg, salt, balance of sugar and yeast mixture. Stir in 2 cups flour. Turn out on floured surface. Knead to incorporate rest of flour, about 10 minutes. Let rise in greased bowl, covered, until doubled (about 45 minutes). Punch down dough, then roll into 10 x 18-inch rectangle.

Make the sticky base: in a 9 x 13-inch baking pan combine brown sugar, butter, corn syrup and ¼ cup water. Slowly cook mixture over very low heat about 3 minutes, or until sugar dissolves.

Assemble the pastry: spread butter over the rectangle to within ½ inch of edges. Sprinkle dough with sugar, cinnamon, pecans and raisins. Drizzle with ¼ melted sugar mixture. Cut rectangle in half lengthwise.

Starting at long side of first 5 x 18-inch rectangle, roll up jellyroll fashion, pinching seam to seal. Cut into 16 slices. Repeat with second piece of dough. Place rolls cut-side-up on melted sugar mixture in pan. Let rise, covered, in a warm place for 30 minutes.

Bake at 350 degrees for 30-40 minutes, or until golden brown. Let cool in pan 5 minutes, then turn upside down, leaving pan in place 15 seconds before lifting it off. Serve warm.

■

ORANGE WHOLE WHEAT STICKY BUNS

Makes 72 buns

Pastry:

4¼-4¾ cups bread or all-purpose flour

½ cup sugar

2 teaspoons salt

2 packages active dry yeast

1¼ cups milk

1 cup sour cream

1 stick butter

2 eggs

3 cups whole wheat flour

Filling:

3 cups packed light brown sugar

3 sticks butter, softened

2 tablespoons grated orange peel

2 tablespoons light corn syrup

⅓ cup freshly-squeezed orange juice

Make the dough: grease two 9 x 13-inch baking pans. In large mixing bowl combine 3 cups bread or all-purpose flour, sugar, salt and yeast; set aside. In small saucepan heat milk, sour cream and butter until very warm. Add dairy mixture and eggs to flour mixture. Beat with hand mixer 3 minutes at medium speed. Stir in whole wheat flour and enough bread/all-purpose flour (¾-1 cup) to make dough pull away from bowl. Turn dough out onto a floured surface and knead for 10 minutes, using more bread/all-purpose flour (½-¾ cup) if needed to form smooth non-sticky dough. Turn into greased bowl, cover with damp towel or plastic wrap, and let rise in a warm place until doubled.

Make the filling: combine brown sugar, butter, orange peel and corn syrup. Divide in half, reserving half. To other half, add orange juice. Spread half the orange juice mixture in each baking pan.

Assemble the rolls: punch down dough. Divide in half, shaping each half into a ball. Wrap each in plastic wrap; let rest 15 minutes.

Working with one ball of dough, roll out into 10 x 22-inch rectangle; cut in half lengthwise. Spread one-quarter of reserved filling to within ½ inch of the edges of each piece of dough. Roll each up jellyroll fashion, starting with long side; pinch seam to seal. Cut each roll into 18 slices. Place cut-side-up in prepared pan (36 to a pan). Repeat with second ball of dough. Let rolls rise, covered, in a warm place until doubled.

Bake at 375 degrees for 20-30 minutes, or until golden brown. Cool for one minute, then invert rolls onto plate or foil.

■

AUNT HELEN'S ORANGE ROLLS

Serves 12

Pastry:

1 cup milk

1 package active dry yeast

3 eggs

½ cup sugar

3 tablespoons butter

1 teaspoon salt

4 cups all-purpose flour, divided

Filling:

½ cup sugar

½ cup butter

grated rind of 2 oranges

Scald milk. Dissolve yeast in milk. Beat eggs slightly and combine with sugar, butter and salt. Add this mixture to milk. Add 1 cup of the flour. Beat until smooth. Let rise 2 hours. Then add remaining 3 cups flour. Mix well but do not knead. Let rise 2 hours more. Roll out on floured board ¼-inch thick and spread with filling. Roll and cut like cinnamon rolls. Bake in muffin tins at 350 degrees for 15 minutes.

Cook's Memory: Aunt Helen Donnelly was the baker of our family. Each year my father would have her come out from North Dakota and train the bakers at Camelback. It was one of those visits when I was about 5 that she taught me how to bake. Soon after, I baked some cookies that I was very proud of because I didn't use a recipe. No one could get their teeth through them either!

■

FRENCH QUARTER BEIGNETS

about 2 dozen beignets

½ package active dry yeast

¼ cup warm (110-115 degrees) water

2 tablespoons shortening

⅓ cup sugar

½ teaspoon salt

½ cup boiling water

½ cup evaporated milk

1 egg

3½ cups all-purpose flour, divided

oil for frying

sifted powdered sugar

In small bowl mix yeast and warm water, stirring to dissolve; set aside. In bowl of heavy-duty mixer combine shortening, sugar and salt; add boiling water and milk, stirring to melt shortening. Let cool slightly, then add yeast mixture and egg. Add 2 cups flour and beat at medium speed until well blended. Beat in remaining flour to form soft dough. Turn into greased bowl, cover and refrigerate overnight.

Preheat oil in deep fryer to 375 degrees.

Turn dough out onto floured work surface. Roll out ⅛-inch thick and cut into 2-inch squares.

Fry in deep hot oil until golden brown, turning once. Drain on paper towels and smother with sifted powdered sugar. Serve 3 beignets to a person.

■

BISCOCHITO-NUTS
(New Mexican Raised Doughnuts)

Makes 35 2-inch Doughnuts

2 packages active dry yeast

¼ cup plus 1 tablespoon sugar, divided

½ cup warm (110-115 degrees) water

1 cup milk, scalded

1 teaspoon salt

1½ teaspoons aniseed, crushed

1 teaspoon cinnamon

¼ cup plus 2 tablespoons shortening

4 cups all-purpose flour

vegetable oil for frying

Vanilla Glaze

Dissolve yeast and 1 tablespoon sugar in warm water, stirring; let stand until foamy.

In large mixing bowl combine milk, remaining ¼ cup sugar, salt, aniseed, cinnamon and shortening, stirring to melt shortening. Cool a bit, then add yeast mixture. Stir, then knead in flour to form soft dough. Turn into greased bowl, cover and let rise in a warm place until doubled, about 45 minutes.

Punch down dough. Turn out onto a lightly floured surface; let rest 5 minutes. Roll out to ½-inch thickness. Cut with floured doughnut cutter.

Lay doughnuts and holes on lightly-floured baking sheet and let rise until doubled, about 30 minutes. Preheat oil in deep fat fryer to 375 degrees.

Fry doughnuts, a few at a time, until golden brown, turning once. Drain well, then quickly dip in glaze. Serve warm.

VANILLA GLAZE

⅓ cup boiling water

2 cups sifted powdered sugar

Mix until sugar dissolves; keep warm.

Cook's Note: In New Mexico "biscochitos" are crispy anise-cinnamon cookies; this is our version in an elegant raised doughnut.

∎

COCOANUT CREAM BUNS

Makes 30 buns

1 recipe Brioche dough (see page 60)

Pastry Cream:

2½ tablespoons cornstarch

¼ cup milk

1 egg

1 egg yolk

¾ cup half and half

½ cup sugar

pinch salt

3 tablespoons butter

½ teaspoon vanilla

1 cup moist shredded cocoanut

Glaze:

1 cup sifted powdered sugar

¼ cup water

Preheat oven to 400 degrees.

Make the pastry cream: in small bowl, thoroughly combine cornstarch and milk. Beat in egg and yolk; set aside. In small saucepan, heat half and half, sugar and salt to the boiling point. Slowly pour half the hot mixture into egg-milk mixture, stirring constantly. Return to saucepan, stirring constantly until it boils. Let boil one minute, take off heat and stir in vanilla. Press waxed paper on surface of cream and refrigerate while you roll out pastry.

On floured surface roll chilled brioche dough into a 12 x 15-inch rectangle. (Let dough rest 5 minutes if it springs back while rolling.)Spread with butter and cooled pastry cream and sprinkle with cocoanut. Cut dough in half lengthwise. Roll up each rectangle jellyroll fashion, starting at long side. Pinch seams to seal. Slice each roll into 15 pieces; place pastries cut-side-up on a greased baking sheet about 1 inch apart, flattening each slightly. Put in a warm place and let pastries rise until doubled, about 1 hour.

Bake at 400 degrees for 15-20 minutes, until tops are golden brown.

Make the glaze: boil powdered sugar and water for 1 minute. Brush warm pastries with glaze.

■

APRICOT BRAN BREAD

1 loaf

½ cup all bran cereal

½ cup whole wheat flake cereal

¼ cup wheat germ

½ teaspoon salt

2 tablespoons butter, softened

¼ cup apricot preserves

½ cup boiling water

½ cup warm water (105-115 degrees)

1 package active dry yeast

2 eggs, well beaten

3 cups flour

½ cup chopped dried apricots

½ cup chopped walnuts

Combine bran and wheat flake cereals, walnuts, wheat germ, salt, butter and preserves. Stir in apricots. Add boiling water and stir to melt butter. Into a small bowl, measure warm water. Sprinkle in yeast and stir until dissolved. Add dissolved yeast and beaten eggs to cereal mixture and stir well.

Add flour, stir to make soft dough. Cover and let rise in a warm place until doubled (about 30–45 minutes). Grease a 9"x 5"x 3" loaf pan. Stir dough down and spoon into pan. Cover and let rise in a warm place for another 30-45 minutes. Bake at 375 degrees for approximately 45-50 minutes or until lightly browned. Cool on rack before cutting.

■

More
from our
Pastry
Basket

LEMON CASHEW BREAD

Makes one medium loaf

Pastry:

1½ cups all-purpose flour

¾ cup sugar

2 tablespoons grated lemon rind

1 teaspoon baking powder

½ teaspoon salt

½ cup unsalted cashews, toasted and chopped

¼ cup milk

¼ cup fresh lemon juice

6 tablespoons vegetable oil

2 eggs

Glaze:

½ cup sugar

2 tablespoons lemon juice

Preheat oven to 350 degrees. Grease an 8½ x 4-inch loaf pan.

In medium mixing bowl combine ingredients in order given. Pour into prepared pan and bake at 350 degrees for one hour. Cool 15 minutes.

Remove from pan. Poke holes in top of loaf with a toothpick. Mix sugar and lemon juice; brush over top and sides of loaf, with special attention to top. Let stand until glaze hardens before slicing.

■

TOASTED ALMOND APRICOT LOAF

Makes 3 medium loaves

1 6-ounce bag dried apricots, coarsely chopped

3 cups boiling water

½ stick unsalted butter

2 cups sugar

2 teaspoons salt

3 cups plus 2 tablespoons all-purpose flour

2 teaspoons baking soda

1 cup whole wheat flour

1½ cups almonds, toasted and coarsely chopped

2 eggs, beaten

1½ teaspoons orange extract

Preheat oven to 350 degrees. Grease three 8½ x 4-inch loaf pans.

In medium mixing bowl mix apricots, boiling water, butter, sugar and salt; set aside. Into small bowl sift flour with baking soda; add to apricots. Stir in whole wheat flour, almonds, eggs and extract. Divide batter among pans, leveling tops.

Bake at 350 degrees for 1 hour and 10 minutes, or until tops are browned and toothpick inserted at center comes out clean.

Cook's Note: This quick bread is at its best baked one day and served the next.

■

ORANGE-PECAN BREAD

Makes 1 large loaf

½ cup packed light brown sugar

¼ cup sugar

½ stick butter, softened

1½ tablespoons grated orange rind

2 eggs, beaten

2 cups all-purpose flour

1 cup whole wheat flour

1 tablespoon baking powder

½ teaspoon salt

1 cup orange juice

¾ cup milk

1 teaspoon vanilla

1 cup coarsely chopped pecans

Preheat oven to 375 degrees. Grease a 9 x 5-inch loaf pan.

In medium mixing bowl cream sugar with butter until light and fluffy; beat in rind and eggs. Sift the flour, whole wheat flour, baking powder and salt into the mixture; add orange juice, milk and vanilla and stir just until blended. Fold in pecans.

Bake at 375 degrees for 50-60 minutes, or until a toothpick inserted at center comes out clean. Let cool in pan on rack 15 minutes before removing.

∎

TROPICAL TEA BREAD

Makes 2 loaves

⅔ cup butter

1⅓ cups honey

4 eggs

4 tablespoons milk

1 teaspoon vanilla

2 tablespoons vegetable oil

4 cups sifted all-purpose flour

1 teaspoon salt

1¾ teaspoons baking powder

1 teaspoon soda

2 cups toasted cocoanut

2¼ cups mashed banana

4 teaspoons grated lemon rind

2 teaspoons fresh lemon juice

Preheat oven to 350 degrees. Grease and flour two 9 x 5-inch loaf pans.

Cream butter until fluffy; add honey in thin stream. Beat in eggs; stir in milk, vanilla and oil.

Into medium bowl sift dry ingredients; stir in toasted cocoanut and set aside. In small bowl blend banana, lemon rind and juice. Add dry ingredients to creamed mixture alternately with banana mixture, blending only until moistened. Spoon into pans.

Bake at 350 degrees for 55 minutes. Cool in pan 5 minutes; remove and cool thoroughly before slicing.

Cook's Note: These loaves slice nicely if stored overnight or frozen and thawed.

∎

TISH'S ZUCCHINI BREAD

Makes 2 loaves

3 eggs

1 cup vegetable oil

2½ cups sugar

2 cups grated zucchini

1 tablespoon vanilla

3 cups all-purpose flour

1 teaspoon salt

¼ teaspoon baking powder

1 teaspoon baking soda

1 tablespoon cinnamon

1 cup pecans, chopped

Preheat oven to 325 degrees. Grease two 9 x 5-inch loaf pans.

In medium mixing bowl beat eggs with oil, sugar, zucchini and vanilla; set aside. Into medium bowl sift flour, salt, baking powder, soda and cinnamon. Stir dry ingredients into wet ones; add pecans.

Pour into loaf pans and bake at 325 degrees for one hour, or until toothpick inserted at center comes out clean.

Cook's Note: This is one of the few recipes for which altitude adjustments are necessary. We have left the recipe at low altitude, as Tish gave it to us. For Santa Fe and altitudes above 5000 feet, we have made these alternations: ⅛ teaspoon baking powder, ¾ teaspoon baking soda, 2 cups plus 2 tablespoons sugar and bake at 350°.

Cook's Memory: Tish Knowland has had her own catering business in Piedmont, California. She is a superb cook and baker. This wonderful bread freezes well and is always a popular item at our Christmas Bazaar.

■

APPLESAUCE SPICE BREAD

Makes 1 large loaf

2 cups all-purpose flour

1 teaspoon baking soda

½ teaspoon baking powder

½ teaspoon cinnamon

½ teaspoon allspice

¼ teaspoon nutmeg

½ teaspoon salt

1 cup sugar

1 cup applesauce

⅓ cup vegetable oil

2 tablespoons milk

2 eggs

¾ cup chopped walnuts

Topping:

¼ cup packed light brown sugar

⅓ cup chopped walnuts

Preheat oven to 350 degrees. Grease a 9 x 5-inch loaf pan.

Into medium mixing bowl sift flour, soda, baking powder, spices and salt; set aside.

In medium mixing bowl combine sugar, applesauce, oil, milk and eggs, beating well. Stir in dry ingredients, combining well with as few strokes as possible. Stir in walnuts.

Pour batter into prepared pan. Sprinkle combined topping ingredients over batter.

Bake at 350 degrees for about 1 hour, covering loosely with foil after first ½ hour. Remove from pan after 10 minutes and cool on rack.

DATE WALNUT BREAD

Makes 1 large loaf

1 cup chopped dates

1½ tablespoons dark rum

1 cup sugar

½ stick butter

¾ cup boiling water

1 egg, beaten

1 teaspoon baking soda

1 ¾ cups all-purpose flour

½ teaspoon salt

1 cup coarsely chopped walnuts

Preheat oven to 350 degrees. Grease a 9 x 5-inch loaf pan.

In medium mixing bowl soak dates in rum 10 minutes; add sugar, butter and boiling water, stirring until butter melts. Beat in egg; set aside.

Into small bowl sift soda, flour and salt. Stir into liquid ingredients, mixing just enough to blend. Fold in walnuts.

Bake at 350 degrees for 45-50 minutes, or until toothpick inserted at center comes out clean.

Let loaf cool in pan at least 15 minutes before removing.

■

WALNUT MOCHA BREAD

Makes 1 large loaf

1½ cups all-purpose flour

2 teaspoons baking powder

½ teaspoon salt

1 cup coarsely chopped walnuts

1 stick unsalted butter

2 teaspoons vanilla

4 teaspoons instant coffee powder

1 cup sugar

2 eggs, separated

½ cup milk

1½ ounces semi-sweet chocolate, chopped

Preheat oven to 375 degrees. Generously grease, then flour, a 9 x 5-inch loaf pan.

Into medium mixing bowl sift flour, baking powder and salt. Sprinkle 1 tablespoon over walnuts in small bowl; stir to mix, then set walnuts aside.

In medium mixing bowl cream butter with electric mixer. Add vanilla, coffee and sugar; beat 3 minutes. Add egg yolks and beat another 3 minutes. Alternately add flour and milk to creamed mixture beating well after each addition. Stir in walnuts. Beat egg whites until stiff but not dry and fold into mixture.

Spoon half the batter into the pan. Sprinkle with chocolate and top with remaining batter. Run a knife through mixture several times.

Bake at 375 degrees for 55-60 minutes, or until toothpick inserted at center comes out clean. Cool in pan 10 minutes, then invert onto cake rack to cool.

■

DUTCH HONEY SPICE BREAD

Makes 1 large loaf

3 eggs

¾ cup packed dark brown sugar

½ stick butter, melted

¾ cup mild honey

2¼ cups all-purpose flour

1 teaspoon baking powder

¾ teaspoon baking soda

½ teaspoon salt

1½ teaspoons cinnamon

½ teaspoon allspice

1 cup chopped walnuts

¾ cup very strong brewed coffee, cooled

grated rind of 2 oranges

Preheat oven to 350 degrees. Grease and flour a 9 x 5-inch loaf pan.

With electric mixer, beat eggs with sugar in medium mixing bowl just to mix. Add butter and honey, again beating only enough to combine ingredients; set aside.

Into medium mixing bowl sift flour, baking powder, soda, salt, cinnamon and allspice. Toss walnuts in small bowl with 1 tablespoon flour mixture; set walnuts aside.

Add flour mixture to creamed ingredients alternately with coffee. Stir in walnuts and orange rind.

Smooth batter into prepared pan; it will be full! Bake at 350 degrees 1 hour and 10-15 minutes, or until top springs back when touched. If loaf is browning too quickly, cover with foil during last 30 minutes of baking time. Cool in pan 10 minutes, then invert onto rack to cool.

■

PUMPKIN RAISIN BUNDT BREAD

Makes 12 servings

3 eggs

1½ cups sugar

1½ cups pumpkin

1 cup plus 2 tablespoons vegetable oil

2 teaspoons vanilla

2¼ cups all-purpose flour

1½ teaspoons baking soda

1½ teaspoons baking powder

1½ teaspoons salt

2 teaspoons pumpkin pie spice

½ cup coarsely chopped pecans

1 cup raisins

Preheat oven to 350 degrees.

In medium mixing bowl beat eggs and sugar until well-blended. Add pumpkin, oil and vanilla, mixing well. Set aside.

Sift flour, soda, baking powder, salt and pie spice into a small bowl. Add to pumpkin mixture and beat. Add pecans and raisins, stirring to blend.

Bake at 350 degrees for 1 hour, until a toothpick inserted at center comes out clean.

■

GINGERYBREAD

Serves 12

1 cup shortening

¼ cup sugar

2 eggs

grated rind of 1 orange

1 cup dark molasses

1 cup honey

2 tablespoons brandy

1¾ cups boiling water

4½ cups all-purpose flour

1¾ teaspoons soda

1 teaspoon salt

2 teaspoons ground ginger

2 teaspoons cinnamon

⅓ cup chopped candied ginger

Preheat oven to 325 degrees. Grease a 10 x 14-inch baking pan.

In a medium mixing bowl cream shortening and sugar until fluffy. Blend in eggs, orange rind, molasses and honey. Stir in brandy and boiling water; set aside.

Into medium bowl sift flour, soda, salt and spices. Stir dry ingredients into liquids, blending well. Fold in candied ginger.

Bake at 325 degrees for about 45 minutes, or until top springs back when touched. Serve warm.

Cook's Note: This gingerbread is similar to the way ginger-bread is made in Scotland—dark and substantial—with the underscoring candied ginger to provide texture.

■

BOSTON BROWN DATE BREAD

Makes 2 small loaves

½ cup rye flour

½ cup cornmeal

½ cup whole wheat flour

1 teaspoon baking soda

½ teaspoon salt

½ cup molasses

1 cup milk mixed with 1 tablespoon vinegar

½ cup chopped dates

Prepare the molds: cut the tops off 2 16-ounce cans, emptying contents into other containers for storage. Peel off labels, wash cans and grease interiors well.

In small mixing bowl combine rye flour, corn-meal, whole wheat flour, soda and salt. Stir in molasses, soured milk and dates. Split batter equally between molds. Cover each mold tightly with aluminum foil, then place on rack in 4-quart saucepan. Pour in boiling water to reach halfway up molds. Cover saucepan and simmer molds 1½ hours, adding boiling water to maintain proper level.

Remove molds from water. Bake at 300 degrees for 20 minutes. Let cool 15 minutes. Cut bottoms out of molds and push bread out. Cut into ¼-inch slices and serve spread with cream cheese and drizzled with honey.

■

CHERRY COFFEE CAKE

Serves 12

2 sticks butter

1½ cups sugar

6 egg yolks, room temperature

2 tablespoons Kirsch liqueur

juice of one lemon

1 tablespoon grated lemon rind

1 teaspoon salt

4 egg whites

pinch cream of tartar

2 cups all-purpose flour

2 cups frozen cherries, thawed, well-drained

powdered sugar for dusting

Preheat oven to 350 degrees.

Butter a 9 x 13-inch baking pan. In medium mixing bowl cream butter, sugar and egg yolks until light and fluffy. Add Kirsch, juice, rind and salt; set aside. In small bowl beat whites with cream of tartar until stiff but not dry. Fold whites into creamed mixture alternately with flour. Scrape batter into pan; distribute cherries on top.

Bake at 350 degrees for 45 minutes, or until golden brown. Dust with powdered sugar.

■

APPLE COFFEE CAKE

Serves 12

Pastry:

½ cup shortening

1 cup sugar

2 eggs

1½ teaspoons vanilla

2 cups all-purpose flour

2 teaspoons baking powder

½ teaspoon baking soda

½ teaspoon salt

1 cup sour cream

2 cups peeled, chopped apple

Topping:

1 cup chopped pecans

1 cup packed light brown sugar

1½ teaspoons cinnamon

½ stick butter, melted

Preheat oven to 350 degrees. Grease a 9 x 13-inch baking pan.

In medium mixing bowl cream shortening and sugar until light and fluffy. Add eggs, 1 at a time; mix in vanilla. Set aside.

Into medium bowl sift flour, baking powder, soda and salt. Mix flour into creamed mixture alternately with sour cream; stir in apple.

Smooth batter into prepared pan; sprinkle with combined topping ingredients. Run knife through batter to "marble" in topping.

Bake at 350 degrees for 35-40 minutes, or until golden brown. Let stand in pan 10 minutes before cutting into squares.

■

PEAR STREUSEL ROLL

Serves 10

Filling:

2 pears, peeled, cored and chopped

½ cup chopped pecans

⅓ cup sugar

1 teaspoon pumpkin pie spice

Pastry:

3 cups all-purpose flour

1 tablespoon baking powder

¼ teaspoon baking soda

1 teaspoon salt

½ cup vegetable shortening

2 eggs, beaten

½ stick butter, melted

¼ cup milk

Glaze:

½ cup powdered sugar

2-3 tablespoons milk

Preheat oven to 350 degrees.

Make the filling: combine all filling ingredients; set aside.

Make the pastry: into medium mixing bowl sift flour, baking powder, soda and salt. Cut in shortening until mixture resembles coarse meal. Add eggs, butter and milk and beat 20 strokes.

Turn out onto lightly floured surface. Knead dough 8 to 10 times, then roll out into 9 x 13-inch rectangle. Spread pear mixture to within ½ inch of each side. Starting at shorter side, roll up jellyroll style, pinching seams to seal. Place seam-side-down in pan. Bake at 350 degrees for one hour. Remove from pan immediately. Cool and glaze with combined glaze ingredients.

∎

JOANNIE'S APRICOT LATTICE CAKE

Serves 4

2 cups all-purpose flour

4 teaspoons baking powder

½ teaspoon salt

1 tablespoon sugar

½ cup butter

¾ cup milk

½ cup apricot preserves

Mix flour, baking powder, salt and sugar. Cut in butter with pastry blender. Add milk and stir with fork. Pat ⅔ of above dough into a buttered 9-inch square pan. Cover with apricot preserves. Roll out remaining ⅓ of dough and cut into strips criss-crossing over preserves. Bake at 425 degrees for about 15-17 minutes until browned.

∎

STRAWBERRY RHUBARB CRUMB CAKE

Makes 2 coffee cakes, about 16 servings

Filling:

3 cups fresh or frozen chopped rhubarb

2 cups fresh or frozen strawberries

2 tablespoons fresh lemon juice

1 cup sugar

⅓ cup cornstarch

Pastry:

2½ cups all-purpose flour

½ cup whole wheat flour

1 cup sugar

1 teaspoon baking soda

1 teaspoon salt

2 sticks unsalted butter

1 cup buttermilk

2 eggs, beaten

1 teaspoon vanilla

Topping:

¾ cup sugar

½ cup flour

6 tablespoons unsalted butter

Generously grease two 9-inch layer cake pans.

In medium saucepan bring rhubarb and strawberries to a boil and cook over medium heat 5 minutes. Add lemon juice; mix sugar and cornstarch and stir into fruit. Bring back to boil and cook another 5 minutes, or until fruit is softened and mixture is thick. Cover and set aside.

Preheat oven to 375 degrees.

Into medium mixing bowl sift flour, wheat flour, sugar, soda and salt. Cut butter into ½-inch cubes and cut into flour mixture with the fingers or pastry blender. Stir in buttermilk, eggs and vanilla.

Divide half the batter between prepared pans and smooth and spread to edges. Divide cooled filling between pans, spreading to edges. Top with remaining batter, smoothing surface; set aside.

In small bowl mix sugar and flour. Cut in butter using the fingers or pastry blender. Divide topping between the pans.

Bake at 375 degrees 40-45 minutes, or until topping is browned and crumb cakes are bubbly. Cool at least 45 minutes before serving.

■

STRAWBERRY-MACAROON PUFF

Serves 10

1 pound Puff Pastry The Easy Way

6 large cocoanut macaroons, crumbled

16 medium fresh strawberries, washed,
hulled and dried

2 teaspoons red currant jelly

¼ cup sugar

1 egg beaten with 1 teaspoon water for glaze

Preheat oven to 450 degrees.

Divide puff pastry in half; refrigerate half. Roll out other half into a circle about 10 inches in diameter. From it cut an even 9-inch circle, using a pie or cake pan as a guide. Slip onto an ungreased baking sheet and chill ½ hour.

Roll second half of dough into a circle about 10½ inches in diameter. From it cut an even 10-inch circle of pastry, using a 10-inch pie pan as a guide. Slip onto an ungreased baking sheet and chill ½ hour.

Remove 9-inch disk from refrigerator. Sprinkle it with cookie crumbs to within 1 inch of edge. Place berries upright on crumbs, then dot with jelly. Sprinkle with all but 1 tablespoon sugar. Brush pastry border with egg glaze.

Cut a 1-inch hole in center of second circle and set pastry disk on top of berries. Seal edges of disks together by crimping all around with tines of fork. Brush top with egg glaze and sprinkle with remaining 1 tablespoon sugar. Chill 20 minutes.

Bake at 450 degrees for 10 minutes; reduce heat to 400 degrees and bake another 20-25 minutes, or until puffed and golden brown. Cool on wire rack; serve warm or at room temperature.

PUFF PASTRY THE EASY WAY

Makes about 1 pound

1½ cups unsifted all-purpose flour

2 sticks butter, ice-cold

½ cup sour cream

¼ teaspoon lemon juice

Place flour in a medium mixing bowl. Cut butter into ½-inch cubes; using a pastry blender, cut butter into flour until mixture looks like coarse meal. Stir in sour cream and lemon juice. Knead in bowl just until dough holds together in ball. Flatten into a rough 5 x 7-inch rectangle; wrap in waxed paper, then in plastic wrap. Chill for at least 4 hours, or overnight. Let stand at room temperature 15 minutes before working with dough; then work quickly!

Cook's Note: Just remember to keep dough chilled; if it warms as you work it, refrigerate 30 minutes, then try again.

■

PEACH POCKET CAKE

Pastry:

2⅓ cups all-purpose flour

3 tablespoons sugar

1 tablespoon baking powder

½ teaspoon salt

4 ounces cream cheese, softened

½ cup ricotta cheese

6 tablespoons butter

¼ cup shortening

½ cup milk

Filling:

¾ cup peach preserves

½ cup walnuts, finely chopped

Glaze:

1 cup sifted powdered sugar

2 tablespoons milk

¼ teaspoon vanilla

Preheat oven to 400 degrees. Grease a large baking sheet.

In medium mixing bowl stir together flour, sugar, baking powder and salt. Cut in cream cheese, ricotta, butter and shortening until crumbly; stir in milk. Knead dough in bowl 20 times.

Cover work surface with a 12 x 16-inch rectangle of waxed paper. Roll dough on waxed paper into 12 x 13-inch rectangle. Spread preserves to cover ⅔ of rectangle; sprinkle with walnuts. Fold bare ⅓ of rectangle over ½ of peach-covered section. Fold remaining third over 2-layer portion. Seal edges.

Bake at 400 degrees for 25-30 minutes, or until "pocket" is golden brown. Cool and frost with combined glaze ingredients.

■

GCI BLUEBERRY COBBLER CAKE

Serves 9

1½ cups sugar

1 stick butter, softened

1½ teaspoons baking powder

1 teaspoon vanilla

1 teaspoon almond extract

4 eggs

3 cups all-purpose flour

½ can blueberry pie filling

Preheat oven to 350 degrees. Grease a 9 x 9-inch square baking pan.

In medium mixing bowl beat together sugar, butter, baking powder, vanilla and almond extract on low speed until moist. Add eggs. Switch to high speed and beat 3 minutes. Stir in flour and blend well.

Spread ⅔ of batter over bottom of prepared pan. Spoon on pie filling and smooth, then drop remaining batter by tablespoons onto filling. Bake at 350 degrees for 45 minutes. Cool 15 minutes, then cut into squares.

■

BLUEBERRY-ALMOND COFFEE CAKE

Serves 10

Pastry:

1 teaspoon baking powder

1 teaspoon baking soda

2 cups all-purpose flour

½ teaspoon salt

1 stick butter

1 cup sugar

2 eggs

1 cup sour cream

1 teaspoon almond extract

⅔ cup sliced toasted almonds

1 can (15 ounces) blueberry pie filling

Frosting:

¾ cup sifted powdered sugar

2 tablespoons hot water

½ teaspoon almond extract

Preheat oven to 325 degrees. Grease and flour a 12-cup bundt pan.

Into medium bowl sift baking powder, soda, flour and salt; set aside. In medium mixing bowl cream butter and sugar until light and fluffy. Add eggs one at a time. Add flour to creamed mixture alternately with sour cream. Add almond extract.

Pour ⅓ of batter into prepared pan. Spread half pie filling over. Cover with another ⅓ batter. Spread remaining blueberry filling over that layer and top with rest of batter. Sprinkle with toasted almonds.

Bake at 325 degrees for 60 minutes, then cool in pan 15 minutes before removing. Frost with combined frosting ingredients, making sure cake is cool.

■

BLACKBERRY CRUMB KUCHEN

Serves 9

Pastry:

½ stick unsalted butter

1 teaspoon vanilla

¾ cup sugar

1 egg

2 cups all-purpose flour

1 ¾ teaspoons baking powder

½ teaspoon salt

½ cup milk

grated rind of 1 lemon

1 pint fresh blackberries or
1 package frozen blackberries

Topping:

⅓ cup all-purpose flour

½ cup sugar

½ stick butter

½ teaspoon cinnamon

pinch salt

sifted powdered sugar for topping

Preheat oven to 375 degrees. Butter a 9-inch square baking pan.

In medium mixing bowl cream butter with vanilla and sugar until fluffy and light in color.

Add egg and beat just until smooth.

Into small mixing bowl sift flour, baking powder and salt. Add flour to creamed mixture alternately with milk, beating just until smooth after each addition. Stir in grated rind, fold in blackberries.

Smooth batter into pan. Combine topping ingredients in small bowl, rubbing butter into other ingredients with the fingers until mixture resembles coarse crumbs. Sprinkle over batter and swirl through mixture with a knife.

Bake at 375 degrees 45 minutes, or until crumb topping is browned. Cool in pan 30 minutes before sprinkling with powdered sugar and cutting into squares.

■

RASPBERRY STREUSEL COFFEE CAKE

Serves 12

Pastry:

½ stick unsalted butter, softened

1 cup cottage cheese

1½ cups sugar

2 eggs

2 cups all-purpose flour

2 teaspoons baking powder

½ teaspoon salt

1 teaspoon soda

½ cup milk

1 teaspoon vanilla

½ pint fresh raspberries

Streusel Topping:

⅓ cup sugar

1 teaspoon cinnamon

1¼ cups all-purpose flour

⅛ teaspoon salt

1 stick unsalted butter, softened

Preheat oven to 350 degrees. Grease a 10 x 14-inch baking pan.

Make the pastry: in medium mixing bowl cream butter with cottage cheese and sugar until light and fluffy. Add eggs, beating well. Set aside.

Into medium bowl sift flour, baking powder, salt and soda. Gradually add to creamed ingredients. Stir in milk and vanilla, beating to thoroughly mix.

Spread batter in prepared pan and sprinkle with raspberries.

Make the streusel: into medium bowl sift sugar, cinnamon, flour and salt. Cut in butter with fingers; topping will be lumpy. Sprinkle over raspberries.

Bake at 350 degrees for 20-30 minutes, until golden brown. Serve warm.

■

CAMELBACK INN SUNDAY COFFEE CAKE

Serves 16

3 cups all-purpose flour

3 teaspoons baking powder

½ teaspoon salt

½ teaspoon baking soda

1 cup butter

1 cup sugar

1 tablespoon vanilla

3 eggs

1 cup sour cream

Streusel Topping:

1 cup brown sugar

1 cup all-purpose flour

¾ cup butter

1 tablespoon cinnamon

Preheat oven to 350 degrees.

Mix dry ingredients and set aside. In large bowl cream butter and sugar. Add vanilla and then eggs. To this mixture add sour cream alternately with the dry ingredients. Grease a 10 x 14-inch rectangular pan. Pour batter into pan and sprinkle with Streusel Topping. Bake for 30 minutes at 350 degrees.

Cook's Memory: This recipe came from Martha Caine's memory. It was one I fondly remember having in the roll warmer on Sundays at Camelback.

■

POPPY SEED COFFEE CAKE

Makes 2 medium loaves

2 sticks unsalted butter

1½ cups sugar

5 eggs, separated

1 teaspoon vanilla

2 cups minus 2 tablespoons all-purpose flour

¼ teaspoon salt

1 teaspoon baking soda

1 cup sour cream

¼ cup poppy seeds

Preheat oven to 350 degrees. Generously butter two 8½ x 4-inch loaf pans. In medium mixing bowl cream butter and sugar until fluffy and light. Beat in egg yolks and vanilla.

Into small mixing bowl sift dry ingredients. Add to creamed mixture alternately with sour cream. Stir in poppy seeds.

Beat egg whites until stiff but not dry. Stir ½ of whites into batter, then gently fold in remainder, using spatula.

Pour into prepared loaf pans. Bake at 350 degrees for 35-45 minutes, or until toothpick inserted at center comes out clean. Cool in pans at least 15 minutes before removing.

■

SUPER CARROT COFFEE CAKE

Serves 12

3 cups (about 1 pound) grated carrots

1 tablespoon lemon juice

1 15-ounce can crushed pineapple

3 cups all-purpose flour

1½ cups sugar

2 teaspoons baking powder

2 teaspoons baking soda

1 teaspoon salt

2 teaspoons cinnamon

½ teaspoon cloves

½ teaspoon nutmeg

½ teaspoon allspice

1½ cups vegetable oil

5 eggs

2 teaspoons vanilla

1 cup cocoanut (preferably the moist, flaked variety)

1 cup walnuts

1 cup raisins

sifted powdered sugar for dusting

Preheat oven to 350 degrees. Grease a 10 x 14-inch baking pan.

Toss carrots with lemon juice. Drain pineapple in colander.

Into large mixing bowl sift flour with sugar, baking powder, soda, salt and spices. Beat in oil, then stir in carrots. Beat in eggs and vanilla. Stir in cocoanut, walnuts, raisins and pineapple.

Pour into prepared pan.

Bake at 350 degrees for 1 hour 10 minutes, or until tester inserted at center comes out clean.

Cool 25 minutes before serving; dust with powdered sugar.

■

SOUR CREAM STREUSEL COFFEE CAKE

Serves 10

Pastry:

¾ cup sugar

1½ sticks butter, softened

1 teaspoon vanilla

3 eggs

2 cups all-purpose flour

1¼ teaspoons baking powder

1 teaspoon soda

¼ teaspoon salt

1 cup sour cream

Streusel Filling:

1½ cups packed light brown sugar

1 cup chopped pecans

2½ teaspoons cinnamon

4 tablespoons melted butter

powdered sugar for dusting

Preheat oven to 350 degrees. Spray a 12-cup bundt pan with non-stick vegetable spray.

Make the pastry: in a large mixing bowl cream sugar with butter until light and fluffy. Add vanilla and eggs, mixing well.

Into a small bowl sift flour, baking powder, soda and salt. Add dry ingredients to creamed mixture alternately with sour cream.

Make the streusel: combine brown sugar, nuts, cinnamon and butter in small bowl, mixing well to distribute butter.

Spread half the batter in prepared pan. Sprinkle with two-thirds of streusel. Spread other half of batter over streusel and smooth. Sprinkle with remaining streusel.

Bake at 350 degrees for 35-40 minutes, or until golden brown. Let cool in pan 20 minutes before turning out. Dust with sifted powdered sugar.

■

KUGELHOPF

Serves 8

2 tablespoons almonds, finely ground in processor

1 cup golden raisins

¼ cup dark rum

2¼ cups all-purpose flour

2 teaspoons baking powder

½ teaspoon salt

2 sticks butter, softened

1¼ cups sugar

5 eggs

1 teaspoon vanilla

2 tablespoons half and half

powdered sugar for dusting

Preheat oven to 400 degrees. Grease a kugelhopf mold (an aluminum mold which resembles a crown, with a tube in the center). Shake almonds around bottom and sides to coat. Soak raisins in rum for at least one hour.

Into medium mixing bowl sift flour, baking powder and salt; set aside. In another mixing bowl beat butter on medium speed of electric mixer until softened. Add sugar and cream mixture until light and fluffy. Beat in eggs, vanilla and half and half. Add flour mixture to creamed ingredients, beating on low speed just until smooth. Stir in raisins and rum.

Pour batter into mold; run through with a knife to eliminate air bubbles. Bake at 400 degrees for 15 minutes; lower heat to 350 degrees and bake another 30 minutes, or until toothpick inserted at center comes out clean. Let cake sit in pan 15 minutes on a wire rack before removing. Dust with powdered sugar while warm.

■

TROPICAL TORTE

Serves 10

Pastry:

2 sticks butter, softened

1 cup sugar

3 eggs, separated

2 cups all-purpose flour

1 teaspoon baking powder

1 teaspoon baking soda

¾ cup sour cream

1 cup walnuts, finely ground in processor

grated rind of 1 orange

grated rind of 2 lemons

pinch salt

Glaze:

½ cup sugar

1 tablespoon orange juice

1 tablespoon lemon juice

Preheat oven to 350 degrees. Butter a 9-inch spring form pan, then coat it with fine, fresh bread crumbs.

In medium mixing bowl cream butter; add sugar and beat on high speed of electric mixer 2 minutes. Beat in egg yolks one at a time.

Into medium bowl sift flour, baking powder and soda. Beat flour mixture into creamed ingredients alternately with sour cream. Transfer to medium bowl and stir in walnuts and rinds.

Beat egg whites with salt until stiff but not dry. Fold into batter. Pour into prepared pan and smooth top.

Bake at 350 degrees for 1 hour, or until toothpick inserted at center comes out dry. Remove from oven and immediately poke top all over with toothpick. Brush combined glaze ingredients over top until all is absorbed. Let torte cool completely before removing sides of pan.

■

ALMOND PUFF PASTRY

Serves 12

Pastry:

1 stick unsalted butter, cold

1 cup flour

2 tablespoons cold water

Topping:

1 cup water

1 stick unsalted butter

1 teaspoon almond extract

1 cup flour

3 eggs

Icing:

1½ cups sifted powdered sugar

2 tablespoons unsalted butter, softened

1 teaspoon almond extract

1½ tablespoons warm water

¼ cup sliced toasted almonds

Preheat oven to 350 degrees.

Make the pastry: cut butter into half-inch cubes. Using fingers or pastry blender, cut butter into flour in medium mixing bowl until mixture resembles coarse meal. Sprinkle with water, stirring with a fork until ingredients are moistened. Shape dough into 2 rolls, each 6 inches long. On ungreased baking sheet pat each roll into a 3 x 12-inch strip, leaving about 3 inches between strips. Refrigerate.

Make the topping: bring water and butter to rolling boil. Dump in flour all at once, add extract and stir vigorously over low heat until mixture forms a ball. Cool 15 minutes, then add eggs one at a time, beating until batter is smooth after each addition. Spread evenly over pastry strips. Bake at 350 degrees for 1 hour, or until puffed and golden brown.

Beat icing ingredients except almonds until smooth. Spread over tops of pastries and sprinkle with almonds. Serve warm.

Cook's Note: This Almond Puff Pastry is one of our most requested and best-loved recipes. Double the recipe and freeze 2 of the pastries for later.

■

PEACHY CORNBREAD

Serves 12

½ cup vegetable oil

¾ cup sugar

2 eggs, beaten

1½ cups all-purpose flour

1 tablespoon baking powder

¼ teaspoon salt

1½ cups yellow cornmeal

1 cup milk

4 ripe peaches, peeled and chunked

Whipped Honey Butter

Preheat oven to 400 degrees. Grease and flour a 9 x 13-inch baking pan.

In medium mixing bowl blend oil and sugar; beat in eggs and set aside. Into small mixing bowl sift flour, baking powder, salt and cornmeal. Add dry ingredients to sugar-egg mixture alternately with milk. Stir in peaches.

Pour into pan and bake at 400 degrees for 25-35 minutes, or until golden brown. Serve warm with Whipped Honey Butter.

WHIPPED HONEY BUTTER

Makes about 1½ cups

1½ sticks unsalted butter

¾ cup mild honey

In small mixing bowl beat butter with electric hand mixer until light and fluffy. Gradually add honey, scraping down sides, and beat until mixture is smooth and creamy. Allow to stand at room temperature for half an hour if refrigerated before use.

■

APRICOT OR RASPBERRY PIROSHKI

Makes about 36 pastries

16 ounces (2 8-ounce packages)
cream cheese

4 sticks butter, room temperature

4½ cups sifted all-purpose flour

2 teaspoons salt

2 tablespoons sugar

¾ cup apricot or raspberry preserves

1 egg beaten, for glaze

powdered sugar for dusting

Beat cream cheese with butter in electric mixer until very smooth. Gradually mix in flour, salt and sugar on low speed. Knead mixture in bowl only until it clings together. Wrap dough in waxed paper and refrigerate 3-4 hours. Cut dough into quarters. Starting with first quarter, roll out on lightly floured surface, shaping into rectangle about ¼-inch thick. Cut into 3½-inch squares. Working quickly so dough doesn't over-soften, fill each square with a scant teaspoon preserves. Bring corners to center of each pastry, pressing down to seal. Refrigerate; repeat with remaining dough. Chill pastries on an ungreased baking sheet 3-4 hours, or freeze before baking.

Brush each pastry lightly with egg glaze. Bake in a preheated 325 degree oven for 30 minutes, or until golden brown. Dust with powdered sugar before serving.

■

JOSEPHINE'S BISCOTTI

Makes about 2 dozen biscotti

1 stick unsalted butter

3 eggs

1 cup sugar

2 tablespoons aniseed, crushed

3 cups all-purpose flour

2 teaspoons baking powder

Preheat oven to 350 degrees. Grease a medium baking sheet.

In small saucepan melt butter. Set aside to cool 5 minutes.

In medium mixing bowl beat eggs and sugar on medium-high speed until mixture is lemon-colored, light and fluffy, about 5 minutes. Add aniseed; slowly add butter until incorporated.

Sift flour with baking powder. Add to egg-sugar mixture slowly, scraping sides of bowl frequently. Spoon batter onto baking sheet, forming into 2 rough 4 x 14-inch rectangles, side by side, about 4 inches apart. Smooth into shape with floured fingers.

Bake at 350 degrees for about 20-25 minutes. Loaves will not be browned, but should feel solid when touched in middle. Remove from oven and cool 5 minutes.

Using sharp, serrated knife, slice each loaf crosswise into inch-wide pieces. Turn each piece on its side and bake until top edges are golden brown, 7-10 minutes. Flip each cookie over and bake again, until top edges are golden brown.

Cook's Note: Finished biscotti should be crisp and dry, yet still tender enough to bite into! Let these mellow a day or two

for fullest flavor. This is the old Italian family recipe of a friend who is one of Santa Fe's best bakers: Josephine Ball. These not-too-sweet biscuits are just the thing with coffee and tea—morning or afternoon.

■

CURRANT SCONES

Makes about 16 scones

½ cup dried currants

¼ cup brandy

2 cups all-purpose flour

3 teaspoons baking powder

1 tablespoon sugar

½ teaspoon salt

¼ cup shortening

¾ cup half and half

1 egg mixed with 4 tablespoons milk for glaze

sieved light brown sugar

1 cup heavy cream, whipped

raspberry jam

Soak currants in brandy ½ hour to plump. Drain and set aside.

Preheat oven to 425 degrees. Lightly grease a baking sheet.

Into a medium mixing bowl sift flour, baking powder, sugar and salt. Using a pastry blender, cut in shortening until mixture resembles coarse meal. Add currants and stir in half and half, using a fork, until dry ingredients are moistened.

Turn dough out onto a floured surface and knead 6 times. Roll out to ¾-inch thickness; cut with a 2-inch round biscuit cutter.

Place rounds on baking sheet. Brush with egg glaze, then sprinkle with sieved brown sugar.

Bake at 425 degrees for about 15 minutes, or until sugar has caramelized and tops are golden brown. Serve with whipped cream and raspberry jam.

■

TENDER BUTTERMILK BISCUITS WITH THREE-FRUITS BUTTER

Makes about 16 biscuits

1 teaspoon baking soda

1½ cups buttermilk

4 cups all-purpose flour

4 teaspoons baking powder

1 teaspoon salt

¾ cup shortening

Preheat oven to 450 degrees.

In small bowl dissolve baking soda in buttermilk; set aside.

Into medium mixing bowl sift flour, baking powder and salt. Using pastry blender, cut in shortening until mixture resembles coarse meal. Stirring dry ingredients with a fork, pour in buttermilk; stir just until ingredients are moistened.

Turn dough out onto lightly floured surface; knead 5-6 times, just until dough holds together in rough mass. Roll out to ½-inch thickness. Fold dough in half; gently flatten a bit with rolling pin. Cut biscuits with a 2-inch cutter or the edge of a juice glass.

Transfer biscuits to a greased baking sheet.

Bake at 450 degrees for about 12-14 minutes, or until lightly browned. Serve with Three-Fruits Butter.

THREE-FRUITS BUTTER

1 stick unsalted butter

¼ cup three-fruits marmalade (Keiller's Dundee is good)

few grains salt

In bowl of electric mixer beat butter until slightly softened. Add marmalade and salt and beat on medium-high speed until light, fluffy and well-combined.

■

GRANDMOTHER STEWART'S RAISIN BISCUITS

Makes 30-36 biscuits

4 cups sifted all-purpose flour

2 tablespoons plus 2 teaspoons baking powder

1 teaspoon salt

1 cup sugar

2 sticks unsalted butter, cut into ½-inch cubes

1 cup whipping cream

¾ cup milk

2 cups raisins

Preheat oven to 425 degrees.

Into large mixing bowl sift first four ingredients. Cut in butter, using the fingers or pastry blender. Stir in whipping cream and milk, then raisins.

Turn out onto floured surface and knead 6 times. Rollout to about ⅓-inch thick.

Cut biscuits with a floured 2-inch cutter. Bake on ungreased baking sheet at 425 degrees for 10-15 minutes.

Cook's Memory: Grandmother Stewart, or "Grandma Stew," was in her eighties by the time I was 5 and was no longer baking. I remember her well though, especially her willingness to play "tea party" with me. Once I fixed her lunch on my doll china...cottage cheese and maraschinos (all I could reach!), and she complained bitterly to my parents that it just wasn't enough lunch for her!

■ CHEDDAR-CHIVE BISCUITS

Makes 1 dozen biscuits

1 cup all-purpose flour

1½ teaspoons baking powder

¼ teaspoon salt

¼ cup vegetable shortening

1 tablespoon chives, fresh or freeze-dried

2 tablespoons Parmesan cheese

½ cup shredded sharp Cheddar cheese

¼ teaspoon white pepper

½ cup half and half

Preheat oven to 450 degrees.

In medium mixing bowl stir together flour, baking powder and salt. With fingers or pastry blender, cut in shortening until mixture resembles coarse meal. Stir in chives, Parmesan, Cheddar and pepper. Sprinkle half and half over dry ingredients, stirring with fork to moisten.

Turn dough out onto floured surface; knead 6 times. Roll dough out to ¼-inch thickness. Fold in half. Cut with a 2-inch biscuit cutter, rerolling scraps. Place on greased baking sheet. Bake at 450 degrees for 10 minutes, or until lightly browned. Serve hot with butter and Red Pepper Jelly (see page 217).

■

BACON PARMESAN POPOVERS

Makes about 12 popovers

2 eggs, beaten lightly

1 cup milk

1 tablespoon butter, melted

1 tablespoon sugar

1 cup all-purpose flour

¼ teaspoon salt

¼ cup cooked, crumbled bacon

¼ cup grated fresh Parmesan cheese

Preheat oven to 400 degrees. Generously grease a 12-popover pan, muffin tin or 12 glass custard cups.

In a medium mixing bowl combine eggs, milk and butter. Stir in sugar, flour and salt. Beat with electric mixer on medium-high speed for 3 minutes. Stir in bacon and Parmesan. Divide batter equally among cups, filling each no more than half full.

Bake at 400 degrees for about 40 minutes, being sure not to open oven door during baking time. Prick each with a toothpick and return to turned-off oven, door ajar, for 10 minutes to dry interiors. Serve hot.

■

GERI'S SOPAIPILLAS

Makes about 16 sopaipillas

4 cups all-purpose flour

2 tablespoons baking powder

2 teaspoons salt

1 tablespoon lard

vegetable oil or a combination of oil and shortening for frying

honey

In medium mixing bowl stir together flour, baking powder and salt. Cut in lard with the fingers or pastry cutter until mixture resembles coarse meal with a few pea-sized lumps. Add 1 cup warm water. Stir to blend, then knead 20 times, until dough is fairly smooth. Cover in bowl and let rest a few minutes.

Roll out dough on floured surface into a rectangle about ⅛-inch thick. Cut into triangles or have some fun—use heart or rabbit-shaped cookie cutters!

Heat about 1 inch of oil in large frying pan to a temperature of 375 degrees. Fry sopaipillas until golden brown on both sides, turning once. Drain on paper towels and serve at once with honey.

■

PINEAPPLE FRITTERS

Makes about 18 fritters

Pastry:

1 8-ounce can pineapple chunks, drained

1½ cups all-purpose flour

1½ teaspoons baking powder

2 tablespoons sugar

½ teaspoon salt

3 eggs, separated

½ cup milk

1½ tablespoons butter, melted

vegetable oil for frying

Topping:

½ cup sugar

½ teaspoon cinnamon

Preheat frying oil to 375 degrees in deep fryer.

Coarsely chop pineapple; set aside.

Into medium mixing bowl sift flour, baking powder, sugar and salt. Beat egg yolks and milk in small bowl; stir into dry ingredients. Add melted butter, stirring just until blended.

Beat egg whites until stiff but not dry. Stir into flour mixture; gently stir in pineapple.

Fry batter by the tablespoonful in hot oil until golden brown, turning once. Drain on paper towels, then roll in topping mixture. Serve immediately.

∎

FRESH APRICOT BEIGNETS

Makes about 2 dozen beignets

1 cup plus 2 tablespoons water

6 tablespoons butter

¼ teaspoon salt

1 cup plus 2 tablespoons all-purpose flour

6 eggs

1 dozen fresh apricots, pitted and chopped

½ teaspoon cinnamon

vegetable oil for frying

powdered sugar for dredging

Preheat oil to 375 degrees in deep fryer.

In heavy saucepan bring water, butter and salt to a boil. Dump in flour and stir vigorously over medium heat until dough is smooth and pulls away from sides of pan.

Remove from heat and beat in eggs one at a time. Stir in apricots. Drop dough by rounded tablespoonful into oil. Fry until golden brown, turning once. Drain on paper towels, dredge with powdered sugar and serve hot.

∎

MOTHER'S JAM CAKE

1 bundt cake

¾ cup butter

1 cup sugar

3 eggs

1 cup strawberry jam

2½ cups flour

1 teaspoon cinnamon

1 teaspoon ground cloves

1 teaspoon ground allspice

1 teaspoon nutmeg

1 teaspoon baking soda

¾ cup buttermilk

Cream butter and sugar until fluffy, beat in eggs, one at a time, beating well. Fold in jam. Sift together flour, spices and baking soda. Add to batter alternately with buttermilk. Blend well, spoon into greased bundt pan, bake approximately 50 minutes at 350 degrees or until tester inserted in center comes out clean. Let cool 10 minutes before removing from pan, sprinkle with powdered sugar.

■

PUMPKIN RAISIN BREAD

Makes 2 loaves

4 eggs, beaten

2 cups sugar

1½ cups vegetable oil

3 cups flour

2 teaspoons baking powder

2 teaspoons baking soda

1 teaspoon salt

1 teaspoon nutmeg

1 teaspoon cinnamon

½ cup sour cream

2 cups cooked mashed pumpkin

1 cup raisins

Preheat oven to 350 degrees. Combine eggs, sugar and oil. Beat in a large mixing bowl until blended. In another mixing bowl blend all dry ingredients. Add dry ingredients slowly to egg mixture. Mix sour cream with pumpkin. Add to batter and blend well. Stir in raisins. Pour into 2 greased 9" loaf pans.

Bake for approximately one hour or until toothpick inserted in center comes out clean.

■

AUNT HELEN'S GRAND MARNIER CAKE

Makes 1 bundt cake

CAKE:

1 cup butter

1 cup sugar

3 egg yolks

1 teaspoon Grand Marnier

2 cups all purpose flour

1 teaspoon baking powder

1 teaspoon baking soda

1½ cups sour cream

grated rind of 1 orange

1 cup chopped walnuts

3 egg whites

GLAZE:

½ cup sugar

1 cup orange juice

1/3 cup Grand Marnier

Preheat oven to 350 degrees. Cream butter and sugar. In large mixing bowl beat in egg yolks, one at a time. Add 1 teaspoon of Grand Marnier. In another mixing bowl sift together the flour, baking powder and baking soda. Add dry ingredients to batter, alternating with sour cream. Mix until smooth. Stir in orange rind and nuts. Beat egg whites until stiff and fold into batter. Pour into greased bundt pan. Bake for 50-55 minutes at 350 degrees until inserted toothpick comes out clean.

Use toothpicks to make holes in top of hot cake while it is still in the pan, so that glaze will penetrate cake. Pour glaze over cake. Let cake cool before removing from pan.

■

CHOCOLATE ZUCCHINI BREAD

1 bundt cake

2½ cups flour

½ cup unsweetened cocoa

½ teaspoon baking powder

¼ teaspoon baking soda

2 cups sugar

1 cup brown sugar

1 cup butter, softened

1 teaspoon vanilla

6 eggs

1 cup yogurt (vanilla)

1 cup zucchini grated, drained

½ cup chocolate chips

In bowl, stir together flour, cocoa, baking powder and soda. Set aside. In another bowl, beat sugars with butter and add vanilla. Add eggs and beat well. Add yogurt. Add dry ingredients slowly beating. Stir in zucchini and chocolate chips. Bake approximately 1 hour 10 minutes at 325 degrees in well greased bundt pan.

■

LEMON MANGO BREAD

Makes 1 loaf

2½ cups flour

1 teaspoon baking powder

½ teaspoon baking soda

1¼ cup sugar

½ cup butter

3 eggs

½ cup lemon juice

½ cup milk

¾ cup mangos, chopped and drained

STREUSEL

½ cup Macadamia nuts, finely chopped

¼ cup brown sugar

½ teaspoon nutmeg

In medium bowl, stir together flour, baking powder and soda. In another bowl, beat sugar and butter. Add eggs. Beat until fluffy. Beat in lemon juice and then milk. Add slowly to dry ingredients. Stir in milk. Set aside.

Stir together streusel ingredients.

Spoon ½ batter into greased loaf pan. Add ½ streusel; then rest of batter and top with rest of streusel.

Bake minutes at 350 degrees. Cool before slicing.

■

Jellies
&
Preserves

LUCY'S APRICOT JAM AND VARIATIONS

Makes about 4 pints

5 cups fresh apricots, pitted and halved

¼ cup lemon juice

1 (1¾-ounce) box Sure-Jel fruit pectin

7 cups sugar

Optional:

1 small papaya

1 small fresh pineapple

In big saucepan combine apricots, lemon juice and Sure-Jel. Bring to a hard rolling boil, stirring constantly. Add sugar, bring back to a hard rolling boil, then boil for exactly one minute. Skim foam, pour into prepared jars, seal, then process for 20 minutes in hot water bath.

Variations: Add to apricots either 1 small fresh papaya, peeled, seeded and diced into ½-inch cubes, or 1 small fresh pineapple, peeled, cored and diced into ½-inch cubes, then proceed with boiling.

Cook's Memory: Lucy Romero spends months every year canning for the Inn's Christmas Bazaar. This apricot jam she has made for her own family for years.

■

PLUM JAM

Makes about 5 pints

7 cups plums, pitted and chopped in ½-inch dice

1 (1¾-ounce) box Sure-Jel fruit pectin

8½ cups sugar

In a large saucepan combine plums and Sure-Jel. Bring to a hard rolling boil, stirring constantly. Add sugar and bring back to a hard boil. Boil for exactly one minute. Skim foam, pour into prepared jars, seal, then process for 20 minutes in hot water bath.

■

STRAWBERRY JAM

5 cups strawberries, washed, capped, and chopped

2 tablespoons lemon juice

2 (1¾-ounce) boxes Sure-Jel fruit pectin

7 cups sugar

In big saucepan combine strawberries, lemon juice and Sure-Jel. Bring to a fast rolling boil, then add sugar. Bring mixture back to a hard rolling boil and boil exactly one minute. Skim foam, pour into prepared jars, seal, then process in hot water bath 20 minutes.

■

BETSY'S ORANGE-STRAWBERRY PRESERVES

Makes about 5 pints

4 cups strawberries, firm and well-ripened

4 cups sugar

1 naval orange,
sliced very thin and quartered

Wash, hull and cut strawberries in half. Drain well. Put strawberries, sugar and orange in large saucepan. Heat slowly, stirring often to avoid scorching. Boil 8-10 minutes or thicken to desired consistency. Skim if necessary. Seal in sterilized jars.

Cook's Memory: My good friend, Betsy Drackett, passed this wonderful family recipe on to Grant Corner Inn.

■

CRAN-ORANGE RELISH

Makes 2½ cups

2 cups fresh cranberries

1 orange, peel removed and saved, white pith peeled off and discarded

1 cup sugar

In food processor grind cranberries until coarsely chopped, using short bursts of power rather than leaving processor on to control grind. Spoon into bowl and set aside.

Into processor container place orange rind, peeled orange and sugar; process with on and off bursts until orange and rind are ground. Stir into cranberries.

Cover bowl; refrigerate 1-2 days to allow flavors to blend.

■

GRANT CORNER INN PEACH BUTTER

Makes about 5 pints

4 pounds peaches, peeled and pitted

1½ cups sugar

2 teaspoons cinnamon

1 teaspoon ground cloves

½ teaspoon allspice

grated rind and juice of 1 lemon

Slice peaches into a large saucepan. Cook peaches in their own juice until soft, about 20 minutes. Add sugar, spices, lemon rind and juice. Continue simmering mixture another 2-3 hours, until peaches are reduced to a smooth, thick puree.

Ladle into sterilized jars, seal and process in hot water bath 20 minutes.

■

BAKED APPLE BUTTER

Makes about 5 pints

6 pounds baking apples (Jonathans
or Winesaps or a combination of the two)

½ cup sugar per cup of cooked pulp

grated rind and juice of 1 lemon

2 teaspoons cinnamon

¾ teaspoon cloves

½ teaspoon allspice

¼ cup brandy

Quarter apples and core, but don't peel them. Place in large saucepan; almost cover with cold water.

Cook gently for 1½-2 hours. Put pulp through fine strainer. Add ½ cup sugar per cup of pulp. Stir in lemon rind, juice, spices and brandy. Bring mixture to a boil. Cook and pour mixture into ovenproof porcelain dish or crock. Set in oven; turn oven to 300 degrees.

Bake at 300 degrees, stirring occasionally, until puree thickens.

■

BLUEBERRY CHUTNEY

Makes about 6 cups

3 pints fresh blueberries or
3 packages frozen berries

2 cups apple cider vinegar

1½ cups seedless raisins

1½ cups sugar

1 clove garlic, minced

1 2-inch piece fresh ginger, peeled and minced

1 medium onion

1 tablespoon yellow mustard seed

1 teaspoon ground cinnamon

½ teaspoon cloves

½ teaspoon allspice

1½ teaspoon salt

Combine all ingredients in 5 or 6-quart Dutch oven and bring to a boil; simmer, covered 1¼ hours. Remove lid and cook another 45-60 minutes, or until thickened. Cool and pack into glass jars for storage.

Cook's Note: This chutney keeps beautifully in the refrigerator for at least 6 months. Serve it at room temperature for most favorful results.

■

PLUM-CHERRY CHUTNEY

Makes about 3 cups

1½ cups fresh or frozen tart cherries

1½-2 cups fresh unpeeled sliced purple plums

1½ cups apple cider vinegar

¾ cup sugar

½ cup currants

1 medium onion, finely chopped

¼ cup minced candied ginger

pinch freshly grated nutmeg

¼ teaspoon ground cloves

¼ teaspoon allspice

¾ teaspoon salt

¾ teaspoon cinnamon

Combine all ingredients in 3 or 4-quart enamel or stainless steel Dutch oven. Bring to a boil, cover and simmer 1 hour. Remove lid and simmer another 40 minutes, or until thick, stirring frequently toward end of cooking time. Cool and pack into glass jars for storage. For heightened flavor, serve at room temperature.

Cook's Note: This chutney will keep virtually forever (at least for 4-6 months) in refrigerator; it also freezes well.

∎

GOURMET CHUTNEY

Makes about 6 pints

3 pounds ripe peaches, peeled and pitted

1 pound ripe mangoes, peeled and pitted

2 quarts cider vinegar, divided

2 pounds sugar

2 tablespoons yellow mustard seed

1 tablespoon ground red chile

1½ cups golden raisins

1 medium onion, diced

1 clove garlic, minced

8 ounces candied ginger, boiled with ½ cup water until soft and syrupy

Into medium saucepan dice peaches and mangoes; add 1 quart vinegar. Bring to boil, simmer over medium heat 20 minutes; set aside.

In small medium saucepan combine sugar and remaining vinegar; boil until thick and syrupy. Drain liquid from fruit into sugar-vinegar mixture. Boil until thick. Stir in fruit, mustard seed, chile powder, raisins, onion and garlic and cook 45 minutes. Add ginger and its syrup. Cook another 30 minutes. Pour into hot sterilized canning jars and seal.

Cook's Note: This chutney should age at least 1 week for best flavor.

∎

RED OR GREEN PEPPER JELLY

Makes 6 half pints

1¼ cups green or red bell peppers,
seeded and finely chopped
(use your food processor)

1½ cups apple cider vinegar

6 cups sugar

1 bottle Certo

Mix peppers, vinegar, and sugar in large stainless steel pan. Bring mixture to a boil, add Certo, then bring back to full, rolling boil. Boil for exactly one minute; remove from heat. Let stand for three minutes, then skim off foam. Ladle into sterilized jars. Seal and process in hot water bath 20 minutes.

Cook's Note: Yes, this is the same jelly we serve with cream cheese and crackers in the evening to our guests. It is also the most sought-after item for sale in our Country Store.

■

PICKLED WATERMELON RIND

Makes 2 pints

1 pound watermelon rind, peeled and diced into
1-inch squares

2 quarts cold water, divided

1 tablespoon salt

2 cups sugar

1½ cups apple cider vinegar

2 cinnamon sticks

2 tablespoons sliced candied ginger

1½ lemons, peeled, sliced thinly and seeded

1st day: Dissolve salt in one quart water. Soak rind overnight.

2nd day: Bring one quart of water, sugar, vinegar, cinnamon sticks, ginger and lemons to a boil in large saucepan. Add drained rind. Let boil until rind becomes translucent. Remove from heat, cover and let sit overnight in syrup.

3rd day: Sterilize 1-pint canning jars by covering with water in large pan, bringing to a boil and boiling 30 minutes. Heat jar lids. Bring syrup-rind mixture to a boil. Let boil 15 minutes. Pour mixture into prepared jars; seal and submerge in panful of water; bring to boil and let boil 20 minutes. Cool and store.

■

GRANT CORNER INN BLACK BEAN SALSA

Makes 3 quarts

1 cup white onion, finely chopped

½ cup jalapeños, finely chopped

4 cups chopped tomatoes

2 cups tomato sauce

1 cup corn

1½ cups fresh cilantro

1 cup cayenne pepper sauce

3 teaspoons salt

1 tablespoon garlic

½ cup red wine vinegar

6 green onions, chopped

1 green pepper, chopped

1 red pepper, chopped

In large stockpot, combine ingredients and simmer for 1 hour on low heat. Ladle into sterilized jars, seal and process in hot water bath 20 minutes.

Cook's Notes: To serve fresh, store refrigerated in tightly covered container for up to 3 days.

Lucy and I concocted this recipe together and made 5 times this recipe the first time, and sold all the jars of salsa within 2 weeks.

Celebrations

219

At Grant Corner Inn we like a celebration. Celebration is our way of giving a little "sparkle" to others. We celebrate God, Country, People and Life in general, hoping to make everyday as special as the last.

Valentine's Day we're all hearts. For brunch we have heart-shaped doughnuts, heart-shaped French toast and flowers for the ladies. Then there are heart-shaped cookies for tea and hearts on each pillow at bedtime.

Easter, of course, is Grant Corner Inn's "hey-day." Bunnies come out of the woodwork. With the staff in bunny costume, a special Easter brunch is served, complete with colored eggs on every table. Following brunch, begins an Easter egg hunt for the children on the front lawn with prizes for all.

Besides the opening of the opera season in Santa Fe and Independence Day, we have two important summer celebrations, Bumpy's birthday and Indian Market (both in August). Each year Indian Market brings thousands to Santa Fe for the judged show and sale of Indian art from across the country.

Then Christmastime is Grant Corner Inn's most eventful time. The first week of December hundreds flock to our charity Bazaar, to buy holiday decorations, gifts, the Inn's jellies and breads. All our staff work for about eight months to prepare for this special occasion. In addition to our holiday brunches, we also serve traditional Christmas Eve and Christmas night dinners.

The menus that follow are offered with ideas for your own special-occasion entertaining.

Cook's Memory: When I was growing up, my mother had what we called "the back closet," a room about 20 x 20-feet, where she stored her specialties for celebration: party hats of all sorts, balloons, doilies, decorations, wrapping and gifts galore. My mother never forgot any occasion. Of all the hotel guests, friends and family, all birthdays, anniversaries, births and marriages were lovingly acknowledged. And we all appreciated her special attention.

VALENTINE BRUNCH

Champagne Cantaloupe With Berries
(see page 23)

Strawberry Omelet (see page 39)

Bacon Twists (see page 103)

Biscochito-Nuts (see page 178)
cut with heart-shaped cookie cutter

Coffee and Tea

Cook's Dec-Notes: Pink and red roses, lots of heart doilies and lace tablecloths.

■

G.W.

To My Valentine

220

EASTER BRUNCH

Fresh Orange Juice
Sour Cream Ambrosia (see page 27)
Pat's Eggs Benedict (see page 52)
Fresh Blueberry Kolacky (see page 167)
Martha's Hot Cross Buns (see page 168)
Coffee and Tea

Cook's Dec-Notes: Easter baskets, pastel floral bouquets, jelly beans, assorted pastel napkins and white linen table-cloths.

∎

BUMPY'S BIRTHDAY BREAKFAST

Spiced Peach Smoothie (see page 16)
Fresh Raspberries Sprinkled
with Granola (see page 26)
Bill Manning's Stuffed French Toast
with maple syrup (see page 116)
Sausage Links
Strawberry-Macaroon Puff
Birthday Cake (see page 191)

Cook's Dec-Notes: Dolls, daisies and pink and yellow helium balloons.

∎

INDIAN MARKET BUFFET

Fresh Fruit Compote:
strawberries, blueberries, melon balls,
sliced peaches and seedless grapes with
fresh mint garnish
Green Chile Strata (see page 55)
with condiments of sour cream and Pat's
Chunky Salsa (see page 94)
Anne's Blue Corn Waffles with

Honey-Orange Sauce (see page 125)
Sausage Pinwheels (see page 103)
Pastry Basket:
Apple Cinnamon Twists (see page 170)
Geri's Sopapillas (see page 205)
Rice-Corn Muffins (see page 146)
Lemon Cashew Bread (see page 182)

Cook's Dec-Notes: Terra cotta serving dishes, baskets and brightly colored woven table runner.

∎

CHRISTMAS MORNING BREAKFAST

Cranberry-Banana Frappé (see page 14)
Omelet Pat (see page 38)
with cherry tomato garnish
Doug's Parmesan Potatoes (see page 96)
Pumpkin Streusel Muffins (see page 145)
Cortés Hot Chocolate with candycanes
(see page 17)
Coffee and Tea

Cook's Dec-Notes: Fir garlands with pine cones, gingerbread men tied with red ribbons, and red napkins.

∎

APRIL FOOL'S BREAKFAST

Serves 1

Place 2 raw eggs on platter with 2 slices of raw bacon and decorate with attractive garnish. Present platter, with a sweet smile, and wait as long as possible for a reaction.

Cook's Memory: One of my most interesting reactions was: "But, I didn't order meat . . . !"

Happy April Fool's Day, Cliff and Ray!

Beyond Brunch

BEYOND BRUNCH

Major holidays and special events have presented a grand opportunity for Grant Corner Inn to expand its horizons to meals other than breakfast/brunch. Our dinners are typically served with one seating, providing a long evening of celebration and camaraderie.

Pat's plates are works of art – sculptures in their own right. Combining his background in art, design and building with a long, self-taught experience in cooking, Pat has created some of the most outstanding culinary extravaganzas.

As you might expect with an artist, Pat's greatest challenge is "actually" writing his recipes, as his talent comes not only with his basic knowledge, but also from that natural passion for food, which means he continually adds a little of "this and that" to taste. And so, the following recipes have been tested; but if you wish, be adventuresome, play, experiment and personalize them to your liking.

■

New Year's Eve Dinner

— Amusé —

Star Crustade with Herbed Deviled Quail

— Appetizer —

Skewered Shrimp, Scallops, Roasted Garlic and Tomatoes

Joseph Phelps Pastiche White Vin De Mistra Napa 1996

— Salad —

Papaya and Melon with Baby Greens
And Juniper Berry Balsamic Vinaigrette
Served with Deep Fried Tortilla Points
And Marinated Goat Cheese

Rosemount Estates Grenache Shiraz Australia 1998

— Entrée —

Filet Mignon Topped with a woven Basket of Plantains
and Fig Flowers
Au Gratin Potato Wheel
Baby Carrot and Jicama Bundles
Ferrari-Carano Sienna Sonoma 1996

— Dessert —

Cricket's Flourless Chocolate Cake with Caramelized Pears
And Homemade Vanilla Bean Ice Cream
Carres Nimrod Porto Tawny

STAR CRUSTADE WITH HERBED, DEVILED QUAIL

Serves 4

STAR CRUSTADE

4 sheets of pastry dough, 4 inches square, at room temperature

4" star cookie cutter

2" circular cookie cutter

Preheat oven to 350 degrees. Cut pastry dough with star cutter, remove pastry star. On cookie sheet, place and space equally 4 stars. Set aside for 20 minutes to let dough proof. Bake in center of oven till golden brown. Set aside.

HERBED, DEVILED QUAIL

1 small quail

3 hard-boiled eggs, cooled and shelled

2 tablespoons sour cream

2 tablespoons minced fresh herbs (tarragon, parsley & basil)

1 teaspoon Dijon mustard

1 teaspoon herb flavored vinegar

1 teaspoon shallots, minced

¼ teaspoon salt

¼ teaspoon Worcestershire Sauce

¼ teaspoon ground black pepper

pinch curry powder

paprika (for garnish)

parsley, chopped (for garnish)

Preheat oven to 350 degrees. Bake quail, uncovered until lightly browned, approximately 30 minutes. Then cover and cook slow at 200

degrees approximately 1 hour.

From hard-boiled eggs, remove yolks and place in food processor bowl.

Combine all ingredients, except quail, with egg yolks and pulse lightly. Remove meat minus skin from cooked bird. Chop lightly and add to mixture. Continue pulsing until mixed thoroughly.

To serve, place crustade in center of small plate. With melon baller, scoop out quail mixture, and place in center of star. Put entire plate in oven to warm. Dust entire plate lightly with paprika and finely diced parsley.

■

SKEWERED SHRIMP, SCALLOPS, ROASTED GARLIC AND TOMATOES

Serves 4

4 large heads garlic

4 tablespoons Brie cheese

1 scallion

3 jumbo shrimp

1 tablespoon sesame oil

½ teaspoon chile oil

16 large scallops

2 eggs separated, whites reserved

¼ cup grated Pecorino or Parmesan cheese

2 tablespoon butter

1 tablespoon fresh parsley, finely chopped

8 wood skewers

1 pint each red and yellow baby pear

tomatoes, halved lengthwise

¼ cup balsamic vinegar

¼ teaspoon Worcestershire Sauce

¼ teaspoon red wine vinegar

½ teaspoon tarragon, finely chopped

Preheat oven 350 degrees. Remove loose skin and top ¼ from heads of garlic. Place in small bake pan, butter top and cover. Bake till tender, about 50 minutes. Spread 1 teaspoon of Brie over browned top. Keep warm.

Cut scallion into 1 inch strips. Shred thin and chill in ice water to curl. Set aside.

Grill shrimp in sesame oil.

Batter scallops in egg whites, roll in grated cheese and coat thoroughly, flash fry in butter till golden. Keep warm.

To serve, place roasted garlic in center of plate. Toss colored medley of tomatoes around plate. Drizzle red chile oil over plate. Thicken and flavor vinegars by adding herbs and Worcestershire Sauce and reducing mixture in small saucepan. Freely drizzle herbed vinegar mixture over plate and tomatoes. Alternate shrimp and scallops on skewers. Lean 2 crossed skewers against garlic and sprinkle scallion curls around plate for color.

■

PAPAYA AND MELON WITH BABY GREENS AND JUNIPER BERRY BALSAMIC VINAIGRETTE SERVED WITH DEEP FRIED TORTILLA POINTS AND MARINATED GOAT CHEESE

Serves 4

1 small ripe papaya

1 small ripe honeydew melon

1 tablespoon lemon juice

⅓ cup orange juice

2 ripe avocados

1 pound mixed baby greens

Peel, seed and thickly dice both melons and avocados. Gently mix in bowl, adding liquids. Set aside in refrigerator.

JUNIPER BERRY BALSAMIC VINAIGRETTE

1 cup balsamic vinegar

1 cup orange juice

½ cup pineapple purée

1 teaspoon lite soy sauce

1 tablespoon juniper berries

2 tablespoons honey

1½ cups olive oil

1 teaspoon fresh sage, finely chopped

salt and pepper to taste

Combine vinegar, orange juice, pineapple purée and soy sauce in a heavy bottomed pot. Reduce by half. Add juniper berries and reduce 10 minutes more. Season and add sage. Slowly whisk in oil and refrigerate.

DEEP FRIED FLOUR POINTS WITH SEARED GOAT CHEESE

18-ounce goat cheese, soft and creamed

1 tablespoon virgin olive oil

1 clove garlic, finely chopped

1 tablespoon rosemary, finely chopped

pepper to taste

2 10-inch flour tortillas (flavored are best)

1 cup vegetable oil

1 tablespoon juniper berries (for garnish)

1 tablespoon black sesame seeds (for garnish)

Cream goat cheese with olive oil, garlic and spices in a food processor. Set aside.

Cut each tortilla in 6ths. Fry in vegetable oil till golden in color.

Using pastry bag with ¼ inch round tip, pipe zig-zag bead of goat cheese on each tortilla point and sear with propane torch.

To serve, toss fruit and greens together, adding dressing to taste. Arrange on chilled salad plates. Lay 2 tortilla points in V shape with approximate ½ of each point protruding off edge of plate. Sprinkle juniper berries and black sesame seeds over salad and serve.

∎

FILET MIGNON TOPPED WITH A WOVEN BASKET OF SAUTÉED PLANTAINS AND FIG FLOWERS

Serves 4

4 filet mignon steaks

coarse peppercorns

5 plantains, ripe yet firm

5 eggs, separated, whites reserved

½ teaspoon garlic powder

2 cups all purpose flour

¼ teaspoon salt

½ teaspoon pepper

3 cups vegetable oil

4 ripe figs

On cutting board, remove plantain skins and slice meat lengthwise by ⅛ inch. Select 4 longest strips from each plantain. Lay in flat pan, coating both sides with egg whites. In mixing bowl, combine flour and garlic, salt and pepper and mix well. Lay battered plantain strips on flat surface and coat both sides with flour mixture. Using 4 plantain strips, weave 2 strips horizontally with 2 strips vertically. Lay each woven plantain basket into a large, bowl shaped wire press, approximately 3 to 4 inches in diameter. Heat oil in deep pan, and fry each until golden in color. Set aside and keep warm.

For fig flowers, cut each fig into 4ths from top to bottom, careful to stop knife ⅔ of the way down. Pull tips back exposing interior. Set aside and refrigerate.

Grill steaks to taste just before serving. Sprinkle with pepper to taste.

To serve, top with inverted plantain basket. Open small hole in basket bottom to insert fig flower.

■

AU GRATIN GRUYERE WHEELS

Serves 4

2 pounds baked, peeled and thinly sliced potatoes

2 cups heavy cream

2 tablespoons green chile, finely chopped

3 cloves garlic, finely chopped

1 teaspoon salt

¼ teaspoon black ground pepper

¼ teaspoon nutmeg

1 tablespoon butter, softened

1 cup Gruyere cheese, grated

Preheat oven 350 degrees. Coat 9" x 12" baking pan with butter and layer potatoes in pan. In saucepan, combine cream, chile, garlic, salt, pepper and nutmeg. Bring mixture to a gentle boil over medium heat. Continue to cook and stir until the liquid thickens slightly, about 5 minutes. Pour mixture into prepared pan. If potatoes rise, press down to submerge. Sprinkle Gruyere cheese over mixture and bake until top is golden and potatoes are tender, approximately 1 hour. When slightly cooled, using a 3" or 4" round pastry cutter, remove 4 circular au gratin wheels from the wheel. Serve warm.

Cook's Note: Au Gratin Wheels presents beautifully served under filet mignon.

■

CARROT AND JICAMA BUNDLES

Serves 4

1 pound carrots, peeled and julienned into 3" long sticks

1 small jicama, peeled and julienned into 3" long sticks

1 leek

Remove 2 to 3 layers of skin from leek. Wash and cut 6 full length strips. Bundle 4 carrot sticks and 4 jicama sticks together, and tie tightly with leek strips. Blanch bundles in deep pan, using enough water to cover.

■

CRICKET'S FLOURLESS CHOCOLATE CAKE WITH CARMELIZED PEARS AND HOMEMADE VANILLA BEAN ICE CREAM

Serves 4

CRICKET'S FLOURLESS CHOCOLATE CAKE

1 pound bittersweet or semisweet chocolate, coarsely chopped

1¼ stick butter, cut into 10 pieces

5 large eggs, separated

¼ teaspoon cream of tartar

1 tablespoon sugar

Preheat oven to 325 degrees. Grease an 8" x 2" round pan (not springform) and line the bottom with parchment or wax paper.

Combine chocolate and butter in a large heatproof bowl. Set the bowl in a large skillet, barely simmering water and stir often until the chocolate and butter are warm, melted and smooth. Remove from heat and whisk in 5 egg yolks.

In another large bowl, beat on medium speed until soft peaks form, 5 egg whites and cream of tartar. Gradually add sugar, beating on high speed. Continue beating until the peaks are stiff but not dry. Use a rubber spatula to fold ¼ of the egg whites into the chocolate mixture, then fold in the remaining egg whites.

Scrape the batter into the pan and spread evenly. Set the pan in a large shallow baking dish or roasting pan. Set the baking dish in the oven and pour enough boiling water into it to reach halfway up the sides of the cake pan. Bake for exactly 30 minutes. The top of the cake will have a thin crust and the interior will still be gooey. Set the cake pan on a rack to cool completely, then refrigerate until chilled, or overnight.

GLAZE

6 ounces semisweet chocolate, chopped

1 stick sweet unsalted butter, cut into pieces

1 tablespoon light corn syrup

Combine all ingredients in top of double boiler over simmering water. Stir until smooth. Remove from water. Cool to lukewarm, stirring occasionally. Pour glaze in pool over center of chilled cake. Using icing spatula, spread glaze over top and sides of cake.

CARMELIZED PEARS

2 medium pears, firm with skins on, sliced thin

¼ cup sugar

On baking sheet, lay out pear slices. Sprinkle sugar on 1 side. Using propane torch, heat sugar until brown. Set aside.

LOUISE'S VANILLA BEAN ICE CREAM

Makes 1 quart

2 cups heavy cream

¾ cup whole milk

½ cup sugar

½ vanilla bean, split

5 egg yolks

In a heavy bottomed saucepan, heat the cream, milk and sugar until sugar is dissolved and the mixture is hot. In a small bowl, whisk egg yolks briefly. While whisking, slowly pour in about 1 cup of the hot cream mixture. Mix until smooth and then slowly pour it back into the saucepan. Cook over medium heat, stirring constantly until mixture thickens and slightly coats the back of a spoon (about 8 minutes). Be sure not to let the mixture boil, or it will curdle. Strain the mixture into a clean bowl and chill. When totally chilled, pour into ice cream maker and freeze.

Cook's Note: I have tried substituting vanilla extract for the vanilla bean, and it just doesn't cut it!

Cook's Memory: I have many fond memories of my mom making homemade ice cream in the summer with the hand crank, using a wide variety of fresh summer fruits. I use this basic recipe for all my fruit ice creams (excluding the vanilla bean). To the above recipe, after chilled, add ½ cup puréed fresh fruit and stir until blended. Pour into ice cream maker and freeze.

To arrange dessert plates, sprinkle white powdered sugar on plates. Lay pear slices around center of plates and top with wedge of cake. For additional fun of presentation, chop white Baker's chocolate into rough even sized pieces. Place the pieces in a dry heatproof bowl and set the bowl over a pan of hot water (not simmering). When the chocolate starts to melt, stir it with a wooden spoon until smooth. Pour into small pastry bag with tiny plastic tip (not metal), draw concentric circles on top of cake wedge.

One day before serving, cover 2 foot area of countertop closest to the stove with parchment or wax paper. Assemble ½ cup sugar, ⅓ cup corn syrup, 1 pastry thermometer and 1 large spoon.

In small heavy saucepan, stir together the sugar and corn syrup, bringing to a boil over medium heat, stirring constantly. Increase the heat and boil until caramel is amber and the thermometer registers 360 degrees. The residual heat will raise it about 10 degrees. If the temperature is below 360 degrees, the caramel will be pale and the spun sugar white instead of gold; over 370 degrees, it will have a brassy color. Immediately transfer the caramel to a heatproof glass measuring cup to stop the cooking. Timing is critical, so work quickly but loosely. Fill the spoon with caramel and pour free form shapes about 4 inches tall with a pointed base onto covered counter. Once you have four shapes you like, stick 1 in the center of each white chocolate circle on each cake wedge. On the side of cake wedges, place a scoop of ice cream, and serve.

■

Santa Fe Spring Luncheon

in the Season of Wisteria and Lilacs

Spicy White Bean Soup

Santa Fe Rolled and Stuffed Sole

with

Linguini and Pineapple Habanero Ginger Salsa

Fresh from the Garden

Cheesy Muffins

Camelback Inn Strawberry Pie

Serve with: Heiss Chardonnay or

Raspberry Iced Tea

"FRESH FROM THE GARDEN" CHEESY MUFFINS

Makes 1 dozen muffins

1½ cups all-purpose flour

2 teaspoons baking powder

½ teaspoon salt

⅔ cup milk

4 ounces (1 package) cream cheese, soft spreadable

1 egg, beaten

2 teaspoons fresh chives, minced

2 teaspoons fresh dill, chopped fine

2 teaspoons fresh basil, chopped fine

Combine flour, baking powder and salt. In separate bowl combine milk, cream cheese, egg and fresh herbs. Stir into flour mixture until moist, spoon into greased muffin cups. Bake at 375 degrees about 15-20 minutes. Serve warm with butter.

Cook's Note: These muffins must be served immediately. They do not freeze or keep well.

■

SPICY WHITE BEAN SOUP

Serves 4 to 6

½ pound white beans

4 cups water

1 tablespoon salt

3 white onions, chopped

4 cloves garlic, minced

¼ cup olive oil

1 tablespoon white vinegar

1 roasted Anaheim chile, chopped

1 small jalapeño, chopped (optional)

1 6-ounce can tomato paste

2 cups vegetable broth

salt and pepper to taste

FOR GARNISH

sour cream

fresh cilantro

paprika

Simmer beans in salted water until soft. In large fry pan sauté onions, garlic, cilantro and red pepper in oil until onions are translucent and slightly brown. Add vinegar, chile, jalapeño, tomato paste and vegetable broth. Stir over low heat to blend. Drain beans, reserving 2 cups of liquid.

Add the 2 cups of liquid and the cooked beans to the pan mixture. Stir, continuing to simmer for several minutes over low heat. Purée mixture in small amounts in blender. Then pour back into pan to reheat and simmer for 5 minutes over low heat, stirring constantly. Serve hot garnished with cilantro leaves, a dollop of sour cream and paprika.

■

SANTA FE ROLLED AND STUFFED SOLE
WITH LINGUINI AND PINEAPPLE HABANERO GINGER SALSA

Serves 8

2 cloves fresh garlic, finely chopped

2 teaspoons fresh cilantro, chopped

1 teaspoon fresh rosemary, chopped

2 teaspoons Parmesan cheese, freshly grated

¼ cup balsamic vinegar

¼ cup olive oil

8 bunches fresh spinach, washed, dried and stems removed

16 small Dover sole filets

2 red bell peppers, roasted, peeled, seeded and very thinly sliced

2 green bell peppers, roasted, peeled, seeded and very thinly sliced

½ cup butter, melted

1 cup olive oil

10 ounces linguini, cooked until it is halfway al dente and drained

4 cloves fresh garlic, finely chopped

8 scallions, thinly sliced

3 tablespoons black peppercorns, cracked

salt to taste

1 pound baby greens

Pineapple Habanero Ginger Salsa

In a large bowl place the 2 cloves of chopped garlic, cilantro, rosemary, Parmesan cheese, balsamic vinegar, and the ¼ cup of olive oil.

Whisk the ingredients together. Add the spinach leaves and toww them in so that they are well coated.

Cover the bowl with plastic wrap and marinate the spinach in the refrigerator overnight.

Preheat the oven to 350 degrees.

On top of each fish filet place, in the order, the spinach leaves (reserve the marinade), red and green bell pepper strips, another fish filet, spinach leaves, and red and green bell pepper strips. Roll the fish up and place it in a baking dish.

Pour the marinade from the spinach leaves and the first ½ cup of melted butter over the rolled fish fillets.

Bake the fish for 40 minutes, or until it is done.

In a large sauté pan place the 1 cup of olive oil and the second ½ cup of melted butter. Heat them on medium high until the butter is melted and they are hot. Add the linguini, the 4 cloves of chopped garlic, scallions, black peppercorns, and salt. Sauté the ingredients for 10 minutes.

On each of 8 individual serving plates place the linguini. Place a rolled and stuffed fish filet on top. Place the Pineapple Habanero Ginger Salsa on top of the fish. Sprinkle the baby greens around the edges.

PINEAPPLE HABANERO GINGER SALSA

Makes approximately 4 cups

1 small fresh pineapple, peeled, cored and diced medium

2 tablespoons red onions, finely chopped

4 Habanero chile peppers, finely chopped

2 tablespoons fresh ginger root, peeled and finally chopped

2 tablespoons fresh cilantro, chopped

1 tablespoon balsamic vinegar

In a medium bowl place all the ingredients and mix them together well. Cover the bowl with plastic wrap and refrigerate the ingredients for 30 minutes.

■

CAMELBACK INN STRAWBERRY PIE

Serves 6 to 8

1 baked pie shell

2 cups sugar

4 cups water

6 cups fresh strawberries, cleaned and hulled

1 ½ cups egg whites

1 ½ cups sugar

1 teaspoon salt

2 tablespoons vinegar

8 tablespoons gelatin

2 cups water

3 cups sweetened whipped cream

Boil 2 cups sugar with the 4 cups of water for 5 minutes. Add berries. Beat egg whites in separate bowl. Add the 1 ½ cups sugar to the egg whites 1 spoonful at a time. Dissolve gelatin in 2 cups of water with the salt and vinegar. When it congeals, add to beaten egg whites. Pour into crust. Refrigerate until set. Top with berry mixture, then refrigerate again. Top with whipped cream before serving.

Cook's Memory: This pie, with enormous fresh strawberries, evokes a special memory of Camelback Inn's famous luncheon buffet.

■

Summer Picnic
at the Conejo Cafe

"The Conejo Café" resulted from Pat and I participating in the yearly
Santa Fe A.S.I.D. Showhouse. We have in years past designed a room
and operated a small café for Showhouse guests to enjoy a light picnic
on the terrace.

Peter Rabbit Garden Sandwich
Or
Western Waldorf Sandwich
Or
Sesame-Orange Turkey Wrap

Sausage Potato Salad

Lucy's Homemade Cookies

Oatmeal Apricot Cookies

Raspberry Lemon Almond Bars

Chocolate Chip Butterscotch Cookies

Grant Corner Inn Lemonade

PETER RABBIT SANDWICH

Makes 4 sandwiches

8 slices homemade 7-grain bread (page 157)

12 medium mushrooms, cleaned and sliced

3 tablespoons butter

2 avocados, peeled and sliced

2 small tomatoes, sliced

¼ pound mixed baby greens

4 slices Monterey Jack cheese

⅔ cup mayonnaise

2 teaspoons chopped cilantro

2 teaspoons chopped parsley

2 teaspoons chopped chives

1 teaspoons minced garlic

Sauté mushrooms in butter. Mix seasonings with mayonnaise. Spread mayonnaise on bread slices. Arrange avocados, tomatoes, mushrooms and cheese over baby greens.

■

WESTERN WALDORF SANDWICH

Makes 4 sandwiches

8 slices homemade whole wheat bread

8 slices bacon, cooked crisp and drained (grease reserved)

3 (unpeeled) medium apples, Red Delicious, sliced

4 slices Monterey Jack cheese

½ head butter lettuce, washed, leaves separated and well dried

⅓ cup chopped walnuts

⅔ cup mayonnaise

Sauté apple slices and walnuts in small amount of reserved bacon grease. Spread mayonnaise on bread slices. Arrange all ingredients on sandwiches.

■

SESAME ORANGE TURKEY WRAP

Serves 4

3 cups shredded turkey breast

2 oranges, peeled and sliced into bite size

¼ cup sliced green pepper

1 tablespoon fresh cilantro, chopped fine

½ cup toasted sesame seeds

½ pound baby spinach leaves

4 12-inch flour tortillas

DRESSING

¼ cup rice vinegar

¼ cup sesame oil

1 tablespoon soy sauce

1 tablespoon lemon juice

1 tablespoon sugar

¼ teaspoon salt

In medium bowl, combine turkey, oranges, green peppers and cilantro. Shake dressing ingredients together and pour over turkey mixture. Chill overnight in a tightly covered container.

Line tortillas with spinach leaves and spoon turkey mixture in center. Sprinkle sesame seeds over turkey. Roll tortillas.

■

SAUSAGE POTATO SALAD

Serves 6 to 8

6 cups diced, cold, unpeeled baby new potatoes,
cooked in jackets

1 large cucumber, chopped

2 medium dill pickles, chopped

2 pimentos, chopped

3 green onions, minced

1 bunch fresh cilantro, chopped

1 sweet red pepper, chopped

1 pound Italian sausage, cooked, sliced

½ teaspoon salt

2 teaspoons Dijon mustard

1 cup mayonnaise

Combine all ingredients in bowl. Toss until well blended. Serve on butter lettuce.

■

OATMEAL APRICOT COOKIES

Makes 2½ dozen

1 cup sugar

1 cup brown sugar

1 cup shortening or butter

2 eggs

1 banana

2 cups flour

1 teaspoon cinnamon

1 teaspoon baking soda

3 cups quick oats

2 cups dried chopped apricots

Mix wet ingredients together. Sift dry ingredients. Add dry to wet ingredients. Drop by teaspoonful onto a baking sheet. Bake at 350 degrees for 15 to 20 minutes.

■

RASPBERRY LEMON ALMOND BARS

Makes 1½ dozen 3"x 2" bars

2 cups flour

1 ½ cups old-fashioned oats

½ cup granola (page 26)

1 cup sugar

⅔ cup chopped almonds

1 cup butter, softened

1 teaspoon almond extract

1 cup raspberry preserves

1 ½ cup Lemon Glaze

Mix together flour, oats and sugar. Cut in butter with a pastry blender until mix resembles coarse crumbs. Stir in almond extract. Reserve 2 cups of this mixture and press the remaining mixture over bottom of 9"x13" baking pan. Spread the preserves over the top within ½" of the edge. Mix the almonds and granola and rest of oat mixture. Sprinkle evenly over the preserves. Press gently to compact the oat and almond mixture into the jam. Bake 25 to 30 minutes at 350 degrees. Drizzle with Lemon Glaze while hot. Cool in the pan and cut into bars.

LEMON GLAZE

2 cups fresh lemon juice

2 teaspoons lemon zest

1 cup sugar

Mix juice, zest and sugar in saucepan and bring to boil. Reduce heat and boil until reduced by half.

■

CHOCOLATE CHIP BUTTERSCOTCH COOKIES

Makes 2½ dozen

½ cup butter

¾ cup brown sugar

¾ cup sugar

2 eggs

2 teaspoons Kahlua

2¼ cups flour

1 teaspoon baking soda

½ teaspoon salt

1 cup chocolate chips

1 cup butterscotch chips

Cream together butter and sugar. Add eggs and Kahlua and beat. Combine flour, salt and soda and add to wet ingredients. Mix in chips. Drop by teaspoonful on greased cookie sheet. Bake at 375 degrees for 8-10 minutes.

■

FRESH LEMONADE

Makes approximately 1½ quarts

1 cup fresh squeezed lemon juice

½ cup sugar

1 quart cold water

Mix, chill and serve over crushed ice.

■

Santa Fe Wine & Chile Fiesta Winemaker Dinner

September

— *Amusé* —

Seaweed Gourds with Salmon and Caviar Salsa
Over Bitter Grits with Quail Egg Snails
De Loach Vineyards Chardonnay Russian River Valley 1997

— *Appetizer* —

Roasted Duck Paté in Filo Dough over a Wild Rice Cake
Drizzled with a Shitake Habanero Coulis
De Loach Pinot Noir Estate 1997

— *Salad* —

Lettuce Cups of Radish Sprouts and
Dual-Colored Ribbon Cabbage
Infused with a Sesame Aioli Dressing
De Loach Vineyards Fumé Blanc 1997

— *Intermezzo* —

Watermelon Sorbet

— *Entrée* —

Poached Chilean Sea Bass in a Banana Leaf Jacket
Atop Herbed Risotto with Fall Harvest Vegetables
De Loach Chardonnay OFS 1997

— *Dessert* —

Lace Cookie Cup with Wild Berries
Over Homemade Fresh Mango Ice Cream and Mint Sauce
De Loach OFS Port 1995

Santa Fe Wine and Chile Fiesta is a celebration of the harvest, started 10 years ago to introduce the excellence of New Mexico's local and national vintners to the Santa Fe community. With the long-standing marriage of food and wine the event soon evolved into a pairing of individual wineries to noted Santa Fe fine dining establishments.

The complexity of the palate in both food and wine is best explored with this September event. Quoted as being, "The Best of the Best."

SEAWEED GOURDS WITH SALMON AND CAVIAR SALSA OVER BITTER GRITS WITH QUAIL EGG SNAILS

Serves 4

1 packet dried Nori seaweed

1 6-ounce salmon filet (sushi grade)

1 3-ounce jar black caviar, drained

1 clove garlic, minced

1 small sweet red onion, diced

3 tablespoons grated ginger root

1 3-ounce jar capers

¼ teaspoon lemon juice

¼ teaspoon red chile oil

¼ teaspoon sesame seed oil

¼ teaspoon lite soy sauce

1 cup quick grits

1 tablespoon bacon reserve

1 tablespoon white vinegar

salt and pepper to taste

4 snail shells (Escargots)

4 fresh quail eggs

cracked pepper (for garnish)

additional lite soy sauce and red chile oil (for garnish)

Preheat oven to 350 degrees. Remove 4 sheets of seaweed and cut 8 four inch squares. Lay flat on counter and dampen with wet towel. Set aside. Cut 4 sheets of aluminum foil 5 inches square. Shape each into a cone with wide end about 1 inch in diameter and the opposite end as tight as possible and spray outside with a vegetable oil spray. Using spatula remove damp seaweed one at a time wrapping each square around a cone. Place standing cones on cookie sheet and bake until crisp, approximately 5-8 minutes. Cool slightly, remove seaweed from each cone and set aside.

For salsa, cut salmon filet into ⅛ inch cubes. Set aside. Combine caviar, salmon, capers, red onion, ginger, garlic, lemon juice, red chile oil, sesame oil, and soy sauce.

Cook grits to direction on package. Add bacon reserve, vinegar, salt and pepper to boiling mix. Set aside. Keep warm.

In empty egg carton, place escargot shells face up and fill each shell with 1 raw quail egg.

To serve, spoon salsa into seaweed cone and lay on small plate, allowing additional salsa to spill onto the plate. Spoon 1 to 2 tablespoons of grits to one side of gourd and garnish with cracked pepper. On other side of plate, place Escargot shell facing up. To finish, drizzle soy sauce and red chile oil around plate.

■

ROASTED DUCK PATÉ IN FILO DOUGH OVER A WILD RICE CAKE DRIZZLED WITH A SHITAKE HABANERO COULIS

Serves 4

PATE AND FILO

1 pound duck liver

1 clove garlic, diced

1 tablespoon sage, chopped

¼ teaspoon black pepper

4 sheets thawed filo dough

½ pound melted butter

In medium skillet, sauté livers, garlic, sage and pepper in 4 tablespoons of butter until tender. Remove from heat and purée in food processor. Set aside.

Roll out filo on cutting board 1 sheet at a time. Brush with melted butter and saturate entire sheet. Lay next sheet on top and continue brushing with butter until all 4 sheets are layered and buttered. With a ruler, divide sheets into 6 inch squares. Using a melon baller, place a ball of the paté in center of each square. Fold corners over paté and twist filo over ball to lock together. Place filo on baking pan and bake at 350 degrees until filo is golden brown.

WILD RICE CAKE

2 cups wild rice cooked in 1 cup chicken stock

2 teaspoons salt

4 baby new red potatoes, boiled with jackets removed

2 green onions, fine chopped

4 cloves garlic, minced

3 tablespoons cilantro, finely chopped

2 eggs, slightly beaten

1 tablespoon flour

2 tablespoons sour cream

½ cup olive oil

In large mixing bowl, mash potatoes with fork. Set aside. Sauté garlic and green onions in 1 tablespoon olive oil. To potatoes, add rice, onions, garlic, cilantro, eggs, flour, sour cream and mix thoroughly. With ice cream scoop, spoon out mixture onto oiled large skillet. Flatten with spatula and fry until golden brown and cooked through. Keep in warm oven.

SHITAKE HABANERO COULIS

3 large shitake mushrooms, washed and patted dry

1 small Habanero chile, diced

2 tablespoons Worcestershire Sauce

¼ teaspoon Liquid Smoke

1 cup chicken stock

2 gloves garlic, minced

1 tablespoon olive oil

2 tablespoons butter

salt and pepper to taste

In small skillet, sauté Habanero in butter until brown. Reserve remaining cooked butter and discard cooked Habanero. Set aside. In medium sauté pan, cook mushrooms and garlic in olive oil, adding reserved butter. Cook till brown. Add remaining ingredients and simmer on low heat for 15 minutes. Remove from heat and pour in blender. Process until thoroughly blended. Return mixture to sauté pan and continue to cook on medium heat for approximately 5 minutes.

To serve, ladle coulis on plate to cover entire surface. Lay 1 or 2 rice cakes in center and top with 2 filo twists.

■

LETTUCE CUPS OF RADISH SPROUTS AND DUAL-COLORED RIBBON CABBAGE INFUSED WITH A SESAME AIOLI DRESSING

Serves 4

1 small head of radicchio

1 small head of purple cabbage

1 small head of green cabbage

1 container fresh radish sprouts

bread sticks for garnish

Peel 4 large leaves of radicchio. Wash and pat dry being careful to preserve round shape. Set aside. Wash and dry full heads of cabbage. Cut approximately 2/3 of each head into 1/4 inch strips. Separate into strands and toss in mixing bowl to mix colors.

DRESSING

5 egg yolks

1 cup sesame oil

1/4 cup fresh cilantro

1/2 cup sour cream

1 clove garlic

salt and pepper to taste

In blender, mix yolks, oil, cilantro, sour cream, garlic, salt and pepper. Set aside.

On cool salad plate, arrange radicchio cup at top of plate, fill 2/3 with cabbage mix. Lay on side and fill remaining plate with additional cabbage. Open refrigerated package of radish sprouts and bunch in top of radicchio cup. Ladle dressing over entire salad and garnish with bread sticks.

■

WATERMELON SORBET

Makes approximately 1 quart

1 cup purified water

1 cup sugar

1½ cup pureed watermelon

3 teaspoons fresh lemon juice

To make simple syrup, simmer water and sugar in medium saucepan until sugar is dissolved. Cool to room temperature and refrigerate overnight in a covered jar. Stir puréed watermelon, simple syrup and lemon juice together and pour mixture into ice cream maker and freeze. Serve in chilled goblets with a sprig of fresh mint.

■

POACHED CHILEAN SEA BASS IN A BANANA LEAF JACKET ATOP HERBED RISOTTO WITH FALL HARVEST VEGETABLES

Serves 4

4 6-ounce Chilean sea bass filets (each about 1 ½ inch thick)

1 package prepared banana leaves

1 inch piece fresh ginger root, peeled and chopped

1 cup Japanese rice wine

½ cup saki

½ cup lite soy sauce

½ cup white miso

¼ cup rice vinegar

chive stalks (for garnish)

To prepare marinade, combine ginger root, rice wine, saki, soy sauce, miso and rice vinegar in blender and purée until smooth.

Arrange sea bass filets in 2 inches baking dish and pour marinade over. Marinade for at least 2 hours or overnight.

Cut 4 banana leaves into squares large enough to wrap around each fish filet. Cut remaining banana leaves into strips, 18 inches x ¼ inch long. Wrap each filet with banana leaf squares and tie tightly with strips. Lay bundles flat in steamer and cook approximately 15 minutes. Remove, drain and keep warm.

RISOTTO

4 cups cooked risotto

2 cloves garlic, minced

1 teaspoon rosemary, finely diced

salt and pepper to taste

Combine all ingredients and keep warm.

To serve, spoon risotto onto center of plate. Place fish bundle on top of risotto and arrange fresh fall vegetables around edge of risotto. Lay chive stocks against fish for garnish.

■

LACE COOKIE CUP WITH WILD BERRIES OVER HOMEMADE FRESH MANGO ICE CREAM AND MINT SAUCE

Serves 4

LACE COOKIE CUP

2 tablespoons unsalted butter

2 tablespoons + 2 teaspoons light brown sugar

1 tablespoon + 2 teaspoons light corn syrup

3 tablespoons + 1 teaspoon bread flour

2 pints mixed fresh berries

In a heavy saucepan, bring brown sugar, butter and corn syrup to a boil over moderate heat. Stir in flour and cook, stirring constantly until dough is thickened (30 seconds to 1 minute). Cool dough to room temperature and set aside.

Preheat oven to 350 degrees and butter 2 baking sheets or use 2 silplats to minimize burning and sticking. Have 2 inverted glasses (3 inch diameter base) on hand for molding cookies. Divide dough into 5 equal pieces (one is a spare). Arrange 2 balls of dough, 7 inches apart on each cooking sheet. With your fingers, press dough into 5 inch rounds and bake, one tray at a time, in middle of oven until golden, 6 to 8 minutes (cookies will spread to about 6 inches.) Let cookies stand on cooking sheets until just firm enough to hold their shape (30 to 40 seconds). Quickly transfer cookie to inverted glasses using metal spatula and gently mold cookies around glasses. Cool. Repeat with second sheet of cookies. Cookie cups may be made 2 days ahead and kept in an airtight container at room temperature.

MANGO ICE CREAM

¾ cup puréed fresh mango, chilled

make Vanilla Bean Ice Cream mixture (Page 232) but delete vanilla bean

Stir mango purée into ice cream mixture. Pour into ice cream maker and freeze.

MINT SAUCE

½ cup mint jelly

5 sprigs fresh mint

Combine in blender.

To serve, arrange cookie in center of dessert plate, add scoop of ice cream inside cookie, sprinkle with berries and drizzle with mint sauce.

■

Thanksgiving Dinner

— Soup —
Sweet Red Pepper Bisque with Fresh Basil Pesto

— Salad —
Baby Field Greens and Watercress
With Vegetable Sticks Radiating from a Jicama Core
Drizzled with Fresh Tangerine Vinaigrette

— Entrée —
Roast Tender Turkey with Tequila Honey Glaze
Mild Roasted Ancho Chile Gravy
Caramelized Onion Green Chile New Potato & Yam Mash
Chinese Green Beans
Cranberry Walnut Salsa in an Endive Boat

— Dessert —

Pumpkin Praline Pie with Chocolate Kahlua Sauce

Du Boeuf Cru Beaujolais Moulin-A-Ven 1997
Pine Ridge Chenin Blanc Viognier Napa 1998

SWEET RED PEPPER BISQUE WITH FRESH BASIL PESTO

Serves 4

4 cups vegetable stock

4 red peppers

2 celery stocks

1 leek, washed and sliced (white part only)

1 medium onion, sliced

2 carrots, peeled and sliced

1 small turnip, peeled and sliced

6 cloves garlic, peeled and diced

1 bouquet of garni (bay leaf, parsley, cilantro, rosemary and thyme bundled in a 4"x4" piece of cheesecloth and tied)

salt and pepper to taste

10 tablespoons sour cream (for garnish)

4 fresh basil leaves (for garnish)

In a medium saucepan, combine all ingredients and cook on medium heat for 40 to 60 minutes or until all ingredients are tender. Remove from heat (leaving garni bundle in pot), transfer to food processor and blend till creamy. Return to pot and cook on low heat for an additional 60 minutes or until reduced by 2 cups. Let stand.

FRESH BASIL PESTO

4 tablespoons virgin olive oil

6 fresh sweet basil leaves

3 cloves garlic, peeled

1 green onion, chopped

8 fresh cilantro leaves

2 black olives, pitts removed

¼ teaspoon red chile powder

Combine all ingredients in blender and thoroughly mix into paste. Set aside.

To serve, ladle approximately 1 cup of soup into each bowl. Whip sour cream until smooth and drizzle over soup. Spoon pesto over sour cream, then stand a basil leaf in thickest part of sour cream and serve.

■

BABY FIELD GREENS AND WATERCRESS WITH VEGETABLE STICKS RADIATING FROM A JICAMA CORE DRIZZLED WITH FRESH TANGERINE VINAIGRETTE

Serves 4

16 ounces fresh field greens

4 small jicamas, peeled

Cut each jicama into a round shape with a flat bottom. On top side, cut 3 evenly spaced holes through each jicama at a 45 degree angle, slanted toward the center. The holes should be roughly ½ inch in diameter. (An apple corer will work well.) Keep jicama in ice water until serving.

VEGETABLE STICKS

Makes 1 dozen

1 cup all purpose flour

¼ teaspoon kosher salt

¾ teaspoon baking powder

1½ tablespoon solid vegetable shortening

¼ to ½ cup carrot or beet juice

1 tablespoon olive oil

Preheat oven to 350 degrees. In the bowl of a food processor, pulse flour, salt and baking powder to combine. Add shortening and pulse until mixture resembles coarse meal. With the machine running, gradually add vegetable juice until dough comes together. Transfer dough to a lightly floured surface. Form dough into a smooth rectangle, 4"x 6". Roll out dough into a 4"x 10" sheet about ¼ inch thick. Cut dough into ¼ inch wide strips. Using your hands, gently roll strips back and forth into 12" long strips.

Arrange the sticks on a baking sheet, side by side. Press ends of sticks down onto baking sheet to keep them straight while they bake. Lightly brush with olive oil. Bake until firm and cooked through, 14 to 18 minutes. Transfer the sticks to a wire rack to cool. These will keep in an airtight container at room temperature for up to 3 days.

TANGERINE VINAIGRETTE

Makes 1½ cups

1 cup olive oil

½ cup white rice vinegar

3 tablespoons fresh tangerine juice

1 tablespoon finely grated tangerine rind

1 clove garlic

¼ teaspoon salt

¼ teaspoon white pepper

Combine olive oil and garlic in blender and mix thoroughly. Pour into mixing bowl, add remaining ingredients and whisk together.

To serve, place jicama in center of plate and insert vegetable sticks in each hole. Carefully cover jicama and remainder of plate with field greens. Generously drizzle vinaigrette over entire salad.

■

ROAST TENDER TURKEY WITH TEQUILA HONEY GLAZE MILD ROASTED ANCHO CHILE GRAVY

Serves 4

8-to-10 pound whole turkey

10 fresh sage leaves

4 sprigs fresh rosemary

¼ cup melted butter

salt and pepper

Preheat oven to 350 degrees. Wash bird in cold water and place on rack in uncovered baking pan with 1 inch of water in bottom. Brush with butter. Sprinkle with herbs, salt and pepper. Bake uncovered 1 hour or until golden brown. Add 2 cups of water to pan. Rebaste bird with butter. Cover with foil and reduce heat to 200 degrees. Cook approximately 3 hours, intermittently lifting foil to rebaste. The last ½ hour, raise oven temperature to 350 degrees, uncover turkey and baste with Tequila Honey Glaze.

TEQUILA HONEY GLAZE

1 cup turkey pan juices

2 tablespoon honey

1 tablespoon tequila

1 teaspoon fresh lemon juice

In a small saucepan, combine ingredients and simmer for a few minutes.

ANCHO CHILE GRAVY

2 cups turkey pan juices (if necessary add chicken stock)

1 whole Ancho chile (quartered and seeds removed)

¼ teaspoon Kitchen Bouquet

3 tablespoons all purpose flour

1 splash Worcestershire Sauce

1 clove garlic, minced

1 tablespoon white onion, finely diced

1 tablespoon unsalted sweet butter

½ teaspoon sage, chopped fine

¼ teaspoon pepper

In medium sauté pan melt butter adding garlic and onion. Cook until onion is translucent. Set aside. In a medium sauté pan add Ancho chile to 1 cup turkey pan juices (to accent gravy flavor) and cook on high for 3 minutes. Remove chile and discard. Add flour to reheated butter mixture to make a roux. Add flavored pan juices to roux, whisking briskly. Add pepper and cook until thickened. Add 1 cup of pan juices and remaining ingredients and whisk till thoroughly mixed. Simmer on low, careful not to burn.

■

CARAMELIZED ONION GREEN CHILE NEW POTATO & YAM MASH

Serves 4

1 white onion, sliced into thick rounds

1 fresh roasted green chile, diced

6 medium red new potatoes, boiled soft and peeled

1 medium yam, boiled soft and peeled

3 cloves garlic, finely diced

salt and pepper to taste

1½ cups milk

2 tablespoons sweet butter

In a large mixing bowl, combine potatoes, yam, chile, salt and pepper. Break and mash with fork, adding milk a little at a time until smooth.

Sauté onion rounds until translucent. Remove and lay on buttered cookie sheet, taking care to keep intact. Transfer mix to large pastry bag using round open tip (½ inch to ¾ inch). Pipe a swirl over each onion round, leaving an exposed outer ring. Serve warm.

■

CRANBERRY WALNUT SALSA IN AN ENDIVE BOAT

Serves 4

8 ounces dried cranberries

½ cup cranberry juice

1 tablespoon walnuts, finely diced

¼ small white onion, finely diced

2 green onions, finely diced

3 tablespoon fresh cilantro, chopped fine

2 teaspoons balsamic vinegar

1 teaspoon red wine vinegar

1 large endive

Soften cranberries by sautéing in cranberry juice. In medium bowl, combine and mix all ingredients except endive. Spoon mixture into each endive leaf.

■

PUMPKIN PRALINE PIE WITH CHOCOLATE KAHLUA SAUCE

Serves 4

1 9-inch unbaked pie crust

2 cups cooked mashed pumpkin

6 tablespoons sweet unsalted butter

⅓ cup brown sugar (packed)

½ cup chopped walnuts

1½ cups eggnog

¾ cup sugar

2 envelopes gelatin

1 teaspoon cinnamon

½ teaspoon ground ginger

½ teaspoon nutmeg

3 eggs (separated)

¼ teaspoon cream of tartar

1 cup heavy cream (whipped)

Preheat oven to 450 degrees. Bake pie crust for 10 minutes. Set aside. Cream butter and brown sugar and add nuts. Pour into pie shell and bake 5 minutes longer. Cool and set aside.

In medium bowl, beat egg yolks into eggnog. Add ½ cup sugar, gelatin, cinnamon, ginger and nutmeg. Pour mixture into medium sauce-pan and heat slowly until gelatin is dissolved. Stir in pumpkin and mix thoroughly. Pour into large bowl and chill. Beat egg whites and cream of tartar in medium bowl. Beat in remaining ¼ cup of sugar. Fold egg whites and 1 cup whipped cream into pumpkin mixture. Spoon into crust and chill for several hours before serving.

CHOCOLATE KAHLUA SAUCE

½ cup heavy cream

3 tablespoons sweet unsalted butter

⅓ cup sugar

⅓ cup brown sugar (firmly packed)

⅛ teaspoon kosher salt

4 ounces semi-sweet chocolate, finely chopped

1 tablespoon Kahlua

In a heavy saucepan, combine the cream and butter. Stir over medium heat until the butter melts and the cream is not boiling. Add the sugars and stir until dissolved. Add the salt and chocolate, whisking over low heat until smooth. Add Kahlua.

To serve, drizzle warm sauce over each pie piece.

Cook's Note: Sprinkle cinnamon over each plate, then white powdered sugar and place pie wedge in center for a elegant presentation.

■

Christmas Eve Dinner

— Soup —

Creamy Fresh Pumpkin-Butternut Bisque
With Toasted Pumpkin Seeds in an Acorn Squash Bowl

— Salad —

Radicchio Cups with Baby Greens,
Crabmeat, Avocado and Grapefruit
With a Sweet Red Pepper Vinaigrette

— Entrée —

Habanero Orange Glazed Roast Duck Breast
With Fresh Chanterelle Mushroom Sauce
Wild Rice Medley with Toasted Pinons
Mint and Cranberry Polenta
Baby Carrots and Roasted Corn

— Dessert —

Fresh Fruit Custard Pie with Lime Grand Marnier
Sauce

R H Phillips EXP Syrah Esparto 1997
Joseph Phelps Pastiche White Vin De Mistral Napa 1996

CREAMY FRESH PUMPKIN-BUTTERNUT BISQUE WITH TOASTED PUMPKIN SEEDS IN AN ACORN SQUASH BOWL

Serves 4

1 small pumpkin, approximately 2 pounds

1 small butternut squash

4 acorn squash, as round as possible

4 cups chicken stock

1½ tablespoons cinnamon

2 teaspoons nutmeg

2 cloves garlic, minced

1 stick sweet unsalted butter

½ teaspoon salt

¼ teaspoon pepper

4 thin slices Gruyère cheese

Wash exterior of pumpkin and butternut squash. Quarter both and remove seeds by separating from pulp. Discard squash seeds. Wash and spread pumpkin seeds on cookie sheet to dry. Set aside.

Preheat oven to 350 degrees. Place pumpkin and butternut squash in deep baking pan with at least 1 inch of water in bottom. Melt butter and brush on all meat surfaces. Sprinkle ½ of combined cinnamon and nutmeg over buttered surfaces. Cover pan and bake until soft and tender, approximately 1 hour. Remove and discard skin and mash meat in mixing bowl. In medium saucepan, add combined mixture to remaining ingredients (excluding acorn squash). Cook over medium heat about 30 minutes and set aside. Keep warm.

For acorn squash bowls, cut and remove tips from squash approximately ¾ inch down, taking care not to cut too deeply into meat. This will allow squash to be stable in soup bowl. On opposite end of squash, cut below the stem low enough to create lidded handles, leaving ⅔ of squash for bowls. Scrape off interior of bowls and lids, discarding seeds and pulp. Using remaining butter, brush on all meat surfaces. Sprinkle remaining combined cinnamon and nutmeg over buttered surfaces. Place 4 hollowed squash standing in deep pan of water. Cover pan and bake at 350 degrees until soft and tender, approximately 1 hour. Set aside and keep warm.

TOASTED PUMPKIN SEEDS

reserved pumpkin seeds

1 tablespoon olive oil

1 teaspoon garlic powder

¼ teaspoon salt

¼ teaspoon chile powder

In mixing bowl, combine all ingredients. Transfer to skillet and toast until golden and set aside.

To serve, ladle bisque into squash bowls, float slice of cheese over soup and sprinkle with toasted seeds. Place lids on squash bowls and serve.

Cook's Note: A serving suggestion that really looks beautiful is a braided bread ring cradling the acorn squash bowls. This braid becomes the edible bread for the soup.

■

RADICCHIO CUPS WITH BABY GREENS, CRAB MEAT, AVOCADO AND GRAPEFRUIT WITH SWEET RED PEPPER VINAIGRETTE

Serves 4

1 large radicchio, washed, with 4 large leaves removed and set aside for serving cups

1 pound baby greens

1 pound fresh crab meat, shredded

2 ripe avocados, peeled, seeded and diced thick

2 medium grapefruit, peeled and sectioned

¼ cup grapefruit juice

paprika (for garnish)

In medium mixing bowl, toss crab, avocado and grapefruit sections with grapefruit juice, and refrigerate.

Take remaining radicchio head, tear apart and mix with baby greens.

SWEET RED PEPPER VINAIGRETTE

Makes 1½ cup dressing

2 medium red peppers, seeded

1 cup olive oil

½ cup red wine vinegar

3 cloves garlic, peeled

4 tablespoons cilantro, chopped

1 tablespoon parsley, chopped

1 tablespoon brown sugar

2 green onions, chopped

1 teaspoon salt

¼ teaspoon pepper

In blender, combine all ingredients and blend until smooth.

To serve, place radicchio cups in center of plates. Arrange greens around cups and drizzle with dressing. Sprinkle with paprika over crab mix.

■

HABANERO ORANGE GLAZED ROAST DUCK BREAST WITH FRESH CHANTERELLE MUSHROOM SAUCE

Serves 4

4 duck breasts

1 12-ounce jar orange marmalade

½ cup orange juice

½ small fresh Habanero, diced

1 tablespoon butter

pepper to taste

In small skillet, heat orange juice and Habanero. Simmer 10 minutes and discard the chile. Add marmalade, a spoonful at a time. Mix thoroughly and keep warm. Score skin side of duck breasts. Brush both sides of duck with sauce, add pepper and fry in butter, starting with skin side down on medium heat. Brown both sides, drain and keep warm.

FRESH CHANTERELLE MUSHROOM SAUCE

10 Chanterelle mushrooms, chopped

1 cup chicken stock

1 cup heavy cream

1 tablespoon Worcestershire Sauce

2 cloves garlic, minced

2 tablespoons sweet unsalted butter

salt and pepper to taste

In medium skillet, cook mushrooms and garlic in butter until brown. Add remaining ingredients and simmer on low heat for 15 minutes. Remove from heat and transfer to blender and purée. Return mixture to skillet and continue to cook on medium heat for 10 more minutes.

■

WILD RICE MEDLEY WITH TOASTED PIÑONS

Serves 4

2 cups wild rice

3½ tablespoons pinons

2½ cups chicken broth

½ teaspoon salt

¼ teaspoon white pepper

4 tablespoons sweet unsalted butter

2 tablespoons olive oil

1 medium onion, finely chopped

1 cup red pepper, diced

1 cup celery, diced

2 tablespoons parsley, finely chopped

Toast pinons in sauté pan with 1 tablespoon of butter until lightly browned. In saucepan, bring chicken broth to boil over high heat. Add rice, salt and pepper and stir with fork. Lower heat and simmer 40 minutes. In medium skillet, heat remaining butter and oil over medium heat. Add onion and sauté, stirring occasionally until soft and clear. Add red pepper and celery and continue to sauté for about 5 minutes.

When rice is cooked add pinons and parsley.

∎

MINT AND CRANBERRY POLENTA

MINT POLENTA

Serves 4

1 cup yellow corn meal

1 teaspoon salt

1 teaspoon sugar

6 ounces mint jelly

butter for sautéing

In medium saucepan, bring 2¾ cups of water to a boil. In small mixing bowl combine cornmeal with 1 cup of cold water; add salt and sugar. Add cornmeal to boiling water, a spoonful at a time, stirring constantly. Add mint jelly and continue stirring. When cornmeal is thick, cover and cook over very low heat without stirring for 10 minutes. Spoon polenta onto cookie sheet, smooth and flatten. Cover and refrigerate for 24 hours. Use Christmas cookie cutters to cut out your favorite shapes. Fry in large skillet with butter. Serve warm.

CRANBERRY POLENTA

Serves 4

1 cup yellow corn meal

1 teaspoon salt

1 teaspoon sugar

1 8-ounce can jellied cranberry sauce

butter for sautéing

Follow instructions for Mint Polenta, substituting cranberry sauce for mint jelly.

∎

BABY CARROTS AND ROASTED CORN

Serves 4

12 baby carrots with stems, peeled and washed

4 fresh ears of corn, peeled and washed

In a large pot, cover corn with salted water and boil until tender 20 to 30 minutes. Pat dry, spear with barbeque skewer and roast until lightly blackened over open flame. Cut cooked corn into approximately 1 inch wide wheels and set aside. Keep warm.

Trim carrot stems to 3 or 4 inches. In sauté pan blanch carrots in 1 inch of water for about 5 minutes.

■

FRESH FRUIT CUSTARD PIE WITH LIME GRAND MARNIER SAUCE

NUT CRUST

Makes 2 8-inch to 10-inch pie crusts

(freeze one for later use)

10 finely chopped almonds

1 stick sweet unsalted butter, at room temperature

$1/3$ cup granulated sugar

3 cups all purpose flour

1 egg, lightly beaten

1 teaspoon vanilla

Preheat oven to 325 degrees. In medium bowl, combine all ingredients. Press evenly into pie pan. Chill at least 30 minutes and bake in center of oven 20 minutes or until partially baked.

CUSTARD PIE

Makes 1 8½-inch pie

$1 1/4$ cup sugar

3 tablespoons flour

4 eggs, lightly beaten

1 stick sweet unsalted butter, melted and cooled slightly

1 cup buttermilk

1 teaspoon vanilla

1 teaspoon nutmeg

Preheat oven to 425 degrees. Combine sugar and flour in large mixing bowl. Add beaten egg and mix well. Stir in butter and buttermilk. Stir in vanilla and nutmeg and pour into partially baked pie shell. Place pie in center of oven for 15 minutes. If crust edge is already golden, cover exposed crust with aluminum foil. Lower heat to 350 degrees and continue to bake for about 40 minutes until filling is set. Cool on wire rack.

FRUIT TOPPING

10 kiwi, peeled and sliced thin

1 pint blueberries

1 pint raspberries

Arrange kiwi on top of pie in rows from out-side to center, overlapping as you go. Hold aside, blueberries and raspberries.

LIME GRAND MARNIER SAUCE

¼ cup lime juice

2 cups vanilla yogurt

¼ cup Grand Marnier

Whip ingredients together in mixing bowl till smooth and creamy.

To serve, ladle plate with sauce. Place custard pie wedge in center of plate. Sprinkle berries loosely over sauce.

■

Pat Walter is known by many as the Inn's Renaissance Man. With a BA in Sculpture and an MFA in Space Design, Pat blends his aesthetic skills as chef, designer, and builder at the Grant Corner Inn. His presence gives new meaning to the quote: "Life is the articulation of our loves, and food is life."

Louise Stewart, is Innkeeper, Interior Designer and most importantly, "Mom." She has a BA in English from UCLA and a BFA in Environmental Design from Arizona State University. Although she studied a year at Cornell Hotel School, her hotel education came mainly from her life at Camelback Inn and her father, Jack Stewart. Jack Stewart was a pioneer and genius in the hotel industry in the 1940s, 50s and 60s. In 1936, with the financial aid of John C. Lincoln, he built Camelback Inn, rapidly establishing it as a resort of international acclaim. The Stewart family owned and managed the Inn until 1967 when it was sold to Marriott Corporation, who has continued and furthered the resort's success.

Louise, her husband, Pat, and daughter, "Bumpy," opened the Grant Corner Inn in Santa Fe, New Mexico in 1981.

Before his death in 1996, Garth Williams lived in Santa Fe and then Mexico City. During his time in Santa Fe, he and his family were frequent breakfast guests at the Inn. Mr. Williams, most beautifully and quite naturally, captured the character of Grant Corner Inn rabbits.